MAKING SENSE
The Acquisition of Shared Meaning

DEVELOPMENTAL PSYCHOLOGY SERIES

SERIES EDITOR
Harry Beilin

Developmental Psychology Program
City University of New York Graduate School
New York, New York

In Preparation

DAN OLWEUS, JACK BLOCK, and MARIAN RADKE-YARROW (Editors).
Development of Antisocial and Prosocial Behavior
PIERRE M. van HIELE. Structure and Insight
EDWARD C. MUELLER and CATHERINE R. COOPER. Process and Outcome
in Peer Relationships
JONAS LANGER. The Origins of Logic: One to Two Years

Published

KATHERINE NELSON. Making Sense: The Acquisition of Shared Meaning
ROBERT PLOMIN and JOHN C. DeFRIES. Origins of Individual Differences
in Infancy: The Colorado Adoption Project
ROBERT J. LEAHY. The Development of the Self
STEVEN R. YUSSEN. (Editor). The Growth of Reflection in Children
ROBBIE CASE. Intellectual Development: Birth to Adulthood
J. BARRY GHOLSON and TED R. L. ROSENTHAL. (Editors). Applications
of Cognitive–Developmental Theory
ALLEN W. GOTTFRIED. (Editor). Home Environment and Early
Cognitive Development: Longitudinal Research
EUGENE S. GOLLIN. (Editor). Malformations of Development:
Biological and Psychological Sources and Consequences
DAVID MAGNUSSON and VERNON L. ALLEN. (Editors). Human
Development: An Interactional Perspective

The list of titles in this series continues on the last page of this volume.

MAKING SENSE
The Acquisition of Shared Meaning

KATHERINE NELSON

Developmental Psychology Program
Graduate Center
City University of New York
New York, New York

1985

ACADEMIC PRESS, INC.

(Harcourt Brace Jovanovich, Publishers)

Orlando   San Diego   New York   London
Toronto   Montreal   Sydney   Tokyo

ACADEMIC PRESS, INC.
Orlando, Florida 32887

United Kingdom Edition published by
ACADEMIC PRESS INC. (LONDON) LTD.
24–28 Oval Road, London NW1 7DX

Library of Congress Cataloging in Publication Data

Nelson, Katherine,
    Making sense.

    Includes index.
    1. Language acquisition. 2. Meaning (Psychology)
3. Concepts. 4. Semantics I. Title
P118.N44   1985   401'.9   84-24174
ISBN 0-12-515420-8 (alk. paper)

To Margo and Laura

All the intellectual labor whereby the mind forms general concepts out of specific impressions is directed toward breaking the isolation of the datum, wresting it from the "here and now" of its actual occurrence, relating it to other things and gathering it and them into some inclusive order, into the unity of a "system."

E. Cassirer (1953, p. 25)

Contents

III.   FROM DENOTATION TO SENSE

Preface

In this book I discuss some of the theoretical issues and empirical research concerned with semantic and conceptual development in early childhood. In doing so I have tried to interweave the different strands of my own prior theorizing in order to provide a new integrated account of the child's development of a system of shared meaning. The goal of this enterprise is a coherent overview of the development of a meaning system that begins as an idiosyncratic two-person game and gradually evolves into a multicontexted conventional plurifunctional system of relationships.

Two caveats are in order with respect to this goal. First, the focus of the discussion is on the acquisition and development of word meaning in contrast to a larger semantic or general language approach. However, I believe the implications of the analysis reach beyond this relatively narrow focus to issues of language acquisition in general and its relation to conceptual development and communicative context. I expect then that the issues discussed here should be of interest to all those concerned with child language development or early cognitive development.

Second, while a resolution of the major problems addressed has been attempted, this is viewed as no more than a tentative resolution, one that accords with the evidence as we currently understand it, but one that will no doubt be improved as new evidence is acquired and integrated. In the hope of influencing others to look at old problems from a new perspective and to carry the investigation further, I present here what may be at best an inadequate account, recognizing that the description put forth will need amending, revising, or reformulating before long.

Like many other such projects, this book was first conceived as a collection of previously published papers, to be amplified by introductions and revisions where necessary. But like many such projects, this form was abandoned when it became apparent that simply recasting old papers, even with modifications and introductory comments, would not result in the integrated theoretical statement that I was hoping to achieve. The result is a complete reworking of ideas in three areas: the conceptual basis of early language, children's event representations, and semantic and conceptual development in early childhood. Although most chapters had their origins in previously published work, none is a complete recapitulation of any other publication. Indeed, most have been rewritten numbers of times in the 6 years since this project was first begun.

The length of time and the variety of topics covered indicate that I have benefited from many sources of ideas and help in carrying the project through. Although I had begun a draft of this work during a sabbatical semester at Oxford University in 1978, it was not until my colleague at City University of New York (CUNY) and the Developmental Psychology Series editor at Academic Press, Harry Beilin, encouraged me to complete it that I seriously began work on it. The book subsequently took shape during the preparation of a review of early word-learning literature for an invited presentation to the Developmental Section of the British Psychological Society at a meeting on the development of language and thought in Edinburgh, September, 1980. My paper included a first statement of the basic ideas that form the core of the theory as it has developed. The paper was rewritten for a volume of collected papers based on the conference on semantic development (which I unfortunately could not attend) held in Darmstadt, Germany, in 1981 (Nelson, 1983a). A different version was presented at an invited address to the Jean Piaget Society Meetings in 1981, organized around the theme of new models of concept development, published subsequently in Scholnick (1983). While work on the manuscript continued during the following years, teaching and administrative commitments, combined with other writing and research tasks (in particular work on children's event knowledge—see Nelson, in press) prevented sustained progress, and the final manuscript was not completed until June, 1984. My assessment of related research (Chapters 5 and 6) was essentially completed in 1981 and work reported since then is covered very sketchily, if at all.

At the present time my students and I are continuing to explore the implications of the conceptual to semantic model outlined here through experiments with children at all 3 points in the developmental sequence, and I hope that a progress report on this research will be available in the not-too-distant future. I can report that as of now we have found no reason to amend our theory in any significant way as a result of our observations.

A final word on the use of pronouns in this book. I have tried to avoid using *he* generically by making statements referring to plural children rather than the universal child. (This strategy has attractive theoretical implications as well.) However, at times this is awkward or misleading. When an instance of child is indicated, I have alternated between *he* and *she*. But on the rare occasions when the universal child is referenced, the reader will find that child referred to when necessary as *he*. While I am as opposed as anyone to sexist language I find the presently available alternatives equally unsatisfactory.

Acknowledgments

Although the present manuscript has been completely rewritten several times, the origins of some chapters in previously published work will be evident to those who are familiar with it. As noted previously, Chapter 3 is largely a revised and expanded version of Nelson (1983a & b) and it has subsequently been enlarged upon in Nelson and Lucariello (in press). Much of Chapter 4 is based on a paper published in *Developmental Psychology* (Nelson, 1981a). Parts of Chapter 7 draw from a chapter (Nelson, 1982) in Kuczaj's (1982) *Language Development* and some of Chapters 5 and 6 from chapters in K. E. Nelson's *Children's Language* (Nelson, 1978b) and from a chapter (Nelson, 1979a) in W. Collins, *Children's Language and Communication, Child Psychology* (Vol. 12). Papers prepared for conferences and symposia, especially the 1976 conference on Schooling and the Acquisition of Knowledge (Nelson, 1977c) and the Minnesota Symposium in 1977 (Nelson, 1979a) were early statements of the thinking reflected throughout the book, but particularly in Chapters 7 and 8. Participants and commentators at these and other conferences were helpful in shaping the present version. My work on the acquisition of children's event knowledge (Nelson, in press, supported by NSF Grants BNS 77–01179, BNS 79–14006, and BNS 82–08904) required me to rethink the role of culture in the acquisition of concepts and to make explicit the contribution of interaction with the language community.

There have been many other sources of support—intellectual, financial, and personal—for the work reported here, which I gratefully acknowledge. My theoretical work in this area first began to take shape during several years spent at Yale University, and this work was greatly influenced by my colleague and mentor there, Bill Kessen, who served as goad and critic, as well as intellectual model and friend. His helpful and critical reactions to my work have continued since then and are reflected in the present report. Our joint work on concept development was supported for 6 years by the Carnegie Corporation of New York, for which support I am very grateful.

Jerry Bruner was my host at Oxford in 1978, and my stay there was enjoyable and productive due largely to his efforts, even though he was himself at the time preparing to move on to new endeavors. I have been fortunate in being able to continue to explore with him our common interest in how the child takes advantage of a structured communicative situation in acquiring early language. Actually, Jerry Bruner's influence on my work long predates my years at Oxford and my personal acquaintance with him, as is no doubt evident from what I have written here and elsewhere.

At CUNY I have been fortunate in finding faculty colleagues and students who have helped to shape and test my ideas. Harry Beilin has led me to reexamine old ground and has introduced me to new problems that needed addressing. Joe Glick has provided not only helpful comments on my ideas but his own deep understanding of theoretical issues. His concerns with culture and context were influential in helping me to formulate explicitly the importance of the social and cultural context of conceptual development. I have benefited also in different ways from discussions with Sylvia Scribner, John Dore, and Arthur Reber of CUNY. Since 1982 a small group known as the New York Language Acquisition Group (NYLAG) has met at CUNY every 2 weeks to discuss theory and data. These discussions have been wide-ranging and provocative and have contributed to my thinking in many ways. The regular members of the group originally included Jerry Bruner, John Dore, Carol Feldman, Dan Stern, and Rita Watson. I am indebted to Carol Feldman as well for reading and commenting on several chapters of this book. Rachel Melkman also provided helpful criticism on early versions of some of the chapters.

I am most appreciative of the interest, skepticism, and contributions of my students. Of my students at Yale, Jane Platt, Helen Benedict, Leslie Rescorla, and Janice Gruendel each contributed in important ways to the early development of the ideas presented here. Many other students, too numerous to name, who attended seminars, research meetings, and summer discussion groups, served as valuable sounding boards for early development of these ideas. Gail Ross worked with me on several empirical studies at Yale after completing her doctoral work at Harvard. These studies contributed especially to the work reported in Chapter 3.

At CUNY I have continued to benefit from the criticism and interest of students and postdoctoral fellows who have attended seminars and research meetings concerned with language and concepts. As a postdoctoral fellow, Lucia French worked on the analysis of the language children use to formulate their script knowledge and in so doing helped us to understand how context and meaning interrelate in the mind of young children (French & Nelson, 1982; in press). Joan Lucariello has been a dedicated associate in research in the investigation of mother–child dialogues in scripted contexts, an interpreter of and contributor to the theory of early conceptual development, and a constant challenger of vague and unclear theoretical statements. This book is much clearer because of her. Tony Rifkin, Susan Seidman, Judy Hudson, Robyn Fivush, Susan Engel, Margo Morse, and Amy Kyratis have all contributed in different ways to the work reported here. Julie Gerhardt came to CUNY from Berkeley as a postdoctoral fellow in 1983 and provided important critical comments on the penultimate version of all chapters of the book.

Needless to say, none of these people is responsible for errors or nonsense that may still lurk in dark corners of the manuscript.

Finally, I am indebted to my family and friends. My husband, Richard Nelson, has supported my work faithfully for many years and has demonstrated both interest in and understanding of it. His backing and encouragement frequently kept me going in the face of doubt. My children, Margo and Laura, have not only served as subjects and as research assistants at various points in their lives, but also gave me my first insights into the problems and possibilities of putting language together to make sense. Laura also prepared many of the figures used here both cheerfully and skillfully.

A special word of thanks to Sally Barnes who was a constant supporter and aide at Yale and a friend through many twists and turns of career paths for both of us. Jill Becker, Brenda Magalaner, and Judith Ghinger at CUNY have each helped to organize and prepare this and many other manuscripts, with conscientious attention to detail as well as substance. The innumerable children who have, patiently or impatiently, served as subjects in my own research and in that of others, but who remain anonymous by the canons of research ethics, must be offered the greatest vote of thanks. Without them we would know nothing more than our own intuitions tell us; fortunately, they have presented us with many surprises and challenges to our theories, as well as occasional verifications of our intuitive speculations.

I

Introduction

1

Problems of Meaning
and Its Development

What Children Say and What They Mean

When children learn to talk they enter into a system of shared meanings. The words that they learn to use have the power to evoke in others a conceptual representation that, ideally, matches the one they intend to express. Through words and their systematic structural combinations we are able to build complex conceptual systems that others can share by virtue of their having internalized the same conventional representations of the meanings of words and the structures of sentences. The existence of such shared systems makes possible for most of us, most of the time, to understand each other when we converse. The infant, of course, does not begin life fully equipped with such a system; rather, years are spent building up knowledge of various language structures—syntactic, semantic, phonological—that are necessary for its establishment.

In this book I explore the conditions necessary for the establishment of one part of this total language system—the system of lexical meanings. As will become evident, this system is itself highly complex and undergoes significant development during the early childhood years. To convey something of the complexity of the problems addressed here, consider some familiar examples of children's use of words between 1 and 5 years of age:

1. "Ball." (said by a 15-month-old pointing to the full moon in the evening sky; Dewey, 1894).

2. "Daddy." (said by a 12-month-old pointing to Daddy's shoe; Rescorla, 1976)
3. "Baby. Truck." (said by a 19-month-old before putting doll in truck; Bloom, 1973)
4. "Yesterday did that. Now Emmy sleeping in regular bed." (said by a 23-month-old talking to herself in her crib; Nelson, 1983a)
5. "What kind of juice do you want?" (mother to 2-year-old at lunchtime)
   "Banana juice." (2-year-old responds; Lucariello & Nelson, in preparation)
6. "What happens when you make cookies?" (interviewer to 3-year-old)
   "She gots something out to bake muffins with. But *first* she has to buy some things for muffins." (French & Nelson, 1982)
7. "Is this an animal?" (interviewer pointing to dog)
   "No, it's a dog." ($2\frac{1}{2}$-year-old responds; Macnamara, 1982)
8. "What else is food? . . . What does food look like?" (interviewer to 3-year-old)
   "Potatoes."
   "Chairs." (Anglin, 1977)
9. "Tell me all the animals you can see at the zoo." (interviewer)
   "Lion, tiger, elephant." (3-year-old; Lucariello & Nelson, in press)
10. "What's the first word you think of when I say 'night'?" (standard word association test)
    "Dark." (standard 5-year-old response)

In each of these cases the question arises as to whether words mean the same to children as they do to adults. The first case is an example of what has been called overextension, which is commonly observed in children during their second year when they are just beginning to learn words. Does such overextension indicate that the child believes that "ball" refers to all round things? That it indicates roundness per se? Or that the moon looks like the child's ball? Or that the child would like to play with the ball (moon)? Each of these suggestions is incorporated in one theory or another of the child's first word meaning but none is consistent with the notion that the child's meaning is the same as that of the adult's for this word.

Some theorists have treated Example 2 above similarly to Example 1, calling both overextensions. From this point of view the child's meaning of "Daddy" would seem to be quite bizarre, incorporating Daddy's possessions as well as his corporal being. Others see Example 2 as expressing a relationship between Daddy and his shoe, the single word "Daddy" being either a *holophrastic* expression (a word used to express a complete proposition) or one component of an implied sentence. Again, while the child's expression seems to make sense in context, the meaning of the word used is at best ambiguous.

Example 3 is also ambiguous. Does the child mean to express an anticipated relationship such as "baby in truck," "baby goes in truck," "I'll make the doll drive the truck," or some other relevant action? Or is the child simply verbalizing the names of the two objects that she sees (the later action and relation being unanticipated at the time)?

Can we conclude from Example 4 that this child's use of "now," "yesterday," and the past and progressive forms of the verb indicates her understanding of relations between past and present actions and states? Against this is the inference that either "sleeping" or "now" or both must mean something different to her from what they do to us (since she clearly is not sleeping when she says this); moreover, the action attributed to "yesterday" actually happened to her the same morning. While her word use seems superficially appropriate and readily interpretable, these words have not been given their conventional interpretations. Thus, her representations of their meaning do not appear to match those of the adult; but how they differ is not clear.

Does the child in Example 5 understand the question? Is he being funny? Is he generalizing from an understanding of a category of juices that includes other fruits to suppose that there must be banana juice as well? In this, as in so many cases, we must decide whether the child's use of words reflects lack of knowledge or ingenuity.

The 3-year-old in Example 6 clearly understands the question and is able to answer appropriately. Moreover, she is able to use appropriate discourse devices to repair her initial statement in order to make clear the proper order of events. The use of temporal terms (e.g., "first," "before," and "after") to establish correct sequence has been shown to be a late development when evaluated through performance on experimental tasks where the child is asked to relate two events that have no natural relation in the child's experience. Should spontaneous production data of the kind evident in Example 6 be accepted as evidence that children do understand the meanings of such terms in contradiction to the experimental data? What does it signify when children seem to understand terms in one context but not another?

Examples 7, 8, and 9 illustrate some of the conflicting evidence on children's understanding of hierarchical category relations between words. The child in Example 7 denies a true class-inclusion relation (dogs are included in the class animal), while a child of the same age in Example 9 provides an appropriate list of subcategory members. Are subordinate relations different from and easier than superordinate ones? If so, the superordinate–subordinate relation must be understood differently by children than it is by adults. Or does phrasing the question in experiential terms ("animals you see in the zoo") somehow make it possible for the child to produce the category information required? In any event, the child in Example 8 who provides a member of a different category than that asked for suggests a more basic failure to understand class relations. But perhaps this child is being funny or changing the subject. If hierarchical relations are essential to the semantic system (as most semantic models assume), these contradictory results imply that young children do not have this system under full control.

The answer given to the word association item in Example 10 is typical of the stage of *syntagmatic* responding, in which words from a form class different from the stimulus word are produced in response (as, in the present case, adjective to noun). A shift to *paradigmatic* responding takes place over the early school years, when the dominant response to "night," for example, becomes "day." Is this shift related to changes within the semantic system? Is it an isolated phenomenon or one reflecting other cognitive changes basically unrelated to language?

These examples illustrate some of the problems encountered in describing and explaining the development of the child's semantic system. The methodological puzzles derive from conflicting results of different research paradigms. Many of our data come from natural discourse, that is, children's use of words in context. As suggested earlier, most of the time such use is readily interpretable and appears appropriate. Yet evidence of appropriate meaning based on production in context is frequently at odds with evidence revealing misunderstanding of the same terms in experimental settings. For example, some researchers have found that children interpret "after" as meaning "before" in experiments (Clark, 1971), while children virtually never make such errors in their spontaneous productions (French & Nelson, in press). Apparently trivial changes in context or question format can have a significant impact on the child's ability to understand or use a term (Carey, 1983). Is it possible, then, to represent the child's "real" meaning of the term or must we assume that the child's meaning is variable and context-bound?

Beyond the purely methodological problems, explaining lexical development is also fraught with difficulties deriving from the role of context in the interpretation of meaning by the child. The child necessarily learns and uses words in context. There are no vocabulary drills in the nursery, although some picture–word books appear designed for this purpose. Whatever meaning the child assigns to a word derives from his or her experience with its use. But we cannot simply track such experience to determine what the child learns. Each context is open to innumerable interpretations by different observers, and the child's working model of the world may produce interpretations that would not occur to the adult. To take the first two examples above, the child might believe that the moon was reachable and could be played with (Dewey's 1894 suggestion), and she might think that Daddy's shoes were as much an integral part of him as any other part of his body. Or to take the famous example "the cat is on the mat," the child might believe that this sentence referred to the fire in front of which the cat was lying and thereafter refer to the fire as "mat" or the mat as "cat," producing intriguing overextensions for the adult to interpret in a theoretical model. Bowerman (1976) reported the interesting case of her own child, who interpreted "hi" to mean any finger covering from its use in a finger puppet game played by her mother. The possibilities of misinterpretation of reference in context appear endless for the beginning language learner, and the remarkable outcome is that so much of children's speech appears appropriate rather than bizarre (see Macnamara, 1982; and Quine, 1960). Indeed, the apparent appropriateness of children's speech in the light of so many probable errors demands a theoretical explanation. Context may continue either to aid or impair the child's understanding of the meaning of a term and his or her ability to use the term conventionally long after a beginning vocabulary has been acquired. Understanding how context of use enters into or supports the child's meaning system is essential to understanding the development of meaning.

As the discussion of these examples has suggested, developing a shared meaning system draws on two major components: the child's cognitive system and the exchange of meaning through language in communicative situations. These two aspects cannot easily be disentangled from one another. The meanings a child assigns to a term reflect the state of his or her own conceptual representations; at the same time, these representations determine how a language exchange within a given situation will be interpreted by the child.

Thus, a theory of semantic development must deal with three problems: the communicative context within which meaning is expressed and learned; the child's cognitive system, which interprets and intends meaning; and development—cognitive, linguistic, social—which changes the parameters of the system throughout the period. Any theory that fails to deal adequately with any one of these will fail to produce an adequate explanation of how the system develops. The outcome of the theory should be a semantic system that reflects what is known about adults' representations of the meanings of words. However, the outcome need not (and I would emphasize should not) determine the analysis of its development.

The Meaning of Meaning

Thus far, I have used the term *meaning* very loosely. I have implied that words have meanings, that sentences[1] have meanings, that meanings derive from discourse, and that they are interpreted in conceptual representations. The looseness with which I use the term and with which it is used by others is not surprising; Lyons (1977) lists 10 different meanings of the term as used by laymen and specialists. Still, if we are to study the development of a meaning system, it is essential to have a better understanding of what that system consists of.

Do words mean or do people mean? Some version of this question has been the center of philosophical, linguistic, and psychological discussion for the past century. To duck all of the important implications of the various arguments put forth by Wittgenstein, Austin, Searle, Putnam, Kripke, and others for the basis of meaning in use may be unwise, but to discuss them properly would occupy a book in itself and would put off indefinitely the psychological consideration of how the child comes to understand the meaning of language terms in the first place. In contrast to the assumptions of a use-based model of meaning, psychological and linguistic models have usually been based on the assumption that words have enduring and conventional meanings that can be represented in static structures reflecting combinations of criterial features or, alternatively, the relations between words in a subjective lexicon.

For the purposes of the present discussion, I take the intuitive position that there are conventional meanings of words that speakers of a language must acquire if they are to use those words in such a way as to be understood by others in the language community, but also that individual speakers may use words in such a way as to convey different meanings on different occasions of use, depending upon intentions and discourse context. Metaphor, sarcasm, analogy, paraphrase, synonym, homonym, formula, idiom, colloquialism, creativity, poetry, oddity, novelty, and plain idiosyncrasy all have a place in considerations of meaning. These are especially important to consider when the problem is to describe how the child comes to master a meaning system that reflects conventional uses even though convention does not always determine use. Thus, it is necessary to accept both sides of the argument: that words mean in conventional ways and that people mean in different ways when they use those words. These two approaches to meaning exemplify semantic models as a structural system on the one hand and as the functional realization of communicative intentions on the other. These in turn are the two sides of the Saussurian (de Saussure, 1915/1959) analysis—*langue,* the language system independent of its speakers, and *parle,* language in discourse. There is a further complication here in that psychological semantic models assume not only that there is a system independent of speakers but that each speaker has a mental representation of the lexical structure, a subjective lexicon reflecting the structural principles of *langue.*

It is evident, however, that children do not begin with well-organized semantic systems. The problem for the child, therefore, is to construct a system on the basis of experience at interpreting meaning in context. *The study of the development of meaning then depends upon determining how internal systematicity emerges from the external experience of meaning in context.* This is the central problem addressed in this book.

In this work, then, meaning is considered to be imposed on words by the speakers in a particular context. This imposition is accomplished through the meaning systems of the speakers involved and reflects, in part, conventional meanings. The subjective meaning system is a complex of interactive component systems used to express intentions and interpret the intentions of others. This complex of systems includes virtually the entire cognitive system, consisting of layers of representations and processes. That is, the interpretation and expression of meaning involve the various language subsystems but draw on much more in the process of making sense. Among the important components is the perceptual system, which establishes representations of the present scene and makes available perceptual representations of previously experienced scenes or of imagined scenes. In addition, meaning calls on the memory system, which keeps track of specific experiences and of spatial–temporal–causal relations. Central to the development of the meaning system is the event representation (or script), which generalizes from experience of events to provide an interpretation of context. At another level, derived from the event representations, is the conceptual system, which represents an organized base of general knowledge relatively unconstrained by specific spatial–temporal context. Finally, the semantic system, which represents knowledge of how semantic relations are realized in the language and of conventional word meanings, occupies a level of its own, dependent upon but separate from the conceptual and event-representation levels. These relations are described in Chapters 7 and 8 in more detail.

Understanding the meaning of an utterance may involve any or all of these systems. Thus, the *meaning system* of the individual includes far more than the semantic system per se, which represents linguistic knowledge or, rather, the interface between linguistic structure (syntax and lexicon) and other knowledge systems. It should be noted that in this book *semantics* and *semantic system* are used in this narrow sense, rather than in the broader sense in which *meaning* is used.

Thus, it is evident that *meaning system* as used here is essentially equivalent to *cognition*. It is assumed that the expression and interpretation of meaning draw, when necessary, on all aspects of cognition. How and when different cognitive components or functions are involved is one of the questions of interest in a developmental model.

For every utterance used in a given context, each speaker and each listener establishes a *subjective meaning* through their respective interpretive meaning systems. Together they come to understand a shared meaning, consisting of those parts of their subjective meanings that coincide. Such shared meanings may range from zero (complete misunderstanding) to one (complete understanding). The greater the degree to which an individual's semantic, conceptual, and script systems correspond to the conventional representations of the cultural (or subcultural) group to which the speakers belong, the greater the likelihood of establishing a high degree of shared meaning on any given occasion. (A subcultural group in this context may consist of only a parent–child dyad.) By extending this proposition we can speak of the individual's development of a *shared meaning system,* that is, an internalized system of knowledge representations—semantic and conceptual—that correspond to those of the cultural group.

The conventional meanings of the cultural group constitute a kind of knowledge that Popper (1972) spoke of as "objective knowledge" or as a third world of reality, distinguishing between the individual's subjective reality, the reality of the experienced world, and the reality encoded in cultural forms—mathematics, logic, literature, and history, for example. The *objective semantic system* is part of this third reality. It is a product of the culture as a whole and is not represented in any one individual, although each individual acquires some knowledge of it.

In this regard Putnam (1975) emphasized the "division of linguistic labor," which sets the linguistic community (not the individual) as the primary repository of meaning. As he puts it:

Everyone to whom gold is important for any reason has to *acquire* the word "gold"; but he does not have to acquire the *method of recognizing* if something is or is not gold. He can rely on a special sub-class of speakers. The features that are generally thought to be present in connection with a general name . . . are all present in the linguistic community *considered as a collective body;* but that collective body divides the "labor" of knowing and employing these various parts of the "meaning" of "gold." (Putnam, 1975, pp. 227–228)

It is important to note that the subjective meaning system may be organized quite differently from the objective system.[2] Given that its acquisition and development are situated in particular contexts of use, its organization no doubt reflects these uses. This is particularly true early in development.

Again, Putnam's view of the matter is relevant to this point:

The grotesquely mistaken views of language which are and always have been current reflect the specific and very central philosophical tendencies: the tendency to treat cognition as a purely *individual* matter and the tendency to ignore the *world,* insofar as it consists of more than the individual's "observations." Ignoring the division of linguistic labor is ignoring the social dimension of cognition; ignoring what we have called the *indexicality* of most words is ignoring the contribution of the environment. Traditional philosophy of language, like much traditional philosophy, leaves out people and the world; a better philosophy and a better science of language must encompass both. (Putnam, 1975, p. 271)

The problem for a psychological theory is to explicate how the individual cognitive system organizes the contributions of people and the world in order to operate within the larger meaning community.

The way in which the language community displays the semantic system to the child is through language in use. The context of those uses is complexly structured and multilayered, as described in Chapter 2. The initial meaning structure that the child derives is bound to reflect the context of use. Some of this context may be highly relevant to the semantic structure of the community and some of it may not be. The latter must eventually be deleted from the system, while the former must become systematized. Moreover, because of its dependence upon context of use, the child's system is bound to be a partial reflection of the adult's system, which is itself a partial reflection of the cultural system as a whole.

We may then speak of three different kinds of meaning: subjective meaning, established within the individual's meaning system as a whole; shared meaning, established between two or more speakers within a given context; and objective meaning, a repository of the culture. These represent, respectively, individual, social, and cultural meaning. In this book we shall be concerned with how the individual develops a meaning system from experience with social meanings reflecting an understanding of cultural meaning.

Given the foregoing assumptions, it is evident that development of the subjective meaning system involves more than the acquisition of a lexicon. It also includes the development of the conceptual system as well as perception, memory, the representation of events, and the interrelations between these systems of representation. Semantic development must then be seen as one outcome of the full complex of cognitive, social, and linguistic development. Moreover, each of the various subsystems may develop according to its own timetable and its own developmental laws.

The eventual solution to this problem involves the subjective representation of the social and cultural worlds. The cognitive system becomes organized in such a way that the individual can coordinate context and culture through the conceptual system. Contexts become understandable through the systems of perceptual representation, specific memory, and general event representations or scripts. The individual's conceptual system derives and organizes general knowledge structures from these contextually based systems. These general concepts are then coordinated with and shared by the lexical uses of the language community to produce a subjective lexical system that reflects that established by cultural convention. This, in a nutshell, is the developmental theory presented here.

The three components of the subjective meaning system—reflecting context, cognition, and culture—are related in an interesting way to the tripartite nature of meaning described in Lyons (1977) in terms of reference, denotation, and sense. Roughly, these terms stand for the relations of words to the world (reference), of words to concepts (denotation), and of words to words (sense.)[3] Although these aspects of meaning have been represented in different philosophical approaches to the study of meaning, in a psychological theory each is a necessary part of lexical meaning. How they work psychologically is the question at issue.

It will help to clarify Lyons' use of these terms and the way they are employed here. *Reference* refers to the relation between a word and what it signifies. The notion seems to be a simple one, but even in early development it may be very complex (see Bruner, 1983, for a discussion of the complexities of reference in early word learning). On the one hand, to refer to a thing with a word is to know, in some sense, what the word means, that is, to know what sort of things may be referred to with the word. To say appropriately "please give me that apple" entails that the object referred to belong to the class of apples. It is this requirement that led Ogden and Richards (1946) to the claim that words refer to concepts and not directly to objects and to construct their famous "meaning triangle" shown in Figure 1.1, illustrating that "words signify things by means of mediating concepts" (Lyons, 1977, p. 110).

On the other hand, reference is a relation established by speakers on a given occasion. The relation is established between words and things signified on that occasion. Thus, the word "apple" may refer to any number of different apples or the class of apples ("the apple is a highly nutritious fruit"), depending upon the speaker's intent. Reference is then a contextualized or deictic relation. Indeed, as will be shown in Chapters 2 and 3, it may be not only contextualized but context-bound. Reference need not involve conceptual knowledge, but only the ability to form an association between a word and a particular object. For example, the child may learn to refer to her pet dog as "Bo" (e.g., "there Bo") but may not have a concept of dogs that provides a basis for referring to any dog seen on the street as "doggie" or "Bo."

Reference fails as a general theory of meaning because it does not necessarily require more than a shared percept (see also Macnamara, 1982, for a recent discussion of reference in child language). Lyons (1977, pp. 112–114) also considers and rejects the usual formulation of conceptualism (as in the Ogden and Richards [1946] model) as a theory of meaning on two grounds. First, there is no evidence that concepts play a role in ordinary language–behavior. For example, on hearing "table" used in a sentence the listener does not need to look up the concept of table in order to interpret the sentence. Second, although the notion of a mediating concept for concrete object words like "table" seems clear, it is not at all clear for other sorts of words (even such common words as "high" or "thank you"). Although he grants the importance of acquiring concepts in order to understand the meaning

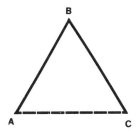

FIGURE 1.1   The "meaning triangle." A = word, B = concept, C = object. (Lyons [1977] based on Ogden & Richards [1946]).

of a word, Lyons rejects the notion that the concept *is* the meaning: "It does not follow, however, from the fact that we must have acquired the concept of a table before we can be said to know the meaning of 'table' that this concept is involved in the production and understanding of most utterances containing the word 'table' " (Lyons, 1977, p. 113).

In Lyons' alternative formulation there are two aspects of meaning, one relating the word to its possible referents (denotation) and the other relating it to other words (sense). Denotation is described as "the relationship that holds between [a] lexeme and persons, things, places, properties, processes and activities external to the language system" (Lyons, 1977, p. 207).

As Lyons (1977) puts it:

> It is obvious enough that the relationship between two lexemes, like "cow" and "animal," is to be distinguished from the relationship that either of these lexemes bears to the class of objects which it denotes: the relationship between a linguistic entity and something outside the language system. . . . But there are serious objections to making either sense or denotation basic. (p. 210)

He goes on to point out that if denotation is assumed to be logically and psychologically basic the problem arises as to how we can know the sense of words such as "unicorn" that have no denotation. Moreover, the problem applies to words that do have denotation. As he notes: "We can learn the sense of 'walrus' (its relationship with such words as 'seal' and 'mammal') without knowing whether it has a denotation or not. Sense, then, in some cases at least is epistemologically prior to denotation" p. 211). But the opposite assumption, that sense is basic, is equally unviable, Lyons argues, since we learn the use of many words in relation to the persons and objects around us before we relate them in sense to other words in the vocabulary.

It is important to note here that denotation in this discussion refers to the applicability of a term and not to its actual reference in an utterance, while sense refers to the relations of a word (lexeme) to other words in the vocabulary and not to, say, a concept.

Although the denotation–sense problem cannot be resolved for the adult language system, it nonetheless seems intuitively obvious that in development reference precedes denotation, which precedes sense relationships. Indeed, this appears to be a basic assumption of most theories, from St. Augustine to Macnamara (1982). In fact, it is difficult to imagine a developmental theory that would posit the reverse.

Note that denotation is not the same as reference; it determines *possible* referents or uses of the term. Sense, in contrast, is defined in terms of all of those relations that can hold between words themselves, such as synonymy, antonymy, and taxonomy. Although Lyons distinguishes between concepts and denotation, the main justification for this distinction seems to be the constitutive structure of the concept. In Lyons' formulation meaning is specified solely in terms of *relations,* not in terms of content, however structured. In this he follows de Saussure's (1915/1959) dictums. The usual view of concepts as constructed of attributes, therefore, does not fit this formulation. As seen above, for Lyons meaning relations are of two types: external to the language system (denotation) and internal to it (sense). However, it is unavoidable that relations relate, and what is denoted by the word through the denotative relation can only be a concept, or a system of concepts, or some other form of mental representation. Thus, the place of the conceptual system in a meaning system would seem to be essential even though the language speaker need not always access it in processing sentences.

It may help to illustrate the ways in which these different aspects of meaning may operate in our everyday discourse. Suppose I ask the question: "Did you eat the apple that was on the counter?" To answer, the addressee, whether child or adult, is unlikely to call up from conceptual storage all knowledge of apples (different types, growing conditions, occasions on which apples are eaten, dishes in which apples are served, etc.), all knowledge about eating (meals, eating habits of people and animals, instruments for eating, etc.) and all knowledge about counters (places where they are found, materials of construction, etc.). What is likely to come to mind in the speech situation is, rather, a particular referent if one is known (a particular apple and counter, for example) and a representation of the action that is appropriate to the referents (apple eating in this instance). Thus, in this speech situation we need a referential model of semantics plus real-world knowledge. Note that the objects referred to are in memory and not in the immediate perceptual array. Nonetheless, we do not need to call on conceptual knowledge about apples and counters but only memory for a specific case. Referential meaning then relates terms to context-specific individuals whether they are present, past, or even imaginary. It is an essential part of meaning in adult language and an essential beginning point for child language.

In contrast, suppose on returning from a trip to my local fruit stand, I ask a friend: "What is a papaya?" The answer I receive from my addressee (presumably better informed than I) should bear some resemblance to a dictionary definition and may contain the essential components of the conventional concept of papaya. It should contain the information I need to identify papayas when I see them, perhaps to tell me what they taste like or when they are eaten. In other words, in this situation we need a denotational theory of semantics. Denotation specifies the possible referents. In this sense it is equivalent to a concept, including both intension and extension. I would become impatient with my addressee in this situation, however, if my informant went on to tell me all about the climatic growing conditions of papayas, the last time he visited Hawaii and ate papayas, the different ways that papayas are used in curing meats, and so on. Thus, we need to make a distinction between a denotational meaning and an individual's total knowledge about a thing. (This point has been made by Katz [1972] as well as Miller and Johnson-Laird [1976] and many others.) It should be noted that a denotational meaning need not be explicitly contrastive or even relational, although usually these are implied in adult usage. It is important to keep in mind that a child might learn to identify and enjoy papayas without knowing that they are a fruit or without knowing any closely related class members. As Lyons (1977) has noted, neither denotation nor sense appears to be *logically* primary in the acquisition of meaning.

But now suppose I asked: "What kind of fruit is a papaya?" Here I would like to know something about the relations between papayas and other fruits. My informant might tell me it is like a mango or it is a kind of exotic tropical fruit or relate it in other ways to other members of the fruit class. While I might find it interesting that we import mangoes from the Caribbean and papayas from Hawaii, that is not really the information I want. Rather, the information wanted is where papayas fit in the conceptual or lexical structure of fruits. Some core of relationships, usually noncontingent (although not implying unchangeable as Putnam [1975] has insisted), enters into these stripped-down, conventional, culturally agreed-upon meaning structures. In brief, we also need a distinction between sense semantics and world knowledge. Sense relations include such relations as hyponymy, synonymy, and antonymy, which reflect organization. Thus, they are paradigmatically contrastive. But in addition, it is important to note that the sense relations holding between words are based on conceptual relations, which in turn are derived from real-world knowledge.

It may be seen that the three components of the subjective meaning system outlined above may be realized in the different ways that words may be said to mean in a linguistic sense. Contextual factors determine reference on any given occasion; the conceptual representation underlying a word (its extension and intension) determines its denotation, and the relations reflected in the lexical system determine its sense, in Lyons' terms. These notions will be discussed in greater detail in subsequent chapters of the book. At this point it may be noted that the tripartite nature of meaning, linguistically and psychologically, suggests that a single set of principles of lexical acquisition and relationships cannot be found to apply to all points in development and that a developmental theory of word meaning may call on different aspects of meaning at different developmental points. In particular, it will be proposed here that the meaning system develops from reference (context) to denotation (concept) to sense (culture).

To illustrate this in a preliminary way, the examples given earlier may be interpreted within this framework. Examples 1, 2, and 3 may all express reference without entailing an underlying conceptual representation applicable to the words used, that is, they may apply only to perceptual representations (prototypes) of familiar objects. Examples 4, 5, and 6 apparently do entail conceptual representations beyond the immediate perceptual array that determine word use. However, Examples 7–10 indicate that a semantic system independent of the conceptual, based on sense relations between words, is not yet developed. These claims will be discussed in detail in subsequent chapters.

The Syntagmatics and Paradigmatics of Conceptual and Semantic Knowledge

A fundamental contrast in the structure of language introduced by de Saussure (1915) is that between syntagmatic and paradigmatic relations. Syntagmatic relations hold between elements that enter into a larger unit, for example, the relations between word classes in a sentence (e.g., adjective–noun) or between phonemes in a (spoken) word. Paradigmatic relations hold between elements that can substitute for one another in a larger unit, for example, between two adjectives. de Saussure considered these relational types to reflect basic properties of human cognition, and this proposition will be explicated in Chapter 6 in terms of a syntagmatic–paradigmatic model of conceptual development. While syntagmatic relations are observable in the surface structure of sentences and analogously in the experience of events, paradigmatic relations are analytic abstractions that are not directly observable.

The syntagmatic–paradigmatic distinction may be related to several other dichotomies that have played a role in discussions of cognition and cognitive development. For example, cognitive psychology has been most concerned with how people understand the physical world in terms of logical relations among objects. The cognitive model that has emerged from this concern has then been extended to the analysis of social phenomena. An alternative to this move has been to suggest that different types of analysis must be applied to social cognition, reflecting the fact that different laws apply to physical and social reality (see Flavell & Ross, 1981). The social world is said to be governed by contingencies, probabilities, and interactions, while the physical world is governed by determinant laws of invariance and conservation.

However, this view is too simple. Not only is the physical world not so predictable as the model suggests, but the social world presents more invariance and predictability than the model claims. More importantly, the social world embeds physical objects and the physical world embeds social relations; the two interpenetrate each other. The interdependence of the two suggests an analogy with the syntagmatic–paradigmatic analysis. Social experiences that people take part in provide "slots" that can be filled by different people and objects on different occasions. The different things that can fill a given slot stand in paradigmatic relation to one another within the syntagmatic structure of the event. The analysis of experience in these terms and the suggestion that it is stored in scriptlike event-representation form (see below) provide the basis for understanding the relation between social events and physical objects in the child's developing knowledge system.

Mental representations of events based on social experiences form one kind of schematic structure. Schemas have been contrasted with categories as organizing structures for the representation of knowledge (Mandler, 1979). Categorical structures can be thought of as grouping together elements on the basis of similar properties to establish equivalence classes of greater or lesser generality. This grouping is obviously based on a paradigmatic analysis. In contrast, schemas bring elements together on the basis of their contextual relationships in time or space, that is, on a syntagmatic basis. For example, while the categories "food" and "furniture" provide one type of knowledge organization, the schemas for "kitchen" and "making dinner" provide a different type that crosscuts the first. The kitchen schema organizes a particular spatial scene that includes a particular set of objects appropriate to the activities that take place there. A subset of the schema type is the script (Schank & Abelson, 1977), an ordered set of events in temporal sequence representing a familiar activity, such as making dinner. The script is a particularly relevant type of schema because of its sequential nature; it represents experience through time and space. It will be argued here (see Chapter 7) that the abstract paradigmatic categories are derived from the analysis of the syntagmatic event schemas.

The social–physical and schematic–categorical contrasts appear to be reflected as well in two general language functions, the interpersonal and ideational (Halliday, 1975; Lyons, 1977). Halliday has claimed that in development the precursors of the interpersonal functions (the pragmatic) precede the precursors of the ideational functions (termed the mathetic). Although this claim would be consistent with the above suggestions of the relation between schema and category (if one associates schemas with interpersonal functions and categories with ideational ones), as will be shown in Chapter 4, the developmental relation may go either way. Both are necessary to the development of a language system.

It seems to be an almost inevitable hypothesis that these distinctions in thought and language may be related to different brain (as well as mind) spaces, the syntagmatic–schematic–interpersonal in the right hemisphere and the paradigmatic–categorical–ideational in the left. However, this is undoubtedly too simple a view of the matter, and neurological speculation of this kind is better left to the neuroscientists. Moreover, these different dichotomies are almost certainly not related in any simple, direct, and lawful way. While theoretically differentiable, they are not differentiable in the real world, instead forming interdependent and interacting systems.

It will be one theme of the story presented here, however, that syntagmatic and paradigmatic analysis work together to construct the conceptual system and subsequently the lexical system from the contextually based event-representation system as semantic development proceeds from infancy to childhood. In this view the development of the subjective meaning system is construed in terms of the emergence of a third level of representation—the lexical—from the contextual and conceptual levels of the presemantic system.

Organization of the Book

Because of the complexity of the subjective meaning system, a theory of semantic development must do more than provide principles of word learning or word meaning in a linguistic framework. Any theory of semantic development must address the following questions:

How is knowledge of the world organized and conceptualized by the child and how does this system develop?
How are language terms learned at different points in development?
How are language terms used at different points in development?
How does use affect meaning?
How are word meanings constructed at different points in development?

How are language terms organized and related to each other at different points in development and how does this organization change?

How are the domains of conceptualization and semantics related to one another and how do these relations change with development?

How do these relations affect performance on language tasks at different points in development?

How does developmental change in the system take place?

In the chapters to follow, these questions will be addressed in the tripartite framework sketched here in an attempt to present a coherent account of semantic development from first words to the point, at about 5 to 7 years of age, where lexical relations seem clearly established. Chapters 2–4 cover the beginning of the system up to about $2\frac{1}{2}$ years of age, and Chapters 5–7 trace further development during the preschool years.

The way this book proceeds is to set forth the research findings and theoretical distinctions that need to be taken into account and on that basis to build an explanation of development that is adequate to the observed complexity. In this way the theory emerges from the phenomena observed. It goes without saying that the theory set forth is probably inadequate. Nonetheless, the aim here is to propose a comprehensive account that can lead to further productive research.

Chapters 2 and 3 and the first half of Chapter 4 lay out research and theory relevant to the emergence of meaning between 1 and 2 years of age, while in the latter part of Chapter 4 an initial integration is attempted. Chapters 5 and 6 likewise survey what is known and thought about semantic and conceptual development in the preschool years, while Chapters 7 and 8 propose a fuller integrative account. Because of this structure, many issues that are discussed in a preliminary way in the earlier chapters are returned to in an attempt at resolution in later chapters. Moreover, the research reviewed derives from heterogeneous sources, including some of the older psychological literature as well as more recent semantic and categorical studies. For an overview and summary, the reader might want to turn first to Chapter 9, where the conclusions drawn and solutions proposed are summarized.

Chapter 2 discusses the context of early meanings. Context is considered as a multidimensional construct that affects the child's understanding and use of terms in many guises. The child's cognitive representation of events is seen as a way of establishing cognitive context that serves to interpret experience, including the experience of language.

Chapter 3 considers theories and data concerning early conceptual representation and early word meaning. Explanations of word meaning based on referential, conceptual, and semantic theories are discussed, and three types of word meaning typically observed in different phases of development during the second year are identified. These are related to the contextual issues discussed in Chapter 2.

In Chapter 4 variations in language-acquisition patterns are reviewed and are related to the contextual and cognitive issues brought out in the previous chapters. A unified account of the development of meaning during the early stages is presented.

Chapter 5 reviews the literature relating to conceptual and semantic development during the preschool years. Different types of concepts are identified. Conceptual structure is discussed in terms of different theoretical perspectives and relevant research. In Chapter 6 research findings with respect to relations between concepts and words are reviewed. Chapters 5 and 6 cover a great deal of research and quite a few theoretical models. Thus, those who are not inclined to dispute the interpretations of this prior research may skip to the conclusions at the end of Chapter 6. Those who are interested in the details or are skeptical will want to read these chapters more closely to see where they conflict with their own interpretations or biases.

In Chapter 7 the syntagmatic–paradigmatic model of conceptual development is outlined, and its implications for the theoretical questions raised in the previous chapters are discussed. This model proposes that the child's conceptual system is based in and derives from the experientially derived event-representation system, resulting in a number of interacting representational levels that provide an interpretive system of meaning and form the basis for the emerging lexical system.

Chapter 8 discusses the specifically linguistic meaning relations such as synonymy and antonymy and concludes that hyponymy, or the superordinate–subordinate relation, also belongs to the class of specifically linguistic relations. This relation is given particular attention in this chapter in the discussion of the emergence of the lexical level of representation. Research findings reviewed in Chapters 5 and 6 are reconsidered from this perspective.

Chapter 9 reconsiders the basic points brought out in the previous chapters and discusses their implications for the basic questions to be addressed by a theory of semantic development, as posed earlier. Chapter 9 provides an integrated view of the proposals elaborated in the rest of the book, and some readers may wish to begin with this chapter before plunging into the more detailed exposition given in the earlier chapters.

Notes

[1]I use *word* and *sentence* here where *lexeme, morpheme, expression,* or *utterance* might technically be more appropriate (Lyons, 1977). Because of the conventional uses of the former terms in psychology, however, I do not adhere systematically to these distinctions.

[2]As a result, knowing the definition of a word is often of little help in identifying it. Crossword puzzle authors take advantage of this asymmetry of words and their definitions. Consider the following set of definitions for one of the most-studied, common terms that young children learn:

> 1. In the rear of; farther back than; following. . . . 2. In search or pursuit of. . . . 3. In relation to; concerning. . . . 4. Subsequent to; at a later period than. . . . 5. In succession to; following repeatedly. . . . 6. As a result of; subsequently and because of. . . . 7. Notwithstanding. . . . 8. Next below in order. . . . 9. According to the nature, wishes or customs of. . . . 10. In imitation of. . . . 11. In honor, remembrance or observance of. . . . 12. Of time by the clock, past. (Funk & Wagnall, 1968, p. 25)

Of these, children are expected to master No. 4 first. Knowledge of the other meanings is not credited in acquisition studies. Few of these definitions of "after" are fully interpretable without their being accompanied by exemplifying sentences.

[3]I apologize to those who are used to using *reference* and *sense* in their Fregian (Frege, 1960) senses. For want of better terminology I have adopted Lyons' (1977) distinctions, which in the case of sense especially are narrower, *denotation* here covering aspects of both reference and sense in Frege's terms. The distinctions, in any case, are somewhat artificial but are useful in the effort to understand important developments in the acquisition of meaning.

II

From Reference to Denotation

2

The Context of Early Meaning

The Context Problem in Early Language Use

Any sample of talk is contexted in complex ways. Indeed, the problem of context is essentially a figure–ground problem. What is focused upon in an analysis—in the present case, talk—may become part of the context when another aspect of the activity, for example, emotional expression, becomes the focus. Thus, without defining the object to be examined one cannot distinguish context from contexted. Moreover, context is multilayered and the layers themselves have interdependencies that need to be examined.

The discussion of context that follows may appear to be far removed from the problem of establishing a meaning system. I include in the term "context" notions of geography, culture, and social class as well as activities and talk.[1] As discussed in Chapter 1, meaning cannot be considered a private matter, a question only of concepts held by an individual. Once the discussion is extended to take into account the world to be understood and symbolized through language, it is apparent that the world itself—social as well as object—must become part of the explanation of the establishment of meaning. How the child understands the world and how language embedded in experience in the world becomes internally represented are key questions in the acquisition of a shared meaning system.

Context is usually interpreted to refer to conditions external to the individual and thus to be objectively defined. A good example of such objectivity is the control that psychologists attempt to impose on the context of their experiments through rigorous laboratory procedures, at best ensuring that the context of observed behavior is the same for all subjects. In this view context is the stimulus array that the experimenter presents to the subject. Of course, the fact that the behavior is observed in a laboratory that itself presents unique conditions of context has long been recognized, and among developmental psychologists in particular there has been an effort in recent years to observe behavior in settings that more closely approach those of the natural environment.

The move to observe behavior in naturalistic settings is generally recognized as increasing ecological validity and thus the generalizability of the conclusions one can draw (see McCall, 1977; see also Cole, Hood, & McDermott, 1982). Why does behavior change when it moves into the laboratory? Aside from such obvious characteristics as impoverished stimulus conditions (ensuring attention to the experimenter's array), notions such as familiarity, expectations, anxiety, and so on are usually invoked. These notions imply an interaction between the subject's internal state and external conditions. That is, it is not external conditions alone that determine behavior but the way that the subject views those conditions, based on attitudes derived from some prior experience. In other words, the subject contributes subjective context to the situation over and above the objective setting arranged by the experimenter. Extrapolating to the problem at hand, the child's interpretation of a situation determines what meaning will be attributed to language used within it. Thus, understanding the child's representation of contexts is essential to understanding the development of meaning.

A widely accepted position, at least since de Laguna (1927/1963), claims that in the development of language, forms are at first embedded in a specific context and later become ''decontexted'' and available for general use. (Variations on this theme have been put forth by Bates [1979], Bloom [1973], and Werner and Kaplan [1963], among others.) The most extreme form of decontextedness obtains in the study of language as an object, for example, in the study of linguistics. It is frequently assumed in the study of child language that the child does not have complete control of a form unless it is fully decontexted. Experiments in the area of semantic development usually make this assumption either explicitly or implicitly. There are two points to be made with respect to this theoretical position. First, if understanding begins and develops within specific contexts, it is misleading to base assessments of understanding solely on performance in presumably decontexted situations. Situational embeddedness may support understanding of a term before that term can be applied generally (Carni & French, 1984). Second, it is important to recognize that no situation is without context. Context varies from providing strong support from the environment for the child's interpretation of a meaning to providing no support, throwing the child on his or her own resources for constructing a meaning. Meaning does not then become decontexted so much as extendable across contexts that provide greater or less support for interpretation. Thus, we might speak of meaning as becoming transcontexted, rather than decontexted.

The move toward generality of contexts is important to the description put forth here, which envisions development from reference to concept to semantic system, each move requiring a further abstraction from the real world. In order to understand the context-boundedness of early meaning, we need to examine the concept of context in greater detail. We begin with an examination of the layers of external or objective context and then consider how they may be represented internally as subjective context.

Objective Context

Objective context consists of multiple layers that partially embed one another. These layers can be independently described, but they are never experienced independently. For the child (or the adult), they define any experienced situation.

Physical Context

The physical environment of the child's life defines many of the things to be talked about and the ways in which they are discussed. The larger physical context includes the geographical setting (island, mountain, desert, and so on) and the architecture imposed upon it (in country, city, or suburb, for example). The more immediate physical context includes places in which the child's activity normally takes place, such as a kitchen or playroom in a suburban American home. The places that the child comes to understand may provide a secure base within which both talk and action can safely proceed and be successfully interpreted. Important to this immediate context are the objects accessible to the child, their relations to self and others, and their known functions.

Children usually begin to learn names for familiar objects rather than novel ones, not surprisingly. However, general understanding of object relations does not appear to be affected by familiarity. In a series of (unpublished) studies concerned with conditions affecting the successful solution of the standard object search problem by infants from 9 to 12 months, Nelson and Kessen found that using familiar or nonfamiliar toys had no effect. Further, children under 1 year do not even notice when one object is substituted for another hidden object (Le Compte & Gratch, 1972), and children between 1 and 2 years seem far more content than older children to substitute one similar object for another. For example, one 15-month-old child I observed watched a ball he was playing with roll under a chair and, rather than retrieve it when asked to "get the ball," he toddled to his toy chest and removed a different ball, then proceeded with the game. (Of course, this general acceptance of substitutability does not apply to *transitional objects* such as a security blanket or favorite stuffed animal.)

Children of this age do appear, however, to be affected by the familiarity of places (Acredolo, 1979). In the same series of studies involving the object search task, Nelson and Kessen contrasted performance in the lab and in the home and found significant differences favoring the home. Thus, unlike objects, places represent specific contexts, and a strange place can be disruptive to talk as well as action, as child psychologists have long concluded. To understand these effects we need to understand the meaning of the strange place for the child.

Cultural Context

At least partially determining and also partially determined by (thus interpenetrating) physical context is the cultural context of learning language. The particular culture in which the child is embedded determines to some degree the physical environment (rain forest or city street) and to a large degree the physical objects the child encounters (hoes and spades, intercoms and computers), as well as the type of social and linguistic interactions considered reasonable or normal both within the family and outside it. The cultural practices prescribed for child care among different social groups have special importance with regard to language and cognitive skills. In American homes across a wide spectrum of socioeconomic classes, babies are given toys to play with from birth. They are frequently left alone in playpens, cribs, chairs, or rooms in the expectation that they will explore spaces and objects. This is not true in many cultures where infants are expected to spend most of the first year sleeping or nursing and are continuously carried on their mother's hip or back or left in a cot in a bare room. While some examination of these differences has been carried out (e.g., Ainsworth & Bell, 1974; Kagan & Klein, 1973; Kessen, 1975; Leiderman, Tulkin, & Rosenfeld, 1977; Mundy-Castle, 1980), a full comparison of the possible variations in developmental patterns is far from complete, and the analysis of their effects on the conditions of language use has only begun (e.g., Schiefflin, 1979).

Although some characteristics are common across our culture (the provision of toys and television sets, for example), subcultural groups within complex societies such as those of the Western world provide their own variations on cultural practices, as has been widely documented by sociologists and anthropologists. Thus, children growing up in the apartment of a Puerto Rican family in upper Manhattan are likely to acquire cultural skills and beliefs that are very different from those acquired by the children of a hog farmer in Iowa of Northern European Protestant descent. That the uses of language to and among the children in each case may be quite different should not be surprising. Of course, these variations may not affect the structural aspects of the meaning systems acquired in each environment. On the other hand, this is a question whose answer cannot be prejudged. For example, the structure of kinship systems varies among different subcultures in the United States, with the definition of "cousin" being based on different relationships depending upon the cultural background of the informants (Kay, 1976).

Equally important to the consideration of the cultural context are the symbolic structures of a culture. For example, in some societies rituals and taboos associated with food—what can be eaten under what conditions and with whom—are very important, while all-encompassing taxonomic categories such as food or animals are not significant (e.g., Douglas, 1978). The meaning structure of a given language—a version of which the child must eventually construct internally—is a symbolic cultural product. In his comprehensive survey of linguistic semantics, Lyons (1977) emphasized the importance of this point in the following terms:

> The denotation of most lexemes [is not] determined solely, or even principally, by the physical properties of their denotata. Much more important seems to be the role or function of the objects, properties, activities, processes and events in the life and culture of the society using the language. Until we have a satisfactory theory of culture . . . it is idle to speculate further about the possibility of constructing anything more than a rather ad hoc practical account of the denotation of lexemes. (p. 210)

The cultural specificity and determinism of the meaning system that the child must internalize precludes attributing any particular type of relational system (such as a hierarchical category system) as an acultural given (cf. Berlin, 1978). This is not to say, however, that universal principles of construction might not apply. The child must rely on some method of relating words to the reality of experience. What these methods are is an essential part of the problem to be addressed here. In any event, while the present discussion is not meant to be culture-specific, it is based upon data drawn primarily from middle-class American children, and this fact and its limitations must be acknowledged.

Social Context

Within the culture the social context that the child encounters and becomes part of may vary between and within families. The structure of a family (presence or absence of father or mother; number, order, sex, and age of siblings; presence of grandparents, aunts, uncles, or cousins) partially determines what kinds of interactions take place. Parental educational and economic status, beliefs about children and child rearing, knowledge and experience with young children, and personality all interact to produce a particular social complex that varies for each child.

For every child, there are also variations in the type of social interactions experienced, depending upon the situation. Being together alone with mother playing with toys, looking at books, or having lunch are very different contexts for the child than are family dinners, trips to the store, or visits with friends, where the child is not the focus (or not the sole focus) of attention, and where different behavioral expectations apply. In order to acquire meaning that spans these different social contexts, the child must be able to transfer the specific contexted meaning of words and sentences to a general system. The silence of the young child in strange surroundings cannot be explained away as simple shyness but must be understood as indicative of the problem that context-bound meaning presents. Language use requires shared context on the part of both partners, and the child must establish familiarity with a variety of different situations in order to achieve sharing status. To accomplish this the child must construct a system of subjective context that can be used to interpret even unfamiliar social situations. A part of this system must be a representation of the social roles that people may play in order that the child may participate appropriately in different situations. For example, talking to teachers requires different discourse rules than does talking to peers. In general, one makes different assumptions about the nature of shared or implicit meanings depending upon the people to whom one talks.

An extreme pole of the social-context dimension is the absence of social partners when the child is alone and talking only to itself. This situation has begun to receive some attention from child-language researchers. There is every indication that the child's speech in these cases differs from social speech (de Forest, 1984; Kuczaj, 1983). Under these conditions the child must supply a subjective social context that is missing from the objective situation (see Nelson, 1984a, and the description to follow).

Activity Context

The physical, cultural, and social contexts together constitute the general framework of the child's world, within which all interaction takes place. Any given interaction, whether it involves language or not, is further defined by the context of the activity within which it is situated. Common child-oriented activities in our culture include caretaking routines such as bathing and eating meals as well as playing games or looking at books. Children also participate in adult-oriented activities such as shopping, visiting friends and relatives, and dining out. The centrality of the child in the activity, the goal of the activity, the number of people involved in the activity and their organization in terms of roles, and the location of the activity are all important variables in defining the activity context. Activity context so defined very often determines not only what behavior can be expected but also what will be said and by whom. Of course, some activities are more determining in this respect than others. For example, Ninio and Bruner's (1978) analysis of a "book reading" routine engaged in by a mother and her 1½-year-old child showed that what is said by both partners is almost completely predictable. On the other hand, in the context of a family dinner, conversation may range quite freely around a number of topics, and the child may or may not be required to participate. Of course, even in this situation certain topics may be recurrent, others may be tabooed, and certain routines of etiquette may be required (see Berko-Gleason's 1978 account of "please" and "thank you"). That is, activities may range from completely predictable to highly variable in terms of the child's permissible role.

Within the general theoretical account that claims that language moves from highly contexted to decontexted over the course of development, the activity level of context appears to be the most relevant one. Meanings that are established in one activity context may not be readily transferrable at first to a different context, precisely because the context itself defines the meaning. In the present view the meaning for the child may be carried in the representation of the activity itself. This thesis will be presented more precisely in the discussion of subjective contextualizing.

Agenda Context

Embedded within the activity context we can identify a level that has no agreed-upon label and that for lack of a better one we can call the agenda.[2] The agenda may shift within the same activity frame and thus needs to be given its own identity. Some agendas may be aesthetic appreciation, expression of affection, game playing, pretense, didactic lessons, testing, pragmatic routines, or problem solving. This list is not meant to be exhaustive but only suggestive of the nature of this type of context. While young children are not exposed to all of these, they clearly experience a number of different agenda contexts. They appear to be easily adaptable to shifts from game playing or pretense to pragmatic concerns and back again, although this facility has received little or no systematic study. Obviously, the meaning that one imputes to a given utterance in different agenda contexts may be quite different. The child's ability to interpret the same utterance in different ways depending upon the established agenda has not, however, been studied.

An important consideration in the study of the agenda context is that the child's agenda may be different from the adult's (this may be true of adult talk as well on some occasions). For example, at the dinner table the child's agenda may be game playing, while the adult's is pragmatic activity accomplishment. Different agendas have the potential for leading to misunderstandings and conflicts and the resultant disruption of shared meaning.

Affective Context

Little has been studied or even conjectured about the affective context of early language use. Most investigators have emphasized the positive affect involved in mother–child interactions, but certainly there are exceptions to this happy picture. Many of the interactions I recorded in my longitudinal study (Nelson, 1973b) were overladen with anxiety about the child's behavior and general progress, and these were certainly not unique. Graves and Glick's (1978) study of mothers in observed and "unobserved" contexts recorded interactions that were at least implicitly punitive and rejecting. Child-abusing mothers and drug-abusing mothers have been observed engaging in highly negative affect-laden interactions where the child's behavior was not the primary eliciting factor.

It may be that a general model of meaning should not be required to account for extremes of the latter kind. However, there is no reason to suppose that "normal" children do not experience a range of affect-laden messages when observers are not present with their tape recorders.

How these messages affect the child's interpretation of language is an open question. While models of language acquisition built explicitly on assumptions of positive and negative reinforcement are no longer acceptable, the possible influence of the affective context on the child's interpretation of meaning cannot be discounted. Many studies have indicated that optimal language and cognitive development takes place in an atmosphere of positive acceptance of the child's interests and activities (Clarke-Stewart, 1973; Nelson, 1973b; Ramey, Farran, Campbell, & Finkelstein, 1978). Theorists should be alert to identify on a micro level what this implies about the affective context of interaction and the interpretation of meaning.

Communicative Act Context

On a more micro level, the meaning of an utterance or of a word may vary depending upon whether it is conveyed in the functional context of a request for information or action or a statement of fact. Such variations have been studied in the framework of speech acts (Searle, 1969) and communicative acts (Dore, 1975, 1978). Shatz (1978a, 1983) demonstrated that even 2-year-olds can interpret indirect directives (such as "can you build a tower of blocks?") as requests for action rather than information. The modal "can" in this statement is correctly interpreted by the child not as an inquiry about ability but as a directive to perform. As Allen (1983) demonstrated, whether or not this interpretation will be given depends upon a variety of context cues to which even 2-year-old children are sensitive. How such sensitivity is acquired is a question that has not yet been addressed.

Action Context

The action that the child and others are engaged in at the time of an utterance is often used by researchers to interpret the meaning of the child's utterance. Implicit in this method of *rich analysis* (Bloom, 1970) is the assumption that what is said is part of a behavioral complex that includes action as well as speech. Similarly, it is assumed that the child may use the mother's actions (gestures) to interpret her meaning, and likewise that the mother uses the child's gestures to interpret his or her meaning. Reliance on gestures decreases as children gain command of the language (Bretherton, McNew, Snyder, & Bates, 1981), and it may be that children gain less information from the mother's gestures than theory suggests (Shatz, 1983). Nonetheless, the action that accompanies an utterance often provides the means by which it can be interpreted, and adult's speech as well as children's continues to be accompanied by nonverbal gestures (including facial expressions) that provide essential contextual cues for understanding. It is, of course, a legitimate question to ask whether children learn to interpret language through action cues or action through language, or a bit of both.

Specific Linguistic Context

The impact on meaning of the linguistic context of an utterance or a dialogic interchange ranges from the role of a word in a sentence construction (as in the difference between "Throw the ball" and "Where is the ball?") to the meaning implied for a novel word in an otherwise understood utterance to the relational meaning encoded in different constructions (e.g., "John kissed Mary" versus "John was kissed by Mary") to abstract notions such as the anaphoric reference of pronouns (e.g., "Mary kissed John then [he/she] ran away"). In longer discourse such as conversations and stories, linguistic context extends over long sequences and includes notions of cohesion as well as topic.

The linguistic context of first meanings depends upon how mothers (and others who take the speaker's role with the child) frame their utterances. Considerable research has shown that even very young preverbal children are often capable of discerning differences between some types of linguistic context, for example, the different implications of "ball" in the utterances "Throw the ball" and "Where's the ball?" (see Benedict, 1976, and later examples). More advanced speakers can interpret novel words in otherwise familiar contexts and acquire new meanings in this way. The study of the acquisition of meaning within linguistic contexts, however, is a neglected one. Werner and Kaplan (1963) explored this topic, but their study had serious flaws in that the contexts provided were poorly defined and unrelated to one another. The area deserves a more systematic investigation. In contrast, we know quite a bit about how children interpret the same familiar word in different linguistic contexts, for example, the agent–patient relationship in active–passive sentences (Bever, 1970; Strohner & Nelson, 1974).

In summary, the context of language use met by the child is a complex of interrelated layers that may be mutually supportive of meaning but may also allow for conflicting interpretations. Thus (contra Wexler, 1982), a given utterance is unlikely to be easily interpretable solely through decoding its context. This complex of contextual relationships is schematized in Figure 2.1, which is designed to illustrate the possible embedding layers. In addition, the objective context must be interpreted through a representational system that is itself in the process of development. This is the other side of the establishment of the context

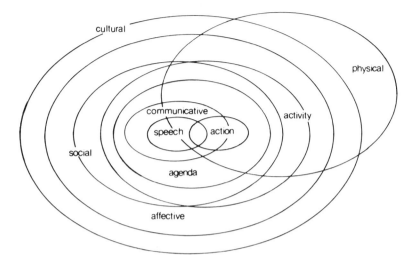

FIGURE 2.1   Embedded layers of context.

of early meanings, the child's contribution to understanding situations and their embedded talk. Some speculations about some of the same dimensions that we have observed in terms of objective context as they may be represented internally and enter into the child's interpretation of language are presented in the following section.

Subjective Context

In any given situation the child manifests an affective attitude, which may very little to do with the adult's understanding of the situation, but which may strongly affect the interpretation of the interaction. As noted in the previous section, the child has an agenda that may match or may conflict with the adult's agenda for the same situation. In the first case this may facilitate understanding; in the second it may inhibit it. The child also brings certain cognitive abilities and skills to the situation, especially including problem-solving abilities that may be activated in the effort to make sense of an otherwise incomprehensible situation. Much of the discussion of nonlinguistic strategies that children employ in experimental tasks concerns efforts that children make to respond appropriately to demands that lack familiar context and therefore call upon problem-solving skills.

Of course, the linguistic knowledge that the child has available constitutes a very important component of the context of the interaction. A child who does not understand grammatical relations and who produces only a few words will be very limited in interpreting and contributing to the verbal exchange. A child who has an extensive vocabulary can take part even before achieving control of the grammatical system. A child still using only single words can utilize many of the basic functions of language, including referring to absent objects, expressing needs, and regulating the actions of others. Up to a certain point in the development of vocabulary, interpreting meaning is primarily a problem for the adult, who must guess at the intent of the expression used by the child. The adult's interpretation in a situation can result in the child's reformulation of the meaning of that expression. Later, when the lexicon has acquired its own systematic character, it may resist this sort of easy reformulation.

Of particular importance to the interpretation of meaning in a given situation is the *cognitive context* provided by the child's representation of that situation. This is the medium of the contribution of world knowledge to the construction of meanings. Prior to the acquisition of any language forms, the child interprets the behaviors of others and responds to them, that is, takes a part in interactions involving reciprocity (Bruner, 1975a, 1975b). This fact implies an internal model of the social world that serves to interpret the meanings of words as well as gestures. What we need, therefore, is an adequate description of the nature of such mental models in order to see how the child can begin to interpret and to use language within them.

Positing an internal model of reality implies an organized level of mental representation in the child beginning to use language. In the view set forth here representation plays a crucial role in both early cognitive and linguistic development, and it is assumed that there is a continuity in representation from infancy to childhood, although what gets represented, how it is represented, and how accessible it is to conscious, deliberate usage may change over time. (See Mandler, 1983, for a more extended discussion of these issues.)

It is also relevant here to bring out the distinction Campbell (1979) makes between cryptic (unavailable to awareness) and phenic levels of representation. In his words, "From the point of view of the experiencing subject: what is evident to the subject is phenic, what is hidden is cryptic" (Campbell, 1979, p. 420f). The overt behaviors that we may observe, both linguistic and nonlinguistic, may be generated by covert processes operating on cryptic representations to produce phenic representations that may be made public through language. Since all we observe are these public manifestations, we cannot make claims about the *form* of the cryptic substrata, although we may speculate on its structure (see Anderson, 1978, on this issue). In particular, when I suggest, on the basis of evidence from the child's early language, that the representation of events at this period has certain characteristics, I recognize that this suggestion is open to challenge. Nonetheless, this suggestion is put forward to account for the available data; challenges to it should offer either a better account or contradictory data. Moreover, when my colleagues and I conclude that young children's scripts are based on well-structured and articulated event representations, we make no claims about the form these possibly cryptic event representations take but only about the structural characteristics they must have.

Cognitive Context: The Child's Model of Reality

The model to be proposed must incorporate both social and physical reality. It must, in fact, organize from the point of view of the young child all those layers of objective context outlined earlier. Social experiences have certain characteristics that the purely physical world does not display, and these must be part of the representation (see Gelman & Spelke, 1981; Glick, 1978; and Kessen & Nelson, 1978). In comparison with most nonsocial objects, people are dynamically more varied, less predictable, less rigid, and produce more stimulus dimensions. People do not appear to obey the same physical laws that inanimate objects do. They engage in independent motion. They can disappear at one place and reappear at another. They produce interesting sounds of a wide variety. They can change the nature of other objects with tools, for example, they can cut things in two and they can cook food. All biological organisms absorb things and excrete other things.

In short, the personal and social world is inherently complex and interactive. More importantly, human action is intentional and thus demands interpretation. Thus, while it is possible to study object knowledge in terms of static, decontexted elements, it is not possible to study social or event knowledge in these terms, because what is an element in a social system depends upon the meaning it has in that system. Rather, it is necessary to consider ongoing relations such as people interacting with other people, acting on objects, or reacting to events. Further, these relational activities take place through time and space. If the child acquires knowledge of them, their characteristics must be integrated over time into a whole representation. This is true no matter what size event we consider, whether the single act of giving or taking objects to and from another or an extended activity such as taking a bath or visiting a friend.

Most studies of perception and cognition in the first year of life have focused on the child's perception, memory, and categorization of discrete forms (or phonemes or colors) (see Chapter 3; for exceptions see Gibson, Owsley, & Johnston 1978; and Spelke, 1982). From these studies we know that babies can form categories of faces, for example, as early as 4 months of age and can remember a particular face for as long as two weeks at the same age. However, these studies have revealed little about the infant's understanding of the social world.

It is not only research with infants that has been concentrated on static objects and relations between objects, or the mental representation of these. Virtually all research in cognitive development, especially in the Piagetian tradition and in adult cognition, has shared this focus. Moreover, traditional theories of cognitive organization have proposed representational schemes relating like elements in linear fashion at different levels of a hierarchy, specified in terms of features or attributes that give rise to coordinate, subordinate, and superordinate relations in taxonomic or paradigmatic schemes (Miller, 1967). While such analytic models may describe well certain aspects of knowledge, it has become clear that they cannot account for many kinds of natural knowledge systems, including those of the social world. Knowledge of such things as spatial layouts, story structures, games, and everyday routines appears not to be taxonomic in any sense but rather *schematic*, relating diverse elements in a holistic structure by means of different types of relationships. Schema structures are more adaptable to dynamic models than are hierarchical structures and thus are more adaptable to cognitive models of the social world.

A particular form of this type of representational model, that fits reasonably well to the young child's understanding of events in the world, incorporating many aspects of social context, is the situational script as a general event representation (Nelson, 1978a; Nelson & Gruendel, 1981; Schank & Abelson, 1977). This model can be useful in describing how real-world knowledge and language fit together and develop as interlocking systems.

Characteristics of Shemas

In general, a schema specifies essential elements in spatial, temporal, or causal relations to one another as well as elements that may be optional. Some elements may be specified in terms of default values that may fulfill a certain function when specific values are not required. For example, a living room schema specifies essentially four walls, a door, and windows (regulated in terms of angles, parallel planes, and so on). It may have as an optional value a fireplace and may specify default values in terms of furniture such as a sofa, chairs, lamps, and a rug. However, if the room is unoccupied, as in a house for sale, these optional values may remain unfilled without destroying the living room schema.

Rumelhart and Ortony (1977) identified four essential features of schemas:

1. They have variables. As in the living room example, there may be both obligatory and optional variables to be filled in, and default values may be specified for each.
2. Schemas may embed within one another. Just as we have a house schema, we have a living room schema, and we also may have a sofa schema, specifying parts in relation to each other.
3. Schemas are generic concepts that vary in their level of abstraction. The living room schema can be seen to be generic (it applies to any and not to any specific living room), but thus far we have not considered different levels of abstraction. It is clear, however, even within the spatial framework we have been using, that the schema for room is necessarily more abstract than that for living room, and it will become clear later that this is a powerful characteristic of schemas of different types.
4. Schemas represent knowledge rather than definitions. They are used to characterize what we know—what is generally true as well as what is only occasionally true.

This discussion of schemas has been in terms of static structures, exemplified by the spatial schema of a living room. Its usefulness for understanding the child's representation of reality, however, depends upon its capability of being extended to structures that are composed in terms of temporal and causal relations as well as spatial ones.[3]

The term "schema" as used here is essentially representational. In contrast to Piaget's (1970) use of the term, it need not represent only the subject's own activities, although it may include them. For example, a 1-year-old may give good evidence of having a "bath schema" (or script) as evidenced by her anticipation of the sequence of bath activities carried out in partnership with the mother. But the child may also have a representation of car driving in which she does not actively participate (see Church, 1966; and Nelson, 1978a).

It is important to note that no position is being taken as to the mode of the schematic representation, whether it is in terms of an image or propositions or is more abstract than either. This problem is not essential to the main argument here. It should also be stressed that the representational schema does not bear any isomorphic relation to real-world objects and events. There is no implication that a representation is a copy of reality; rather, it is a model of experience, and each person's experience of a situation or event will be different. This, of course, applies particularly to the young child whose experience of an event is limited by both knowledge and prior experience.

Event Representations

Scripts (Nelson, 1978a; Schank & Abelson, 1977) are a variation on the schema notion, in this case a schema specifying a sequence of actions related temporally and causally. Because the representation of events plays a central role in the theory of conceptual and semantic development proposed here it will be examined in some detail.

A script is a general event representation derived from and applied to social contexts. Scripts are built up as a person participates in (or in other ways gains knowledge of, for example, through television) social routines. As script knowledge develops, the regularity of the routine projects meaning onto the parts of the whole and, at the same time, regularity invokes necessity: what is becomes what ought to be (see Nelson, 1981b).

According to the Schank and Abelson (1977) model, the script is basically an ordered sequence of actions appropriate to a particular spatial–temporal context, organized around a goal. The script is made up of slots and requirements on what can fill these slots. That is, the script specifies roles and props and defines obligatory and optional actions by actors who fill reciprocal roles. For each slot there are default values that are assumed if the person, object, or action is not specified when the script is instantiated in a particular context. For example, in the prototypical restaurant script a waiter or waitress is assumed, as are a menu, food, a bill, and a tip. Persons hearing a story about a restaurant can readily fill in these items from their general script knowledge.

Before considering whether and what kind of event representations children might have before learning to talk, we need to distinguish between weak and strong scripts and between scripts and scenes (Abelson, 1981). According to Abelson a weak script prescribes what objects, roles, and component events can be expected in a situation but does not prescribe the precise sequence of events, usually because these are inherently variable as, for example, in choosing food items in a grocery store (although the layout of any particular store usually defines the order of choice). A strong script, however, also prescribes the sequence of events, usually because there is a causal dependency among them. For example, in a restaurant one must order before the food is served and the food must be served before one can eat. Order in a strong script may, however, be simply conventional. For example, in an American meal soup comes at the beginning, while in a Chinese meal it traditionally comes at the end. Although not causally based, each such conventional order also constitutes a strong script.

What is sequenced in a script are its *scenes*. A scene cannot be precisely defined anymore than can a script, but roughly it may be said to be a coherent series of actions that take place in a single setting, involving the same goal, people, and objects. Thus, if any of the components—goal, place, people, or objects—change, the scene changes. In a restaurant ordering, eating soup, the main course, and dessert, and paying the bill would all be separate scenes because they involve different objects.

While the psychological reality of script structures has been demonstrated for adults (Bower, Black, & Turner, 1979; Graesser, Woll, Kowalski, & Smith, 1980), it may be questioned whether young children also have event representations in scriptlike form. Certainly preschoolers appear to find it natural to report their knowledge of everyday activities in a form remarkably similar to the script format (see Nelson, 1978a; Nelson & Gruendel, 1981; Nelson, Fivush, Hudson, & Lucariello, 1983). From the reports of a large number of children at one day-care center, for example, we abstracted the common events of a "lunch at the day-care center" script as shown in Figure 2.2.

The events at the left-most side in this figure were those most frequently mentioned. These appear to be the scenes of the lunch script. They are temporally and causally linked and involve changes primarily in location (L) or subgoal (G). Objects (O) and people (P) are less scene-specific.

We know from our script studies that children as young as three know a great deal about the activities they participate in and can articulate that knowledge. We also know that their script knowledge influences their memory for stories and personal experiences. What about the 1-year-old who has not yet acquired language? What evidence is there for the suggestion that general event representations are the conceptual foundations onto which language is first mapped?

If children understand the ongoing activities of their world such that they can take appropriate roles within them, they must have formed a representation of these activities. Evidence for such representation can be found in the child's *anticipation* of the next step in a sequence (examples of such anticipation are given in later sections of this chapter) and in response to statements such as "time for lunch" that produce crawling to the highchair in the kitchen. In order to participate appropriately in social activities, young children *must* represent their own

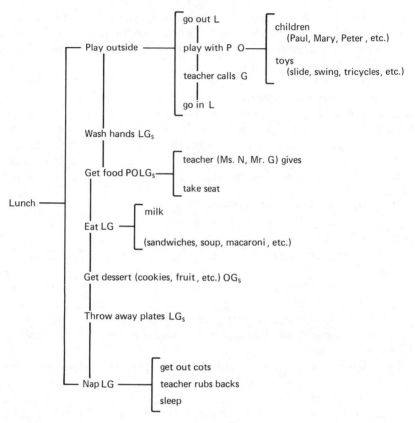

FIGURE 2.2   Script for lunch at the day-care center. L, location; P, people; O, object; G, goal; G$_s$, subgoal.

roles and the roles of others and be able to reciprocate the actions of others with appropriate actions of their own. That is, event representations must be built up to guide interactions in recurrent situations. This is not to claim that the 1-year-old child can think *about* these representations; the first event representations may guide action only, that is, they may be cryptic.

The present proposal is that the child's earliest event representation or script includes action schemes such as throwing, banging, and much more: objects, persons and person roles, and sequences of actions appropriate to a specific scene. In other words, it includes the specific social and cultural components essential to carrying through a particular activity. It embeds in one cognitive structure many of the contextual layers outlined above.

The social world is not static; its presentations are extended in time. In order to represent these presentations, therefore, the child must "chunk" experiences. The claim is not that the child strings together discrete percepts into an integrated whole.[4] On the contrary, the claim is that aspects of the experience are represented wholistically; for example, feeding, bathing, and going for a walk are known as whole events. While the parts are not indiscriminable, they are indissociable. That is, the child recognizes that getting out a coat is a part of the whole walk sequence and expects the rest of the sequence to be carried through; indeed, the child is upset if it is not.[5]

In brief, the proposal here is that the 1-year-old child's mental representations are largely in the form of such scripts for familiar events, involving roles that people play and objects that they interact with in the course of the activity. These are general representations of activities that have occurred more than once rather than collections of particular experiences. The event representation provides the *cognitive context* of the situation; it contains all of the elements of context outlined earlier to which the infant is sensitive. It stands, moreover, between the perceptual representation (or image) of a specific experience and the individual concept of the elements that enter into it. It is derived from the former and is the source of the latter. Thus, it is neither perceptual nor conceptual but serves as an interface between the two and, importantly, as a representation of different aspects of reality. This will be discussed further in Chapter 7.

At this point in our understanding of event representations, it is not clear whether there is a limit on the size of the young child's scripts or whether larger scripts are constructed from smaller ones.[6] The present hypothesis is that the initial event representation is represented as an unanalyzed whole on the basis of the child's participation in (or observation of) an activity, such as eating lunch. The boundaries of the event are assumed to be defined in terms of spatial locations. Subsequently, presumably with the aid of another who names or otherwise identifies parts of the event, the event representation is analyzed into differentiable (and nameable) components. These components may then be reconstructed into the same or different whole events, in play (Bretherton *et al.*, 1981), in language, and through anticipation or action in real life.

It might be noted here that the whole event as a basic unit in the child's initial cognitive representations was implicit in my original model (Nelson, 1974) of the functional core concept (see Chapter 3), in which objects were said to be represented in terms of the relations—primarily actions and reactions—into which they entered. The concept as outlined there was essentially an event representation or, rather, the abstraction of relationships across a number of different scripts. The present description can be viewed as a simple extension of that model; this point will be made explicit in Chapter 3.

It is important to note that events and event representations come in different sizes. The child's throwing of a ball is an event (it is also an action scheme); the reciprocal game of rolling a ball back and forth to another is also an event. The latter can be considered a script because it involves roles that people play, in this case the interchangeable and reciprocal roles of rolling and catching; actions that in fact define the roles and are sequentially and causally related; and an object, ideally a slot for a class of objects that can take different particular objects as instances. (Recall the example of the child who readily substitutes one ball for another.) But ball-rolling is still a small and simple script. Larger scripts that may be mentally represented include meal-eating, bed-going, dressing, and outings of various kinds. We don't know at the present time how large or small a child's scripts typically are at the age of a year, or how many scripts a child of this age may have. (Some illustrations of scripts in action from 1-year-old children will be presented in later sections of this chapter.)

Let me emphasize at this point that the proposal is that at first events themselves are represented as wholes, not as part constructions. That is, playing ball is an *activity*. Adult observers can specify its parts—its roles, props, and so on—but for the child there is no evidence that these are separable, at least initially. Ball implies throwing as book implies reading (or chewing) and cup implies drinking. The child's actions on these objects indicate their place in the appropriate scripts.

Conceptualizing the parts of the script as separate entities—that is, reifying objects, actions, and properties in order to treat them as mental units that can be manipulated (Chapter 3)—requires analyzing the original script into its component parts and the relations between them. This is a development that takes place during the early language development period over the second year.

Let me summarize this tentative proposal and give some rough estimates of ages as indicators of when these developments take place. In later infancy children form global representations of events in which they take part. These are wholes whose parts are initially embedded within them and are not decontextualizable. Over a period of several months from sometime before the first birthday until sometime around the middle of the second year, children partition their scripts, forming separate concepts of objects, people, and actions. (These concepts will, of course, contain as important components the relationships represented in the scripts from which they were disembedded.) During this time most children learn to use some basic language within scripts and may also learn to use words to refer to concepts that have been formed. In the second half of the second year, most children take the enormous step forward of mental manipulation of concepts: they learn to recombine them into new formulations. This step is accompanied by the increased symbolization of concepts in words, the partitioning of new concepts to fit words, and the formation of rules for recombining words into relational statements. This formulation enables the further analysis of how the object and social worlds embed each other and how the child's language in use determines the development of a meaning system.

Up to this point we have considered in a general way the representational model that the child uses to interpret the context of talk. At this point some examples of contextualized language and thought of the 1-year-old will help to illustrate how this model may work.

Contexted Talk

The context of talk is so multilayered and so dependent itself upon interpretation that only bits of it can be studied systematically. Alternatively, we can use the insights provided by the analysis above to examine samples of children's early language use to gain a feeling for how objective and subjective context work in particular instances. I will present here some sample protocols that illustrate both the richness and the sparseness of the interpretive context. (The richness lies in the context; the sparseness lies in the clues to the interpretation.) These samples come from studies that have been carried out by me or by students and former students of mine over the past decade and a half. Each is provocative in different ways although, of course, they do not provide strong evidence for any particular conclusions. I present them for their illustrative and heuristic value with respect to the points considered here.

Billy

The first set of examples is from a child, whom I will call Billy, whose development I followed from the age of 8 months to 2 years. I visited this child, sometimes with an assistant, each week over the first 6 months and then biweekly for approximately 1½ hours at each visit, including a play period and lunch each time. The focus of the study was on the relation between language development and other cognitive developments. It was undertaken as a hypothesis-generating pilot study. (Unfortunately, because Billy was unusually slow in acquiring productive language, its usefulness in this respect was somewhat diminished.)

The social–cultural world in which Billy was enmeshed was relatively complex. He was a first-born child, but both parents came from large families who lived in the area and with whom they spent a good deal of time. His home was a well-kept-up Victorian mansion with innumerable rooms arranged in a complex maze of patterns. His early development was normal and both his social and object schemes appeared well developed by 9 months. By 10½ months he had a recognition vocabulary of about 20 words as reported by his mother and tested in observation sessions. They included some object terms as well as places ("toys" for a cabinet where toys are kept), routines (when mother said "lunchtime" he crawled to a highchair in the kitchen), and procedures (responding differentially to "Where's the ball?" and "Throw ball").

Several object-hiding tests were administered in the early months with varying success. Although he solved the Stage IV "hide at A then B" problem[7] at 10 months, at 11 months he failed to find an object hidden under two screens, and at 12 months he failed the $A\overline{B}$ test when a small box was used for hiding. These results suggested an interdependence of complex physical and social knowledge and language that was further revealed in a hiding test administered at 11 months. In this test his own play space served as the testing space, the hiding places being one of 7 doors (see Figure 2.3). Four doors (back hall, diaper room, front hall, and kitchen) were open as was customary. The storeroom, laundry, and closet doors were closed. The following was recorded immediately after the session, summarizing from detailed notes recorded by the assistant (L):

> The first sequence was performed with M [Mother]. While B [Billy] sat near the kitchen, she walked into the laundry room (1) and remained there with the door closed for 30″ [seconds]. K and L successfully distracted B, who showed no signs of upset. At the end of 30″ K asked, "Where is Mommy?" B crawled directly to the laundry room. A second trial followed the same format. On this trial, B tried to crawl after M, who disappeared into the diaper room (4), but K stopped him, distracted him for 30″, and then asked, "Where's Mommy?" He crawled to the front corridor doorway (5), then turned to the diaper room and found her inside.

Two similar trials with K hiding followed, one successful, one not. Next:

> K then took the new red clutch ball (not allowing him to touch it first, but only to look and hear it) into the laundry room (1). After 30″ L asked, "Where's the ball?" He picked up his own ball, which was in sight. L hid his ball behind her, asked, "Where's the ball?" He crawled directly to the laundry

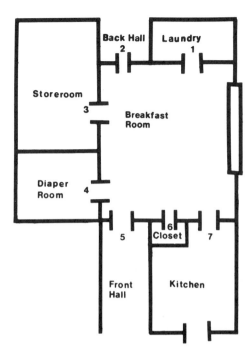

FIGURE 2.3   Billie's play space.

room door. After letting him have the ball for a moment, K took the new ball again into the storeroom (3). A 1-minute delay followed during which he played ring and stick with L and M. M then asked, "Where's the ball?" and B responded by immediately crawling to the store room. Approximately 5 minutes later, a last trial was given. This time, K took the clutch ball to the store room (3) and L took the telephone to the diaper room (4) while M played with B. After 30″ M asked, "Where's the ball?" B moved directly to the store room. After getting the ball M and K asked, "Where's the telephone?" B was distracted by the ball and needed approximately 6 repetitions of the phrase and approximately 30″ longer but then responded by moving directly from his position near the window to the diaper room to find L and the telephone.

My commentary at the time was:

This sequence demonstrates B's remarkable facility to respond to language discriminatively and his memory for objects and places, both social (mother) and nonsocial, familiar (telephone) and nonfamiliar (ball), place in which people and toys are often or frequently found (diaper room and kitchen) and those in which they are not (store room and laundry room and both corridors and closet). The delay through 1 minute and the discrimination of two objects are longer and more complex than have been previously reported at this age and seem to conflict with Piaget's notions of object permanence, represen-

tation, and image at this age. Unless B is in a very extreme advanced stage
of development.

As was subsequently shown, the last explanation was not the case,
and although a good deal of research has recently revealed greater representational capacity at 11–13 months than previously attributed, this
performance nonetheless appears to be unusual. The score of 7 out of
8 successes after delays of 30″ and longer is quite remarkable at this age
(11 months). The reasons for success seem clear enough: Billy was operating in a situation where he had a well-established schema for all the
components and their relationships. We can therefore assume that this
representational schema could be called up to aid in memory. Moreover,
he was used to interacting with people in ways that were quite similar
to this game. He had frequently been sent from one room to another
in search of a toy and had two months earlier first been observed to
crawl after his mother to find her in another room. The fact that he
responded to a few object terms enabled him to locate correctly the
objects and people in the appropriate rooms. Of course, one could argue
that finding K and L involved people rather than objects. Although
this is at least partially true, the cueing question was in terms of the
small object (where's the ball?) rather than the person's name. In addition to familiarity, size, and social status of the stimulus objects, this
test also differed from the standard object test in using language cues.
Which of these factors was of central importance to the result cannot
now be determined although, as previously noted, subsequent research
(Acredolo, 1979; Nelson & Kessen, 1978) has indicated that familiarity
of place is important at this age.

The interpretation of these tests is complicated by the fact that shortly
after this performance at the same session we tried another test in which
a ball was hidden under one basket and a soft toy under the other. In
this test Billy's responses were positionally determined, even though he
had given clear evidence of understanding "Where's the ball?" in the
previous situation. The contribution of different aspects of context to
his understanding the situation and relating language to it is clearly
important here even though we cannot be certain exactly which contextual factors are aiding and which may be hindering interpretation.

While the interplay of context and cognition seems clear in this example, a more direct effect of context on lexical acquisition eludes analysis. This involved Billy's first object term, produced at 11 months.
"Tick tock" was used initially only for his grandmother's clock but by
12 months was extended to two novel toy clocks. The report on the use
of this word at 12;23 is of interest

M reports that he uses "tick tock" now consistently. They have acquired a clock in the living room that chimes. B says from kitchen or playroom "tih toh" and heads in direction of living room. When clock chimed, he was in kitchen, said "tih toh," and started toward living room. He also points now to clock over stove and says "tih toh." Note that M uses the word "clock," B uses "tih toh." K observed word used for kitchen clock 3 times during this session. M reports and later demonstrates that she plays "What does the____ say?" and he replies with "tih toh" for clock . . . K showed B her watch, letting him finger it. He says very tentatively, "t, tih tih." M says this is not really "tih toh." Is it some approximation designed to fit the approximate object? B says "t, t" while pointing out window. M mentions the birds that go "tweet tweet," as before. This sound seems quite definitely a part of the schema of the window (usually but not always while M is holding B).

At the next visit (13 months) a generalization test with pictures of clocks was attempted, but Billy threw all pictures on the floor without naming them. The form of "tih toh" changed toward "tah" (compromise between mother's "clock" and and his own "tick tock?"), and "tih" was used while pointing out window at trees and birds (that go "tweet tweet"). Note that while "tih toh" was used to name an object and was generalized to a few other similar objects, it was also part of an action sequence in response to the chime and of a verbal sequence in response to "What does the clock say?"

For a month or more thereafter Billy ceased to produce "tih toh" or any other words (he had used "hi" and several protowords such as "deh" in pointing to objects). However, "tih toh" reappeared strongly at 14;10 and was used then for watches as well as clocks. Two weeks later he was observed to say "tih toh" while hunting through toys *before* he found the toy clock, indicating the possible use of the word to guide or plan the search. That is, the term had become conceptualized to the extent that it could lead to the object rather than the reverse. Unlike other words that came and went in Billy's vocabulary (by 19 months 20 words had been counted but few persisted), "tih toh" continued to be used throughout the year. Why? What sort of mental representation of the meaning of this term could we propose to explain the ins and outs of its usage and its continuance in contrast to others? He did not overextend the term (except to watches, which is arguably part of the child-basic category and accepted by adults as such), and the picture generalization tests were uniformly unsuccessful. Thus, speculations about the defining features of the concept are not feasible. Why should "tih toh" persist as a term and not, say, "ball" or "telephone," which were at least as attractive and familiar play objects?

Could a theory of cognitive context based on partitioning of event representations help us to explain this phenomenon or others like it?

We can only speculate in particular cases, but it appears that the use of several different event contexts may have led to the early conceptualization of "tih toh." Note, however, that this process was slow and jerky and that it did not generalize to other object terms.

Specific context effects were also evident in Billy's early comprehension of terms. At 15;10 a comprehension test involving novel and familiar objects with old object *terms* (comprehension) and well-formed and scrambled sentences (e.g., "Put on the ball," "Throw me the clock," "Ball me the throw") led to this generalization: "*Throw me* is obviously an important concept to B, and so is *put on*, but they seem to be object specific. That is, it may not be syntax (i.e., word order) alone that is operative but the effect of certain combinations. The semantics of the whole sentence is understood (as is the object word alone), but the elements cannot be recombined. Sentences and words are whole units." The evidence for this conclusion was that Billy responded appropriately to "Throw me the ball," "Look at the shoe," "Look at the clock," and "Put on the shoe" but did not respond at all to "Clock at the look," "Throw me the clock," "Ball me the throw," "Put on the ball," or "Shoe on the put." That is, he seemed to respond to familiar combinations but not the same words in different combinations whether these were across or within the original sentences. In other words, *he did not appear to be able to break these syntagms apart.* The whole construction was necessary to its interpretation, and without that context interpretation was not possible. This situation is precisely comparable to the apparent inability of the child to break apart event sequences and give meaning to the elements at a similar developmental point. The results of these comprehension tests are in accord with Benedict's (1976) subsequent results (see Chapter 3), while the evanescent appearance and disappearance of words was a central theme of Bloom's (1973) report on her daughter Allison. Thus, these phenomena appear to be general ones that occur in many children. Decontexted theories of meaning cannot explain them; a well-worked-out model of the role of cognitive context at different points in development is needed for this purpose.

Rachel

In this example the early generalization of language terms across contexts is examined more directly. Rachel was the subject of a study by Susan Engel in which the focus was on the development of the meaning of words within a particular event context, the morning routine of getting up and having breakfast (Nelson, Engel, & Kyratzis, in press). This situation was highly routinized and predictable, and both Rachel and her mother had well-established scripts for it, providing the event context within which talk could take place. Visits starting at 16 months were made weekly and tape recordings of 30 to 45 minutes were transcribed, together with context notes recording all mother and child speech and the relevant activities surrounding them. Most words used by Rachel in the first session were used in specific contexts (e.g., "shots" for shoes and socks in the dressing situation only). The apparent generalization of several terms across contexts was analyzed in detail. One example is her use of the name of her dog. Each morning Rachel was encouraged to pat the family dog and say "Hi Bo." At first this term was used only in the greeting and petting situation. After a few weeks, however, she said "Bo" on sighting the dog at the other end of the room while eating breakfast, and then used the term many times more during the session (practicing a term newly partitioned from its script). Not all of Rachel's words, even in the early sessions, were context-specific. For example, "mine" said in a whining tone and used with a grasping reach gesture was used cross-situationally.

Rachel's mother provided both verbal routines and action routines within which Rachel could take her part (see Braunwald [1978]; Bruner [1975b]; and Ferrier [1978] for similar observations). In addition, she talked about past and future events and encouraged Rachel to respond accordingly. In anticipation of immediately succeeding events, she talked about what could happen next. For example: "After we get your shoes on, we'll go downstairs and get you some breakfast. Would you like that? Some cereal and juice?" This sort of talk appears common and even banal, but its importance in alerting the child to the use of language to plan, as a vehicle for displaced reference (reference to objects and events not present in the here and now), and as a context-establisher itself should not be underestimated. At the outset, the script knowledge mother and daughter shared made it possible for Rachel to begin to understand references to parts of the script that were not yet perceptually evident.Engel noted that by 18 months Rachel had not used language to plan, but responded to her mother's planning talk appropriately either by expressing pleasure or displeasure at a proposal for action or by using her mother's talk to direct her movements. For example, when her mother asked "Are you ready for some breakfast?" Rachel turned immediately and walked toward her high chair.

Rachel's mother also often referred to past events, as in: "Tell Susie about your trip to Vermont. Did you have fun in Vermont? These references to single past events presumably were not as well understood by Rachel as were the immediate script references, and she did not generally respond to them, although when her friend Matthew was mentioned ("Did you play with Matthew in Vermont?") she did, saying "Matt? Matt?" with some excitement. Of course, it is not possible to know what meaning Rachel attributed to "Matt"—whether she remembered the trip to Vermont and his place in it, for example—but her recognition of his name and repetition of it seemed to indicate at least that she associated it with a person whose company she enjoyed or with an interesting experience.

What these examples from Rachel demonstrate is that talk itself may be used to provide cognitive context for interpretation of meaning even very early in the game. The complexities of dealing with this kind of talk and the problems it raises for the child have scarcely been touched on in our theories of meaning.

Emily

In the next example we note characteristics of uncontexted monologues. The older of two children of professional parents, Emily's pre-sleep monologues were tape-recorded two or more times per week, beginning when she was 21 months old and continuing to 3 years. Being advanced in both language and cognition, Emily's nonsocial speech reveals a great deal about the relation of meaning and social context early in development. In the early months of this study Emily's speech was often difficult to decipher. Fortunately, her mother provided both a preliminary transcript and notes on the context of obscure referents.

The tapes are extremely rich in suggesting what sort of organization of knowledge young children may have (Nelson, 1983a,b). For example, we have been able to trace how Emily integrated the meaning of new terms with her own prior understanding, sometimes successfully, sometimes not. These observations are most revealing when they are related to parental talk before bedtime. For example, in one early transcript after she was told that "mormor" (grandmother) would come to take care of her after her nap, when alone, she said to herself:

21;12   Mormor come afternoon. Read my books. *So* mommy–
         daddy to cocktail party.

Emily had no personal experience of or reference for "cocktail party" except having been told the previous week that mommy and daddy were going to one when she went to stay at her grandmother's. Thus, her only context for it had been verbal. Here she appears to have assimilated its meaning to something like "where mommy and daddy go when I stay with grandmother in the afternoon." Later she apparently follows up on the meaning of "cocktail party," learns that it involves drinking, and turns it into a fantasy game. It next appears in the following:

> 22;23 Tomorrow morning when my wakes up then Daddy [helps] Emmy [washes the dishes.] Morrow morning when my wake up then Daddy [all clean] then put some juice and cups then Emmy have cock- party, then Emmy drinked the cocktail up.

At the time these transcripts begin Emily was long past the stage when she had acquired her first object-term vocabulary, the point where Billy and Rachel were in the above accounts. In fact, she was now being introduced to new concepts and a new understanding of the world through language. Yet, to solidify that understanding she often seemed to need to talk to herself about it and also, when possible, to act it out in play. Consider an unsuccessful effort a month later after her father had told her that on Saturday they would go to Child World (a children's supplies store) and buy an intercom so that they could hear her baby brother crying when they were in another part of the house. Emmy demanded that he repeat this explanation 3 times and he patiently did so. Then when alone:

> 23;15 Daddy said buy diapers for Stevie and Emmy and buy something for Steven plug in and say "ahah" [high-pitched imitation of baby's cry] and put that in . . . on Saturday go Child World buy diaper for Emmy and diaper for the baby and then buy something for the Emmy see for that baby plug in and that diaper for anybody.

In this attempt Emily has managed to get some of the pieces right (for Steven, crying, plug in), but the relations are inaccurate and we would have to infer that her notion of an intercom is vague at best. (Even after seeing an intercom and observing the results it seems probable that her concept of it would be sketchy.) As this example shows, learning object terms through verbal explanations is not a simple matter. The learner must have the appropriate real-world knowledge structure (the cognitive context) in order to map the explanation accurately into a relational framework. Seeing an intercom would be of only minor help here; it might enable Emily to identify another one somewhere else but it would not help her to understand its function.

This example of the intercom takes us far from the usual discussion of the learning of "ball," "ticktock," "car," and "doggie," each of which can be reasonably described in terms of its perceptual features, its function, its place in the child's script, and a semantic hierarchy.

Over the first 5 years children learn many terms for technological artifacts like intercoms, as well as for events like cocktail parties. These differ from the first object terms in that they are cultural products that depend upon demonstration and explanation rather than upon direct unmediated experience. They do not belong to either Putnam's (1975) class of "natural kind" terms or to Rosch's (1978) "basic object" terms (see Chapters 3 and 5). Their place in a semantic hierarchy is not clear. The child's use of such terms draws our attention to the necessity of defining more precisely the difference between knowledge of a thing and the semantics of a word for a thing. In the case of Emily's understanding of "intercom," there does not seem to be any way to make these distinctions. This problem will be returned to in subsequent chapters.

One of the most striking things to emerge from Emily's monologues is her gradual mastery of past and future, together with her acquisition of lexical terms and inflections for marking them (see Nelson, 1983b). As noted above, her parents described for her the things that they would do after nap or the next day, just as Rachel's mother talked to her about plans. They also, but less frequently, discussed with her things that had happened recently as she was being put to bed. It may not be too surprising then that Emily first (at 22 months) began talking about future activities, marking them with "after my nap," "next week," "not right now," "in morning time," "tomorrow morning," "next day," "pretty soon," "afternoon," "Saturday," and even "next year," all of which were used to refer to future events, although not necessarily accurately, before her second birthday. At the same time, she clearly marked the present as distinct from the future—"now" and "right now," "now time" in opposition to "not now." Marking of the past appeared with frequency a month later (at 23 months) by the use of "yesterday," "one day," and "different time" as well as the increased use of the past tense. (See Nelson, 1984b, for a more extended consideration of this development.) At 24 months the use of the generalized present and the recounting of miniscripts appear together, for example, in the following sequence:

> 24;4   In the nightime I only put big girl pants on. But in the morning we put jamas on. In the morning gets up. But afternoon I wake up and play.

In this sequence she has the parts a bit confused ("big girl pants" go on at nap, not night, and "jamas" at night, not morning), but in other respects it appears to resemble the scripts we have obtained from older preschool children in the use of the generalized present and the general "we" (Nelson & Gruendel, 1981).

Given the claim that meaning is a social construct, what significance can we ascribe to Emily's talk to herself? This nonsocial speech (divorced from the context of both reference and conversation) emphasizes the various essential components that enable the child to learn words and establish meaning. In her monologues Emily tells herself what she knows, what has happened, what has been said, what will happen (based on what her parents say), and what she thinks may happen (based on what she knows). Thus, the *real-world knowledge base* is clearly revealed as it changes and develops, sometimes within a single monologue. Her *concepts* of particular things, people, events, and relations are displayed in part, as in the cocktail party and intercom examples. The *social basis* for the language she learns to use to express herself is also clearly revealed in her attempts to integrate what her parents tell her into her knowledge system. It is particularly revealing in her talk about the future and the past as she reiterates what will and what has happened, emphasizing the linguistic markers that distinguish these times from the present. Thus, the context that enters into her meaning system in all its layers is revealed as she recapitulates for herself what she has heard and experienced with others.

Christine

In a final example we can see most clearly how internalized event context supports understanding and use of early language. This example involves a 2-year-old girl who was one of the children who participated in my longitudinal study of learning to talk (Nelson, 1973b). Christine was the younger of two children of professional parents. Her older brother Johnny was in kindergarten. Christine's language and general progress were within the standard norms. She was highly imitative and socially attuned and was classified as expressive (see Chapter 4). For the excerpt here, the physical–social context is initially the child's home, a townhouse with an open floor plan allowing observation of the child in the living room from the dining room. The mother, whose attitude toward child care as well as other matters was unusually casual, habitually carried on a conversation with the visitor regardless of what Christine did or said. (This is not to say she was neglectful; indeed, she was quite warmly interactive with both children. She did not, however, engage in those language teaching tutorials that many middle-class mothers do and that have become the model for some theories of language learning. Rather, her style was to engage the children in play, particularly in fantasy games.) This excerpt begins as mother, child, and visitor leave the house for the car to pick Johnny up at kindergarten:

Child	Adult/context
	(M in dining room has referred to pick- ing Johnny up)
1. Mommy wait n John	(C in living room)
2. Wait John?	
3. Wait John. Wait wait John? Up. Se goes.	(C points at coat)
	K: Oh, you want me to put my coat on?
4. Seven sen coat	M: 2, 4, 6, 8, (counting money)
5. Up	(K and M converse in background)
6. Down	
7. Com' on	
8. Wait John? Wait John? Wait John? Huh? Wait John?	(C agitated)
9. Wait John?	
10. Wait John? Wait John?	
11. Wait John up!	
	K: Pick Johnny up?
	(M talks to K)
12. Yeh. Pick Johnny up.	
	K: Do you pick Johnny up every day?
	M: Okay, com on.
13. Un yeah	
	K: yeah
14. Un yeah. Un yeah.	
	M: Com' on, let's go. Let's go.
15. Mommy. Mommy, me. Mommy.	
	M: Hey, you don't have any rubber pants on. You don't have any pants on!
16. No 'v any pants on.	
	M: No, what happened?
17. Co-ats	
	M: What? Don't touch that pencil. That's a no-no.
18. Wan penny. A check.	
	(C looking at M's pocketbook)
19. Check	
	K: Check?
	(M putting pants on C)
	M: Get your other foot up.
20. Uh pants on	
21. Rubber pants on. Uh want wubber pants on.	
	M: Woops. Do you wanta carry my pocketbook?
22. Yeh. My pocketbook.	
	M: No that's mine.

Child	Adult/context
23. That's mine. It. That mine.	
	M: Now you walk downstairs, okay?
	(In car at school. Bell rings.)
62. Ding, ding, ding. Okay.	
63. Ding, ding.	
	(M talks to K)
64. Get John	
	(Children come out of school)
	M: Oh there they are. Where's Johnny? I see him.
	(K and M converse)
	(C sees John outside)
65. Johnny. Hi John. Hi Johnny. Hi John.	
	(M and K converse)
66. EE	
	K to C: How'd you hurt your nose, Christina? Where'd you get this little scab on your nose?
67. Uh kere scab. Johnny did it.	
	M: Oh you little fibber. Every scratch she has on her—she said to my mother the other day "Johnny did that!" My mother said "Did he?" I said "no she just says that."
	K: Yes.
	M to C: Where's John?
68. Where's John? Where's John?	
	M: And Maria. Did you see Maria today?
69. Johnny. Johnny!	
	M: Call Johnny.
70. Can't . . . call Johnny.	
	(M and K converse)
71. Oh.	
72. Johnny!	
73. I make it. (honks horn)	
74. Baby. Hi John. Ah hah. I was calling John. John.	
	(John arrives at car)
	(M talks to John)
	K: Hello.
	J: lo.
	M: John, this is Mrs. Nelson. This is my son John.
	K: How are you? How are you John?
	J: Okay.
	K: Good.
75. Hey Mommy. My son Nels.	

At the outset of this excerpt Christine responds to Mother's comment to the visitor that it is time to pick Johnny up with an immediate pickup on the meaning of this statement and its *implication*. She repeats with variation the central proposition over and over and also shows K what this involves by pointing to the coat. "Wait Johnny" appears to be some amalgamation of "pick Johnny up," "wait for John" (at school), and perhaps "wake up John" (notice "wait Johnny up!"). "Wait John" appears to be in some sense a name for the entire script of picking up Johnny at school.

In addition, Christine demonstrates well-learned routines for various activities: getting dressed, counting money, carrying the pocketbook, all embedded within the "getting ready to go out" script.

In the last part Christine carries out her role in what is apparently a well-practiced script; that is, waiting for John. This involves imitating the bell, calling John, and honking the horn. When John arrives, Christine has a note of triumph in her voice as she says "Ah hah. I was calling John. John."

Now, clearly much of what Christine contributes here is original: Mother does not say "wait Johnny up" or "seven sen coat." Clearly, some of it is purely imitative: "No -'v any pants on." This child was one of the more imitative and repetitive of those I studied. Yet, clearly also her verbalizations were used within this well-known situation to indicate what would happen next and to try to influence it (call Johnny, put on coat). She shared her mother's goal and took delight in taking her role in the event structure that ensued. Many of her words seem to fit their conventional meanings only loosely (as in "wait John," "that's mine"), but there is a sense that meanings are being extracted from the event context so as eventually to match those of her mother. What we see here is that at this stage (24 months) the event language is embedded in a whole event context, the structure of which takes over and determines what can and will be said. This is not to say that the structure is rigid—putting on rubber pants may be inserted in an un-expected place—nor that it is not partitionable, but only that it seems to be a compelling whole for the child, as indicated in both her action and language. In this example Christine is not learning any new words nor any new meanings for old words. Rather, her words are largely de-termined by the well-practiced routine where they take on meaning from the situation itself. Note that her mother does very little interpretation of what Christine says; nor does she provide any input to be practiced. Indeed, she rarely addresses the child. Yet, the meaning of the child's talk is for the most part clear because it is embedded in a well-under-stood (by child and adult) event context.

Context and Talk

Together, these examples—neither random nor particularly representative—demonstrate some of the many ways that context enters into the establishment of meaning in the early stages. In the first case, the case of Billy, it is clear that a well-understood physical–social context enables him to put together cognitive demands and language directions. He was able to distinguish between "where is the ball?" and "where is the telephone?" and look for each in the appropriate place. His word for clock at first appeared to follow a classic contexted to decontexted route, used first for only the chiming grandfather clock. But very early it was extended to other examples, then was dropped and reappeared to become the most reliable and generalized of his object words during the second year. Indeed, he had few other productive object terms, so that he in no sense could be said to be in a general decontexted *stage*.

In Rachel's case her terms became gradually generalized across activity contexts. At first they were used ("Bo," "shots" for shoes and socks) only in the context of the ongoing related activity. Then they began to be used in anticipation of that activity (e.g., going to see Bo) and then outside of the activity frame altogether.

Christine's talk demonstrates the way in which a well-understood activity frames the interaction in such a way that the child can carry on her part without the active participation of the parent. It is noteworthy that only in segments of that transcript where an interruption of the expected sequence occurred (e.g., noticing the lack of rubber pants) did the mother take an active part in the exchange. Here the child provides her own context for the talk appropriate to the activity, whereas Rachel's mother took an active role in providing the frame for Rachel to take part in. Probably when the routine was new—and when no one else was present—Christine's mother did the same for her. However, clearly the child can take on the framing function herself when she is sufficiently familiar with it.

Emily's bedtime talk takes this framing function further. Here the child can be seen to use her own experience and what her parents have told her to construct increasingly differentiated and abstract representations of the world within which terms become defined and concepts (such as past time) worked out.

It may be noted that little emphasis has been placed on the parents' role in these case-study fragments. Both Billy's and Rachel's mothers did engage in considerable framing of the child's speech productions. Billy's mother showed him pictures of clocks and asked "what does the clock say?," urging him to use his "word." She also showed him real and toy clocks and named them for him. Rachel's mother continuously talked to her about what they were doing, what they would do, and what they had done and urged her to participate verbally (e.g., "say hi to Bo"). On the other hand, neither Christine's nor Emily's talk depended upon parental framing. Of course, the latter children were at a more advanced stage of language and cognitive development. And this, no doubt, was at least partially responsible for their greater ability to provide their own representational frames, that is, their cognitive context for carrying on talk within or about the event. The ability of the child to do this by the age of 2 years supports the proposal that taking part in an activity leads to a representational schema for the activity, a script, which in turn makes external support for the child's part superfluous. When the child has internalized her own experiential frame, she is then no longer dependent on the close guidance of another for taking an appropriate role within that context.

It is also true, however, that caretakers may vary in the degree to which they make explicit the script and the child's role within it, and the event itself may provide greater or lesser support for such training. These variations will be considered in Chapter 4.

Context and Meaning

What can we then conclude about the role of context in the establishment of meaning? Has this discussion added anything to the generally asserted thesis that with development words and their meanings become decontexted?

First, let us reaffirm that words mean in context. Words are only decontexted in dictionaries. The notion that words become decontexted in the course of development can mean only that they can be extended from their original context of use and be given an interpretation in a number of different contexts—eventually in *all possible* contexts.

Second, we have emphasized that context is a highly complex construct with interleaved layers, some specifically linguistic (the role of a word in a sentence), others cognitive, social, or cultural. A beginning suggestion for viewing the role of the different layers of context in the child's construction of meaning is that the effects of each on the child's understanding will be proportional to its magnitude. At the macro level (geographical, cultural, and socioeconomic) major shifts in context may disrupt speech altogether. (There are, in fact, many anecdotal reports of children who have stopped talking for many months on being moved to a foreign environment.) At the median level (specific social, agendas, affect, activities) the interpretation of meanings may depend on the place of the word in the child's script representation, and the same word used in different scripts may be given an entirely different interpretation. Moreover, a familiar word in one script context may not be used or understood in a novel context. At the most micro level (speech act, semantic role) the effect of context must first be mastered before it can affect the meaning of the word. That is, the child must become capable of interpreting the implications of an utterance context (for example, the difference between an active or passive subject) before that context can affect the interpretation of the meaning of the word.

In terms of word meanings, then, contextual generalization applies primarily to the median level. Moreover, it is at this level that we have posited the child's representation of the world in terms of events. How the word is used in the event context provides the basis for the child's interpretation of what it means. Here decontextualization is redefined to mean becoming interpretable across different event contexts. But in another and fundamentally more important sense, contextual generalization entails establishing the cognitive context that will provide the interpretation independent of external objective context. Ultimately, the cognitive context will provide the basis for giving an interpretation in all possible contexts as well as the basis for establishing a lexical system.

The basic thesis here is that development of early word meanings depends not on the word's place in an abstract scheme (based on features, nodes, or contrasts) but on how the word is used by others in the child's social–cultural world. The more general problem, then, is to trace how the representation of the real world that initially embeds the word gets transformed into a lexical representation with its own connections to other words. This is a story for later chapters. The first part of this story—how the child uses cognitive context to establish concepts for early words—is presented in Chapter 3.

Notes

[1] It may be noticed that on these grounds the discussion relates well to the constructs of Soviet psychology based on the work of Luria (1976) and Vygotsky (1962, 1978), although the theoretical language is not precisely the same (see Wertsch, 1985).

[2] My apologies to John Dore who has used this term for a somewhat different (more micro) reference.

[3] It is probably necessary to note here that this use of the schema notion departs from its typical use in developmental psychology taken from Piaget. In Piaget's sense a schema derives from an action that can be applied to a range of phenomena in the world, for example, initially sucking and grasping and later, in the sensorimotor stage, pulling, pushing, and so on. At the end of the sensorimotor period, children have at their

command a set of action schemas that form the foundation for the development of representational thought but are not themselves representational. In some writings and translations Piaget also extended the term to highly abstract structures such as the schema of the permanent object, the number schema, and the operational schemas of the various conservations (e.g., Piaget, 1970). These abstractions, although based in the subject's actions, are very different from the use of schemas that has been set forth here.

[4]Kessen and Nelson (1978) suggested such a model. It might indeed be the case that early perceptual development depends upon the integration of discrete "take-ins." However, at the point being discussed here the integration of perception seems to be well established. It is the coordination of perception into a cognitive model that is at issue.

[5]The fact that much of this description of the anticipation of familiar sequences is true of other mammals as well (for example, domestic pets) is irrelevant. We are concerned here with the notions of how to eat, how to play, and so on that the human child initially builds up. For the child this is not the end point of development, although it may be for a dog or cat.

[6]Work investigating these issues is underway by Mandler, Bates, and their colleagues. Preliminary results by O'Connell and Gerard (in press) using an imitation paradigm suggest that children under 2 years have the components of simple scripts (e.g., bath) represented but not the sequence.

[7]This problem (Piaget, 1963; Le Compte & Gratch, 1972) involves hiding an object under one screen (A) one or more times and allowing the child to find it, then hiding under a different screen (B). The child in stage IV of sensorimotor development typically does not search under (B) but returns to (A), where the object was originally found. According to Piaget (1963), this indicates that the child does not yet conceive of the object as having an independent, permanent existence but, rather, as being at the disposal of his own actions.

3

Concepts, Categories, and Words: First Steps

The Problem of the Meaning of the First Words

A persistent problem in semantic development has been how to characterize the meanings of the first words that children use (see, e.g., Bloom, 1973; Bowerman, 1976; Clark, 1973; Nelson, 1973b; 1974a). This problem is essentially related to those of how children learn their first words, what functions they use them for, and what their cognitive categories are. In order to come to an understanding of how meaning begins, we must consider all these issues. In the previous chapter we discussed the context of early meaning; here we consider its content in more detail.

Theoretical proposals about the acquisition of meanings of the first lexicon can be roughly divided into three groups: those relying on a perceptual match, or *reference* theories; those relying on a conceptual match, or *denotation* theories; and those relying on semantic features or contrasts, or *sense* theories. As discussed in Chapter 1 (based on Lyons, 1977), these three aspects of meaning all enter into the adult's understanding of a word, but they cannot be simply assumed in developmental theories. With respect to the child's language, reference picks out the particular instance—the object, event, or idea—that is the focus of attention on a particular occasion. As Bruner (1975b, 1983) has discussed, mothers employ nonlinguistic devices to ensure joint attention. Denotation delimits the domain of possible referents through a conceptual structure specifying either the intension or the extension, or both, of the concept associated with the word. Sense relates the word to other words in the lexicon either directly or through relations established within the conceptual structure.

The discussion here proposes that these three aspects of meaning are realized within different levels of the individual's cognitive system: reference through perception, denotation through concepts, and sense through the semantic component. Forming the context for interpretation at all levels is the event representation. Although this is an oversimplification and needs fuller discussion, that discussion will be deferred until more of the story has been presented. In this chapter the major proposals under each of these headings will be considered first. Next, the cognitive system of the language learner, with an emphasis on categorization and concepts, will be described in order to put these proposals into perspective. Following this, relevant research on early lexical development will be reviewed. Finally, a theoretical proposal for the development of lexical meaning in this early period will be presented that reconciles the contextualized view of meaning laid out in the previous chapter with the cognitive system described in the present one.

Throughout this discussion the focus is on words for objects and categories of objects. There are several theoretical and pragmatic reasons for this. First, early vocabularies tend to consist to a large degree of object terms. Secondly, most studies of perception and cognition have focused on the static object world and most lexical and semantic theories in linguistics, psychology, philosophy, and anthropology are concerned largely with object names and their hierarchical relations. This object bias in the literature is at odds with the proposal set forth in Chapter 2 that event representations serve as cognitive context for early meaning. An attempt is made in the last section of this chapter to reconcile these two points of view.

Theories of Meaning in the First Lexicon

Referential–Perceptual Theories

Most theories of early lexical acquisition fall under the heading of perceptual or referential theories. For example, the classic description of word learning taken from Augustine (see Macnamara, 1982) has a tutor pointing to objects while uttering the object name. The young learner forms an association between the label and the object, and on future occasions when the object appears applies the label himself. Brown's (1958) version of this general approach has the learner forming a hypothesis as to what category of objects the name may refer to and testing his hypothesis through production of the label in questionable contexts. E. V. Clark's (1973) variation proposes that the learner extracts perceptual features from the examples named and uses them to identify new referents of the label. Bowerman's (1976) version utilizes the notion of the perceptual prototype, as formulated in Rosch's (1975) work, and suggests that the first referent of the name serves as a prototype for future referents.

What all of these theories have in common is the notion that the essential problem for the child is to learn what the word refers to in the real world, that is, to form a word–object bond. For this purpose a perceptual category, a collection of perceptual features, a perceptual prototype, or paradigm (Miller & Johnson-Laird, 1976) may each serve to identify appropriate referents.

The evidence for the referential–perceptual position rests primarily on the analysis of children's extension of terms after they are first acquired (see E. V. Clark, 1973; Bowerman, 1976). Clark analyzed data from diary studies carried out by linguists and psychologists in the early years of this century, usually tracking their own children's language development. She showed that most of the cases in which children used a term to refer to objects that would not be included in the term by an adult could be explained on the basis of the perceptual similarity of the novel object to others in the class. She suggested that the child extracted perceptual features (such as shape and movement) from examples of the referent class and attached the name to one or a few features. Thus four-legged would be attached to "dog," and the word would be extended to other four-legged animals such as cows and horses. She stated: "As soon as he has attached some feature(s) of meaning to it [the word], it simply has that meaning for him" (Clark, 1973, p. 72).

Much research has been undertaken to investigate this position. With respect to extensions and overextensions of early words, the case seems overwhelming that children rely on perceptual features for applying the word to new referents (Anglin, 1977; Bowerman, 1976; Rescorla, 1980). Moreover, children apparently learn many new words from two-dimensional representations such as photographs or other pictorial forms (e.g., Ninio 1983; Ninio & Bruner, 1978; Rescorla, 1980). Thus, it seems indisputable that, where reference is concerned, children rely on some kind of perceptual representation, whether featural or prototypical.

But is reference all there is to meaning in the early period? Clearly, as Miller and Johnson-Laird (1976) have argued at length, it will not do for a complete theory of meaning in the adult language. For one thing, many words do not have clear real-world referents. These include not only unicorns and manicores but also abstract terms such as "peace" and "justice" as well as relational terms that are acquired early by the child. (To what does "all gone" refer, for example?) Moreover, even object terms that appear to have clear referents can be sensibly used to refer to objects that do not fit the canonical perceptual paradigm. Miller and Johnson-Laird's example is the use of "table" to refer to a tree stump in the woods when one is looking for a spot on which to spread a picnic lunch. In order to interpret the statement "That stump would make a fine table" appropriately, one needs to know about the uses of tables as well as their appearance. Evidence that such knowledge is available to the language-learning child is found in examples such as the child putting a wastebasket on his head and exclaiming "hat" (Gruendel, 1977). Thus, the simple form of the word–object match, whether it rests on simple associations, abstraction of perceptual features, or formation of categories around prototypes and hypothesis testing, will not do for all that the child must learn (and must learn fairly early) about word meaning. What else is there?

Denotational-Conceptual Theories

In an early paper (Nelson, 1974a) I outlined an alternative theory centered on the notion of the functional core model (FCM). Essentially, I argued that before learning words children had constructed concepts about the familiar things in their world, and that their early words were attached to these concepts rather than to perceptual features abstracted from examples named by adults. Furthermore, I argued that the concepts children constructed had a functional basis in their own experience and that this functional basis was evident in the kinds of things children chose to name, the vast majority of which were things that did interesting actions (such as "ball," "car," or "dog") rather than "just sitting there" waiting to be named (such as "tree" or "kitchen").

I proposed that the child's concepts were formed on the basis of experience with objects in functional situations and that they included information about actions and reactions of objects in relation to people, especially including the child himself. I suggested that this resulted in a concept formed around a functional "core" and that less critical information about the object (including perceptual features used for its identification) lay outside the core. For example, the concept of a ball was said to be represented along the lines of Figure 3.1.

The notion of function was initially described as what things do or what can be done with them. Later (Nelson, 1979a), it was elaborated as follows to include:

1. actions of things (e.g., dog runs),
2. actions on things (e.g., pet dog),
3. reactions of things (e.g., ball rolls when pushed),
4. conventional uses of things (e.g., drink from cup).

Note that these functional specifications are all from the point of view of the child. The usual course of concept formation in the early language period proceeds from the identification of a single interesting object in a functionally important (to the child) context to identification of critical features for recognition to attaching a word to the resulting concept.

Several lines of evidence were presented to support this conceptual theory in contrast to perceptual reference theories. The fact that children often underextended early words (i.e., not including some cases that adults would) as well as overextending them (Nelson, 1973b; see also Anglin, 1977) was taken as evidence that the child's concepts were derived independently of language use. Although most of the overextensions of words are apparently based on perceptual features (which the FCM as well as the perceptual models predict), some extensions on the basis of function independent of perceptual similarity have been reported in the literature (see Gruendel, 1977; Rescorla, 1980; Benelli, D'Odorico, Livorato, & Simion, 1977; Anglin, 1983), and these are hard to account for with a simple perceptual model. (Both the evidence and the theory will be considered in more detail and brought up to date in Chapters 5 and 7.)

Many other conceptual models of the basis for early language are possible and have been proposed. Rescorla (1980) outlined a componential model that views early word meanings as complexes in Vygotsky's (1962) sense. Piaget's (1962) description of early word meanings is schematic and preconceptual, but only in the sense that the young child is claimed to be prelogical. In other respects, his model is clearly conceptual rather

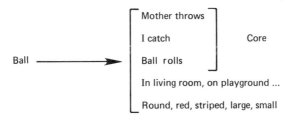

FIGURE 3.1   The Functional Core Model of the child's concept *ball*.

than perceptual. Rosch, Mervis, Gray, Johnson, and Boyes-Braem (1976) argued that the child's early words referred to "basic object categories." Basic object categories in this model are those that are found at the level of semantic hierarchy in which the perceptual and motor-movement components of the category have greatest "cue validity," that is, they have a large number of common identifying features that distinguish the category from other closely related categories. In the "clothes" hierarchy, "pants" and "skirt" are basic object-level terms. Mervis & Mervis (1982) extended this concept in their study of the naming practices of mothers and children to distinguish between "child basic" and "adult basic" levels. For a young child the term "kitty" may refer to a basic category that includes tigers and leopards as well as cats. Rosch (1975) also suggested that categories have internal structure reflected in prototypical members, instances that share the greatest number of features common to the category. For example, "robin" is a prototypical bird, while "chicken" is not.

The notion of a categorical prototype as the basis for early concept learning was relied on by Bowerman (1976). Anglin (1977) proposed a conceptual model combining the functional claims of Nelson (1974a) and the prototype model but accepted the Piagetian claim that at the outset intension and extension were not coordinated. At the other end of the spectrum, Fodor (1981) has put forth a claim about the word–concept relation in which all concepts are "primitives" (i.e., do not have internal structure) and are therefore innate. These alternative models have all been described and critically analyzed elsewhere (see Carey [1982], Clark [1983], Smith & Medin [1981] and the discussion in Chapters 5, 6, and 8). None has been found to be wholly adequate in accounting for either adult or child concepts, for reasons that will be made clear at a later point.

It should be emphasized that the difference between these conceptual models and the first (referential–perceptual) type is that the conceptual models attempt to explain what words *can* denote as well as what particular real-world objects they can be used to refer to. The denotation of a word in this sense *is* the concept and eventually involves a specification of both its extension and its intension. Because the intension specifies more than how to identify an example by reference to a canonical form or perceptual stereotype it can be used to interpret utterances that do not refer to familiar real-world objects.

The acceptance of some version of the denotational–conceptual model of word meaning is well-nigh universal in cognitive science, although there are linguistic arguments against it (see Lyons, 1977, and Chapter 5). There is no reason to accept these models as developmental models, however, without further support. Moreover, a major class of developmental models remains to be specified.

Sense-Semantic Theories

E. V. Clark's (1973) semantic feature model (SFM), which was described in part under referential–perceptual models, was set forth in terms of the acquisition of semantic (not necessarily perceptual) features. Semantic features are based on componential analyses of meaning in analogy to the distinctive features that make up the set of phonemes in any given language (e.g., voiced–voiceless, labial–dental–glottal). Bierwisch (1970, 1981) has been the most articulate contemporary theorist who has defined this approach. As with phonemes, semantic features are defined in terms of *contrast* and can be expressed as ± pairs. For example, many pairs of size adjectives (such as "big," "little") can be expressed in terms of a small set of features including that of [+ size] and [± polar], where the [+ polar] is said to indicate the positive end of a scale ("big") and [− polar] the negative end ("little").[1]

It is apparent that semantic features are abstractions based on common dimensions from a set of terms that form a semantic domain, such as size, movement, or time. The effort to extend the theory to the earliest vocabularies acquired by young children with the claim that children learn meanings component by component led to the confusion of perceptual features (such as "four-legged" or "barks," which depend not on comparison of a set but on the perceptual analysis of a single object) with semantic features and to the perceptual theory outlined above (E. V. Clark, 1973). Barrett (1978) saw clearly the implications of contrast implicit in the semantic feature model and put forth a lexical contrast model that relied not on the acquisition of components but on the differentiation of a semantic field in terms of contrasts. The child is seen as first defining a semantic field (such as animals) and then picking out perceptual dimensions along which members contrast (e.g., size). Contrasts are not componential but relational. There is still a question as to whether perceptual contrasts can do the semantic work for which they have been drafted; clearly they cannot do all of it, since contrasts such as domestic–wild are not perceptually based. Thus, it is clear that some move to a more abstract system has to be posited.

Clark (1983) has recently outlined a theory much like Barrett's, resting on the same principles. Both versions, positing abstract semantic relations, assume that children's vocabularies are organized from the outset along lines similar to adults'. In particular, word meanings are assumed to be defined in terms of relations among terms within a semantic domain. The question of how such a domain is established as a domain has not been addressed (although Barrett speculated that the FCM might be useful for this purpose). The alternative view, taken here, is that both establishing domains and finding dimensions of contrast are developmental achievements and are not the basis on which lexicons are acquired, at least at the outset. This view is elaborated in this and succeeding chapters.

To summarize this section: the three aspects of lexical meaning are each represented in theories of early lexical development. Reference is addressed by a variety of perceptually based theories relating objects and words. Denotation is found in a number of theories positing a concept–word bond. Sense is utilized in theories of semantic features and lexical contrast. In the next sections the evidence regarding early lexical development and its cognitive basis is examined in order to determine whether one of these approaches is better able to explain the data than any other.

Concepts and Categories

Even those theories that are not based on a notion of concepts as word meanings recognize that categorization is essential to the establishment of language (Brown, 1956). Sounds, language forms, and meanings must all be grouped into categories. Therefore, the consideration of the cognitive foundation for language in infancy must include the examination of categorization abilities. This examination is obscured, however, by the interchangeable usage of the terms "concept" and "category" and the attribution of different senses to them depending upon the theoretical purposes of the investigator. The lack of agreement on the meaning of these terms is a problem that has been noted by many authors and that received an extensive analysis in Flavell's (1970) review of concept development research. Confusion on this subject lies behind many of the disputes about the relation of language and concepts. For clarification, I will specify the way in which I use the terms. The term "concept" is used here in the sense of a mental unit. In this unitary sense concepts are easily related to language terms. As Bronowski and Bellugi (1970) stated: "What language expresses specifically is the reification by the human mind of its experience, that is, an analysis into parts (including actions and properties as well as objects) which, as concepts, can be manipulated as if they were objects" (p. 670). There are two essential interconnected aspects to this important observation.

The first is that parts must be mentally separated from the whole; the second is that stable elements are mentally constructed (at least temporarily) from a less stable, more dynamic context.

Implicit in this view is the assumption that experience is first represented holistically; concept formation and language are the result of processes that separate out certain aspects of the whole and make them accessible to mental manipulation as if they were objects. This would seem to be the most important and basic function of conceptual development.

This view of the concept rules out the use of the term in the sense of a cognitive principle or structural framework, a frequent usage. For example, Flavell (1970) stated: "The concept may have only the status of a vehicle or instrument of adaptation, or it may also have in varying measure the status of a well-articulated and fully coded object of thought. An individual could not be said to have a concept if he could not in some sense think *with* it; he might well be said to have it, however, even though he could not in the slightest degree think *about* it" (p. 989). Unfortunately, this view of the concept conflates a tool of thinking with an object of thought, a distinction that seems important to maintain. The conflation of the two has pernicious consequences; for example, when the child is said to have a concept of the permanent object, it is obvious that this concept is in no sense an object of thought as the child's concept of *mother* or *cup* may be. Flavell was quite clear in stating that the child does not think *about* such a concept, although he may think *with* it. However, applying the term "concept" to principles of this kind has the unfortunate effect of objectifying them, and thus giving them the status of mental "thingness," a status that in turn unwarrantedly suggests their final achievement in some definite and fixed sense. Confining the term "concept" only to units of thought—stable wholes that have at least the *potential* (during the same period of development) of being made explicit through language—avoids these problems.

It is important to note as well the implications contained in the assertion that the concept is a unit of thought, a whole that is indivisible. It is not a collection or a category of equal members. The examples of a concept based in experience do not ordinarily retain their individuality in the mind but are assimilated to the general concept. Their identity is merged with the whole. The concept may have internal structure (just as an object does), but this internal structure specifies the conditions under which the concept applies—the functions, perceptual attributes, and relationships of the things conceptualized. It should be noted here that the prototype concept referred to is the basic object concept in

Rosch's (1978) terms. Further, I distinguish concepts from hierarchical *categories,* whose exemplars do retain their individual identity as part of the mental representation. Indeed, it is claimed that such categories are composed of basic concepts. This distinction implies that conceptual structures differ at different levels of semantic hierarchies. The importance of this proposal will become apparent in Chapter 7.

Concepts, then, are considered here to be cognitive wholes with structure but not individuated members. This is not to claim that a concept such as *dog* is not applied to different instances of the dog class but only that, as a cognitive object, it is not a collection of dogs but a single unit. (I should note in passing that the notion of a prototype fits easily here, although it is not necessary.) It is because of this wholistic status that the basic object concept (Rosch, 1978) or natural kind term (Putnam, 1975) has more in common with such cognitive abstractions as *justice* and *peace* than with general concrete category terms such as *furniture.*

A concept has been defined here in terms of a single cognitive unit that can be manipulated as though it were a mental object. Concept instances do not retain their individuality but become merged into the conceptual whole. This is definitional only; it has no implications for what can be thought of. That is to say, it is perfectly possible for a person to conceive of and think about a number of different dogs and also a number of different *types* of dogs. However, when *dog* is the object of thought, it is not a collection of dogs but the unitary concept of dogness, whatever that may be.

In contrast, a conceptual category (or collection, as we shall see) combines a number of different concepts into a larger set or group. In the case of a category the members retain their individual identity; they do not merge with the whole. For example, *animal* dominates or points to a large number of members, such as dogs, cats, cows, horses, tigers, giraffes, and even snakes. It represents a cognitive combination of concepts. In this respect the category can be seen to be the result of a different acquisition process than the concept. The basic concept is differentiated out of its appearance in events (more correctly, in event representations), whereas the category is synthesized from diverse concepts that share some aspects of similarity. This distinction will be made explicit in Chapter 7.

A concept as defined here is not equivalent to everything you know about *x* as Anglin (1977, p. 27) asserts. The concept is a generic unified whole that may be related to other concepts in different ways, reflecting what is known about it. Thus, my concept of *dog,* for example, does not include the knowledge of my childhood dog, although it may point to that knowledge in some way. The concept is more general and less inclusive than all one's specific and episodic knowledge. This is not to say that a concept does not develop over time and with experience; however, it does not simply accumulate new facts, although it may acquire new connections.

Natural lexical categories have been the object of considerable study and theorizing in recent years, but the distinction between concept and category as set forth here has not generally been drawn, nor its implications considered. Two further distinctions must be pointed to. The term "category" is also used ambiguously, and it is necessary to distinguish between at least two types of categories (there may be more)—perceptual categories (category 1) and conceptual categories (category 2). All perceptual categories (e.g., phonemes, colors, faces, etc.) appear to be defined simply in terms of similar responses to perceptually distinguishable stimuli. For such categories to be claimed there is at least one criterion that must be met, namely, that the organism can discriminate between the stimuli that are being grouped categorically. Perceptual categories differ from conceptual ones. Perceptual categories are not accessible to conscious manipulation or reorganization into new categories; they are cryptic, not phenic (Campbell, 1979). Such categories exist, but it takes experimentation by an objective observer, not subjective intuition, to demonstrate them. In contrast, lexical concepts and categories are readily accessible to the conscious level and can be manipulated, changed, defined, and analyzed by the individual.

Perceptual categories (of phonemes, colors, faces, etc.) are represented somewhere within the cognitive system in such a way that when a color, sound, or face is encountered it is assigned to an appropriate category. However, this representation is not accessible to conscious thought. No matter how much we study phonetics or psychophysics we will never be aware of the criterion we ourselves use to distinguish between /t/ and /d/ or green and blue. We simply know. Just as I simply know that the person I met on the street yesterday was Jane Jones, who I knew in high school 30 years ago, although I haven't seen her since and she is now 30 pounds heavier with gray hair. Introspection or rational thought cannot tell us what cues we use to determine these things. Experimental science is needed to tease out the answers.

However, if you ask me what a dog is—or if you ask a 4-year-old child what a dog is—you will get an answer that bears some relation to the criteria that science can show does determine the assignment of objects to that category. In this respect verbal concepts differ from perceptual categories.

On the other hand, we can distinguish both perceptual categories (category 1) and concepts from type 2 categories that organize a group of known concepts into higher-order "packages." The best examples of category 2 are superordinates like *clothes, food, animals,* and *furniture,* whether these are collections or classes (see Lyons, 1977; Markman, 1981). How these type 2 categories are constructed or learned and how they are related to the child's concepts are important aspects of semantic development that will concern us throughout this book. One question to be addressed in this chapter is whether children form type 2 categories at the beginning of language learning. To answer this question, we need to keep in mind that in such categories the subordinate concepts retain their identities (and their verbal labels) in the categorical structure; they are not merged with the whole as in a basic concept. This distinction can be seen in the different uses of the terms "insect" by adults and "bug" by children. The extension of these terms may be precisely the same, but in the adult lexicon the term "insect" dominates the terms "bee," "ant," "fly," and so on, while in the child's lexicon the term "bug" refers to an undifferentiated (and unnamed) group of small crawling or flying things. (That this may not be the case for a particular child or over time does not vitiate the point, which will be further clarified and extended in Chapter 7).

Categorizing in the First 2 Years

As noted above, categorization of some sort is essential to all aspects of language learning (Brown, 1956). The child needs to categorize sounds and to form grammatical categories as well as to classify the object world appropriately. The first two of these seem to be in some sense far more abstract than the last, where we have palpable substantial reality to observe, analyze, and assign to appropriate categories.

Yet, until recently categorization even of objects had not been given much attention in discussions of infant development and the basis for language acquisition. Instead, general knowledge of objects, formalized in Piagetian terms as the concept of object permanence, has been proposed as the essential cognitive achievement. Many studies of language implicate such general knowledge, and several investigations have been designed with the aim of relating stages of object permanence to stages in the acquisition of language (Bates, 1979; Corrigan, 1978; see the review by Corrigan, 1979). Surprisingly few relationships have been found between performance on tests of object permanence and language measures in the second year when age is partialled out of the relation. (It is surprising because one expects most measures of cognition and language to correlate with one another.)

In contrast, studies using a number of different paradigms have supported the claim that preverbal infants categorize the world similarly to adults and that they form concepts of specific object classes as well. In one such study Freeman, Lloyd, and Sinha (1980), using an object search paradigm, demonstrated that infants as young as 10 months were influenced by the canonical function (containment) of the object (a cup) used for hiding. They conclude that "the cognitive bases of language development are to be sought not in a generalized representational or semiotic function—thought by Piaget to emerge at Stage VI of sensorimotor development—but in specific encoding strategies for representing canonical relational information, whose emergence may be traced to around 9 months of age" (p. 261). In other words, they claim that infants form *concepts of cups* that specify a canonical function of containment. When that canonical function is violated (when an object is placed under rather than in), the infant's behavior is disrupted. The important thing to note here is that a function of a *class* of objects, cups—neither a specific object nor objects in general—produces the effect. It follows that infants of 10 to 12 months must be capable of forming general object concepts. That this is in fact the case is evident from other recent work in infant perception and cognition.

Following the early work of Ricciuti (1965) and later Nelson (1973a), a number of studies have recently demonstrated some form of categorization by children as young as 4 months. Between 1 and 2 years infants give evidence for having categories such as *men* and *food items* (Ross, 1980; Reznick and Kagan, 1983), and in play they act on objects that display similar qualities in order to group them together (Sugarman, 1983). In his studies of infants younger than 1 year, Strauss (1979) demonstrated the formation of categories of human faces based on prototypes such as those proposed by Rosch (1975) and Posner and Keele (1968). These studies, following on earlier ones of categorical perception of phonemes (Eimas, 1974), color (Bornstein, 1975), and taste (Nowliss & Kessen, 1976), suggested that categorization is a process that is similar across the human age span and is basic to all cognition.

Unfortunately, the term "category" has been applied loosely to all evidence that infants respond similarly to dissimilar stimuli. That is, the distinctions between type-1 and type-2 categories has not been made, nor have these categories been distinguished from basic concepts. In their studies Cohen and Strauss (1979; Strauss, 1979) demonstrated that infants can distinguish between the stimuli presented prior to forming a category. Thus, they can claim that there is some sort of rule or configuration that is being invoked to ignore the differences and act on the basis of similarities. What they have not shown is that these differences retain any cognitive reality. Thus, it is not yet clear where in the typology outlined here the categorical perception of faces by human infants falls.

All of the categories that have been demonstrated in the first year of life (phonemes, color boundaries, faces, etc.) have a basis in perceptual similarity, even though the criterion for categorization rests on the demonstration that members will be grouped together that are less similar in physical terms than members that are grouped into different categories. For example, in studies of color perception, green and blue light are reacted to differently, although the wavelengths that distinguish the categories are physically no more different than those that occur within the green and blue categories themselves (Bornstein, 1978). One noteworthy characteristic of both the color and phoneme categories is that they tend to erase differences within categories. The difference between the phonemes /d/ and /t/ is categorical; we do not hear /d–t/ but either /d/ or /t/, regardless of when voice onset occurs. Thus, such categories do not meet the discriminability criterion for categories that Strauss and Cohen's studies do.

To summarize the discussion thus far, there is good evidence that perceptual categorization is a pervasive and basic human cognitive function even in infancy (and no doubt in infrahuman organisms as well). Whether or not it is sufficient to support language learning has not been shown. In this regard, Sugarman's (1981, 1983) work on the development of object-categorizing behavior between 1 and 3 years is of great interest. In her studies she used a simple object-sorting task in which children were presented with an array of objects that varied on one or more dimensions. Studying successive and simultaneous grouping behaviors, she found that at 12 months children tended successively to group similar objects and by 18 months they grouped objects according to similarity into one discrete class (e.g., all dolls grouped together); at 24 months and older children made two class groupings, indicating an ability to consider two or more categories (and dimensions) at once. Verbal reference to the items grouped followed a similar progression. Eighteen-month-olds tended to refer to one instance or one class only, while older children (2½ and 3 years) referred to two classes or two dimensions of similarity in the same utterance.

These findings are important for indications of the correlated progression of language and thought expressed in action during the second and third year. However, although they indicate an ability to notice the similarities among things by 12 months, they do not suggest, as Sugarman emphasizes, the ability to coordinate two discrete different classes of objects, as required by word–object symbolization. Nor is a level of categorizing beyond the perceptual during the first half of the second year indicated, since the basis for grouping is perceptual similarity. It seems probable, on the basis of Sugarman's (1981) and other relevant research, that a major change takes place in the child's categorizing ability around 18 to 20 months (for most children) and that this change is reflected in the use of both language and action. Just such a shift is suggested in Piaget's theory as sensorimotor intelligence gives way to representational intelligence and the symbolic function emerges. But Sugarman's analysis suggests that there is considerably more power to the child's thought both before and after this shift than Piaget suggested. Moreover, the nature of the shift does not appear to be best characterized as from sensorimotor to representational but rather to a different and more advanced approach to categorization.

In this discussion little evidence has been presented to show that children have concepts as defined earlier, and as distinguished from categories (type 1 or 2), before beginning to talk. It is difficult to study the establishment of concepts as mental units prior to learning language. The studies by Freeman, Lloyd, and Sinha (1980) of the *cup* concept, demonstrating the effect of the canonical function of an object on behavior with respect to that object, is as convincing evidence as has been brought forth to show that at least some specific preverbal object concepts exist. That children do not always behave as though they did have specific object concepts is indicated by the fact that prior to 12 months children are very often not disturbed when one object is substituted for another in an object-hiding game (Le Compte & Gratch, 1972; Nelson, 1979a). By 1 year, however, children do notice such changes and find them bewildering, thus indicating that they expect objects to retain their characteristics. But it is not individuality that is thus established—children readily substitute objects of the same class for one another. An example was cited in Chapter 2 of a 15-month-old child who, in a game of ball-rolling, was observed to go to his toy box to get another (perceptually distinct) ball when the first one rolled out of sight. This suggests that at this age any ball is as good as any other so long as it can be used in the game.

In summary, this discussion, combined with that in the previous chapter, implicates several prelinguistic representational structures that may form the conceptual basis for word learning. General event representations are assumed to embed object representations as well as actions and actors. Generic concepts of objects and general higher-order categories have also been proposed as basic representational structures. The research on categorization in the first 2 years demonstrates that there is a basic disposition to treat similar things categorically rather than individually, but the ability to classify similar things develops in significant ways over the first 3 years. If categorization is essential to language, changes in language—in particular, changes in meaning structures—may parallel those in the cognitive realm. Studies of early lexical development are next surveyed to determine what implications they have for the existence and development of representational structures.

This approach may seem somewhat circular. We first posit certain conceptual types that are claimed to form the basis for word learning and then look at word learning to find evidence for the types. However, there are two things to be said in favor of this strategy. First, it might be that no evidence is found for these types, thus casting doubt on their existence or efficacy. Second, given that there is no way of viewing the infant's mind directly, the alternative would be to look for evidence in another system, namely, action. However, there is no compelling reason to believe that action has the same cognitive basis as language (although the two *may* reveal similar processes, as in Sugerman's studies). Thus, the absence of evidence in action would not be convincing. Indeed, I suggest that action does not provide an adequate basis for the development of language; that is, meaning in language is on a different plane than meaning in action, and this realization on the part of the child is one of the fundamental achievements necessary to the acquisition of language.

The Beginnings of Language: Learning to Understand

Whereas most children do not begin to use a few words until they are about 12 months old, the majority give evidence of responding to words several months before that time. Few systematic studies have been made of this period. Huttenlocher (1974) observed 4 children over a period of months and concluded that their understanding of object terms developed from context-bound to context-free understanding during the latter part of the first year and the beginning of the second.

The most thorough study of this development was carried out by Benedict (1976) with a sample of 8 children followed from 10 months to 27 months. She recorded and tested all cases of the understanding of language terms and probed children's understanding of sentences of various kinds throughout the period. She described the development of receptive language in terms of 4 stages covering the period from 8 months to 2 years and moving from no indication of response to language terms; to (1) response to a few terms in a particular game context (e.g., "peekaboo," "patty-cake," "thank you"); then to (2) response to a number of single terms not necessarily in context or spoken when the referent is present; followed by response to (3) more than one word in a sentence but not necessarily in correct relation (for example, the recipient might be substituted for the possessor in "give mother your shoe"); and, finally, response to (4) more than one term in a sentence in the appropriate relation. Most children had reached the third stage by 15 months, long before they combined words themselves, but had not reached the final stage until they had themselves begun to construct sentences (at about 19 months). There were wide individual differences in the ages when these achievements were made. What is interesting about this pattern is that it documents very early mastery of the referential meaning of words, but not mastery of the sentence structure, in comparison with the child's own productions.

Benedict found a discrepancy between the types of words understood and those the children produced (a discrepancy also noted by Huttenlocher). Children understood a large number of action words very early, while they tended to produce primarily object terms. The latter finding is consistent with most studies of early lexical acquisitions (e.g., Nelson, 1973b). On the other hand, their comprehension vocabularies increased exponentially as they learned object names, as is usually the case for productive vocabularies, but many months later.

In the Nelson (1973b) study, based on longitudinal data from 18 children, productive vocabularies of 50 words were achieved on the average at 19 months of age, and word combinations began at about the same time. Nominals (terms for people and objects, including pronouns and proper nouns) comprised 65% of the vocabularies on the average, while only 13% were action words and 8% were personal–social expressions. There was considerable individual variation in both the age of acquisition and the composition of the lexicon in this sample (see Chapter 4); however, the relation between comprehension and production for the group as a whole was similar to that found by Benedict.

The discrepancy between production and comprehension can perhaps be explained in terms of the kinds of language appropriate for adults to use with children (comprehension)—primarily directives for action—and the terms children may be inclined to use in play (object terms). Although this is plausible, it is not completely in accord with all of the data on the course of development observed in early productive speech (see below). Moreover, it is not known whether we can attribute the same meaning to words understood as to those produced. There are some reasons for believing we cannot in that children may overextend words in production and not in comprehension, for example. Thus, while the precise relation between the child's early comprehension of language and early production cannot at present be specified, development of word meaning does appear in some sense to advance from interpretation to expression.

Three Types of Early Language Production

The earliest phases of productive language use in children are not easy to identify. First words emerge from and merge with prelinguistic vocalizations and gestural communication. Different criteria for identifying early words and meaningful vocables no doubt account for much of the discrepancy in the attribution of first words between different observers. Despite a large number of generally very careful studies of early word learning and use, there is also disagreement as to the characteristics of the words produced. These disagreements center on issues of pragmatic function, grammatical category, and conceptual content and make it difficult to form an overall picture.

However, from the many studies now available it is possible to discern three phases of early productive speech that appear to follow a developmental course. It should be emphasized, however, that this summarization is an idealization from data that comes from many sources and that by no means are uniform stages of development being proposed. Not all types or phases are observed for any given child, and the types may overlap in development rather than representing discrete steps.

Phase 1: Prelexical

Protolanguage is the term used by Halliday (1975) to characterize his son Nigel's early use of what Dore (1974) termed "phonetically consistent forms" (PCFs) for communicative purposes. Carter (1979) traced in some detail the evolution of some similar forms—which she terms sensorimotor morphemes—in the single subject she studied. These earliest forms are characterized as "pure performatives," as used interpersonally, pragmatically, or communicatively; or, in Grieve and Hoogenraad's (1979) terms, they are used as a means of *sharing experience* rather than a means for talking *about* experience. Common examples of such uses include utterances such as "ta," said when giving or taking objects; "hi" and "bye-bye" and their variants, said to people and objects; "da," said in a questioning tone when pointing to objects; and so on.

However, these recognizable PCFs do not seem to be the *only* kind of protolanguage used by children during what we can term the pre-lexical period. Consider the phenomenon Peters (1977) noted with respect to Minh, the Hawaiian child she studied throughout his second year. Minh, a second-born boy, displayed two distinctive types of speech almost from the beginning. The first type was characteristically poorly articulated but prosodically clear, in some ways resembling those forms identified by Dore and Carter, although many of them were longer and more complex. They included not only "uh-oh" but "open the door" and "I want read Moon good night." Peters characterized these as *gestalts*, involving learning the tune without the words (see also Dore's [1974] description of an "intonation baby"). Brannigan (1979) observed similar gestalts that he called "compressed sentences" (see Chapter 4). As these observers have all noted, gestalts are neither words *nor* sentences. They occur throughout the second year, accompanying both the second (lexical) and third (relational) phases of development as well as the first. Even the more complex phrases resemble the protolanguage forms in being only loosely related (through intonation and vowel quality) to conventional language forms and in being used procedurally (rather than referentially) within clear, socially defined situations.

Peters termed the other type of language form that Minh used analytic—it consisted of clearly articulated single words, and its greatest use was in the context of a naming game, that is, in looking at picture books with mother in response to her query "what's that?" Ninio and Bruner (1978) have provided a detailed description of the interaction that takes place during book-reading situations and the way in which the mother's formatting behavior changes over time as the child's ability to take his part increases. Because of its procedural, routine quality, this stereotyped object or picture naming is classified here as being essentially prelexical in the same way as the interpersonal procedural forms. Dore (1978) refers to these uses as "indexical."

However, in a third type of early use, labels appear to be acquired not only *within* contexts such as picture naming, but to *refer* to contexts from within those contexts. One example is the use of "car" only in the context of standing at the window and watching cars on the road (Bloom, 1973; Nelson, Rescorla, Gruendel, & Benedict, 1978). Christine's use of "wait John" (Chapter 2) is another example. My original notion that "ball" referred to the relations it entered into could be reconceptualized as using "ball" to refer to "ball contexts" (Nelson, 1974a). In the terms introduced in Chapter 2, these words may be viewed as referring to a whole event, or an event representation.

It is probable that these two types of object-term uses (picture naming and event reference) account for most of the earliest object words found in the first 20 or so words of the young child's vocabulary. Although they are clearly identifiable as forms modeled after the adult term, they seem to differ *only* in form from PCFs. In function they too are procedural rather than declarative.

In addition to these uses, some early words appear to be attached to the child's own general object or action schemes. Bloom pointed this out in her 1973 monograph, and many others since have noted the attachment of words to actions early in the second year. For example, McCune-Niccolich (1981) provided an analysis of the use of terms expressing *relations,* that is, neither objects nor action nor social formulas. She observed a common set of terms expressing aspects of sequential transformations of objects among the 5 children she studied longitudinally between 15 months and 2 years. The terms in question are those such as "all gone," "more," "here," "open," and "up," which express general object relations of the type assumed to be established during the sensorimotor period, involving temporal, spatial, and causal notions. They were used primarily in relation to the child's own actions on objects (this is also in accord with Greenfield and Smith's [1976] and Huttenlocher, Smiley, and Charney's [1983] findings). That is, they seem to accompany actions rather than naming them. Gopnik (1982), Gopnik and Meltzoff (1984), and Tomasello and Farrar (1984) each provided additional analyses of these terms and related them to the child's achievement of a general understanding of object relations during the second year. It is of interest that the expression of these simple, general object relationships appears to decline with linguistic advance—they play a decreasing role in early sentences. Thus, they also seem to belong to a particular (early) phase of development.

To summarize, then, there appear to be at least the following subtypes of language forms, used during the first part of the second year, that are prelexical (i.e., not symbolic) in nature: use of words and phrases in social interaction within contexts, naming routines, use of words to refer to events, and attaching words to general action schemes. We can think of these types as different routes into or at least toward language (see Chapter 4). Different children appear to rely on these different routes to differing degrees. Some children, in fact, do not actively participate in any language use at all during this period, although they appear to understand a great deal. Following Grieve and Hoogenraad (1979), it can be said that while all of these uses have *purpose* (that is, to communicate or to accompany action), they do not have *meaning.* Or, to put it another way, they have a perceptual or actional but not a conceptual base. In this sense they may *refer* within a given communicative context but they do not *denote*. As suggested in the previous chapter, children's first excursions into language are supported by their understanding of and participation in routine events. During this phase words have no meaning outside these events. Adults rely to a large extent on formulaic uses of language in well-scripted social situations rather than on original constructions, much as the beginning speaker does. That is, older children's and adult's discourse is sometimes communicative (of intent, emotion, or sociality) without being, strictly speaking, conceptually based, just as is that of beginning speakers. In contrast, the substantive terms that children learn through naming games have at least the *potential* to invoke concepts, even if they do not do so at first. And, words used to refer to undifferentiated events may be closest to being truly conceptual. Although they refer to larger representational structures than is appropriate for the term in the language being acquired, they are not based solely on a perceptual paradigm. This point will be elaborated in the next section.

The implication of this analysis is that when children begin to understand and use a few words themselves at the end of the first year and the beginning of the second, they do not yet have any firm ideas about either the uses of or the structure of language. Therefore, they may hit on different assumptions about language, based on their experiences with it. Some of these uses (including formulaic speech) will continue to be incorporated into later uses and structures, while others (terms referring to action schemes) will drop out. Some of them will develop fuller conceptual meanings, while others will not.

Phase 2: Lexical Symbols

The mental representation of a lexicon requires that words be established as symbols. As I have just indicated, there is little evidence in the studies now available that the majority of words used in the first half of the second year are symbolic in this way. This is a point implicit in the various discussions of a protolanguage, as in Bates' (1976) statement that first words are not something that children "have" but something they "do" (although her recent [Bates, 1979] attribution of "naming" to gestures as well as words seemingly contradicts this position), and in Grieve and Hoogenraad's (1979) suggestions that they are used to share experience rather than meaning. How do children get past this point into the use of words as symbols?

This problem has been addressed by both John Dore (1978) and John McShane (1979) as the problem of the *designation hypothesis* or the *naming insight*. In addition to the evidence just reviewed, suggesting that early word use is procedural rather than meaningful, there is also the fact, frequently underplayed in discussions of early language, that most children acquire few words between 10 and 20 months and use those they have infrequently in specific contexts. There is often a long plateau between acquiring the first few words and an acceleration of vocabulary acquisition around the middle of the second year (McCarthy, 1954; Nelson, 1973b). This acceleration is illustrated in Figure 3.2, taken from Nelson (1973b), showing the rate of acquisition of words by months prior to the achievement of a vocabulary of 50 words, based on a sample of 18 children. This acceleration often seems to be accompanied by what has been called the naming insight. This phenomenon was given its most dramatic account by Helen Keller in her autobiography, where she described how the water from the pump and the "word" being rapped into her hand suddenly came together in a symbol–object relation. Both Dore and McShane have argued that the naming insight is the key to real language, representing a realization on the part of the child that language is a *system* of using words as symbols, symbols that can be recombined in different ways to stand for different relations between things in the world.

It is significant that most of the words acquired in this explosion of learning are words for familiar objects and that many overextensions and other mismatches of meaning are observed around this time (Rescorla, 1980). Experimental studies of early concept formation have also suggested that there is an important cutoff in the middle of the second year prior to which children do not readily learn words for novel objects, whereas after that point they usually do. The only study of this kind

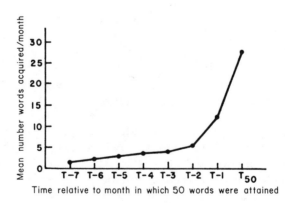

FIGURE 3.2   Rate of word acquisition by months prior to the achievement of a 50-word vocabulary. (From Nelson, 1973b.)

that has been reported for children under 18 months (Oviatt, 1982) showed that up to sometime between 15 and 18 months children could learn a receptive name for a novel object but could not transfer it to new exemplars. In my laboratory an attempt to teach children of 17 months the names for a set of objects met with no success. Even with 20-month-olds we were successful with receptive but not productive naming in many cases (Ross, Nelson, Wetstone, & Tanouye, in press). Together with the data from diary and natural observation studies, this finding supports the suggestion that the basis for the application of words shifts during the middle of the second year, a suggestion also consonant with Sugarman's (1983) studies of classification. The evidence indicates that not until the second half of the second year can discrete concepts of objects and actions be formed and named.[2]

Another important finding that has emerged from these concept studies is that from 18 months or so children can learn names for generalizable object concepts on the basis of exposure to one exemplar (K. E. Nelson & Bonvillian, 1978; Ross et al., in press). If children learn and generalize from one exemplar, they must be engaging in the formation of a unitary concept (rather than a category), as defined earlier. Moreover, in the Ross et al. (in press) study the importance of distinctive functions as a basis for concept formation was supported. Objects that had many distinctive functions (actions that could be performed on or with them) were more readily learned than those with few. This implies that the conceptual development underlying the lexical shift has a functional component, consistent with the proposal that concepts are initially partitioned from event representations.

If words in the prelexical period may refer but do not denote, what can we say about word meanings in the symbolic period? What are words symbolic of? To assert that they symbolize objects cannot be correct, because children readily extend them to novel objects, thus indicating that the word is a symbol of something more abstract than the concrete object itself or a set of familiar objects. That abstraction, moreover, cannot be only a percept or a perceptual paradigm, since words are extended on the basis of their functions and relations as well as perceptual similarity. (Although such extensions are much less frequently observed than perceptually based extensions, they are reported frequently enough to warrant consideration as evidence [e.g., Anglin, 1983]). Thus, a referential–perceptual theory is insufficient; at least beginning in the middle of the second year we need more than a percept to account for naming behavior. The choice is then between a concept and a semantic representation as the symbolized element. While it is too soon to rule out semantic representation at this point in development (either in terms of semantic features or contrasts), it is not unreasonable to posit that when words first acquire symbolic significance it is concepts that they signify. The reasons for holding to this view depend upon understanding later developments as well as early ones; thus, the full case cannot be made until a later point. That words come to symbolize concepts sometime in the second year will simply be asserted for the present.

The symbolic step is essential in order to make possible the *communication* of mental recombinations of concepts. That is, as long as experience is being merely shared, so that the language the child uses is understood in context, that language need not be symbolic of particular concepts. But when the topics are new or nonpresent states of affairs, for example, when the talk is about past events or plans for the future, new combinations of old concepts are wanted, and symbols with shared conceptual meaning are needed to effect communication. In short, symbolic language is essential to the communication of conceptual thought.

Consistent with this observation is the finding that multiword utterances usually begin to be formed shortly after the acceleration of vocabulary acquisition (Nelson, 1973b). This indicates that the child has acquired the notion that words refer to concepts that can be formed into new combinations. From this insight the child subsequently maps words onto all her available concepts and partitions new concepts to fit words used around her. As Halliday (1975) noted, real dialogue also seems to begin about the same time in the latter half of the second year. That is, as concepts are partitioned, words can be acquired as symbols for them; in turn, the concepts (and the words) can be recombined to express new meanings that can be communicated (through dialogue) to the conversational partner.

There is an additional complexity that I must note here. Not all children are observed to have a naming insight or to undergo a marked acceleration of vocabulary during the second year. Often these are children whose early language use has emphasized social–procedural (rather than substantive naming) forms, forms which no doubt continue to be effective at least in limited contexts. The significance of different ways of learning and using early language forms will be considered in Chapter 4.

Phase 3: Relational Constructions

As just noted, most children around the middle of the second year begin to form two-word (or morpheme) constructions. These constructions have received much scrutiny in recent years as indications of the beginnings of a grammatical system. They seem to provide the first evidence that the child is forming rules for using (either for interpreting or producing) language. As noted earlier, the comprehension of sentences during the second year before production of two-word utterances does not appear to reflect systematically the semantic or syntactic categories that have been used to describe adult grammar in either transformational or case-grammar terms (Bloom, Lightbown, & Hood, 1975; Braine, 1976; Brown, 1973).

Bowerman (1978a) analyzed the regularities that do appear as following two different routes for the formation and use of relational categories, that is, categories that determine how concepts may be combined. In one route the child may start with a lexically based rule system that attaches relational terms to lexical concepts (for example, "hat on," "here doggie"). This route is essentially similar to that described earlier by Braine (1963) and others in terms of pivot–open grammar. It has been shown that such grammar is not adequate for the description of most child language but, as Bowerman points out, some children do appear to use small-scope lexical rules of this type early on. The other route depends upon the formation of semantic categories of large or small size that are then combined relationally (for example, "Mommy eat," "baby [in] bed"). The combinational *rules,* rather than relational *terms,* indicate the relations between the concepts. Both of these types of relations appear in adult languages. Word order is used in languages like English to indicate semantic relations. Inflections and grammatical morphemes (such as prepositions) are also used in English to indicate relations among terms. In some languages (such as Latin) case inflections are relied on to the exclusion of word order. Thus, as Bowerman points out, the two routes that she discusses can be seen to represent two possible types of relational encoding in natural languages.

There is a puzzle in this brief overview of early language developments that can be seen more clearly if we accept the view put forth by Bowerman and others that the early combinational rules are essentially semantic or lexical rules for combining concepts, concepts that have an existence independent of the language terms used to express them. The early combinations can then be viewed as a *primitive syntax,* to use Moulton and Robinson's (1981) term. In primitive syntax, lexemes (i.e., words) are mapped directly onto concepts. Relations between the concepts are generally apparent from the pragmatic information available in the real world or in the previously encoded information about the concepts in question. But if lexemes are mapped directly onto concepts and concepts represent states of the world, why should there by a prerelational period and even a prelexical phase of language use? Why does the child not begin by talking relationally (although perhaps with unordered strings, as is apparently the case in understanding during this period)? In fact, Greenfield and Smith (1976) and others have argued that relations *are* apparent in one-word utterances, although one part of the relation is not realized in the language. Their argument has been challenged on a number of grounds (see Barrett, 1982). Here the question is: Why not relation *in* language?

I propose that the notion of the unanalyzed event representation as a conceptual source (as described in Chapter 2) provides a framework within which to view this problem. To recapitulate, during the first half of the second year the child is learning to use language forms *purposefully* to name actions, pictures, familiar objects, and whole scripts, but not to symbolize *concepts*. Mental representation remains wholistic, consisting of integrated events, which can themselves be named, although their parts—not yet partitioned from the whole—cannot. It is only when the event representation is partitioned into its parts and the parts can be analyzed into concepts that can themselves be manipulated and named that relations between concepts can be established and talked about.[3] Interpreting words used by others may play a key role in these developments. Recent studies have shown that comprehension is the best predictor of later language advance (Bretherton *et al.*, 1983; Nelson, 1973b; Rescorla, 1976), supporting this supposition.[4]

As far as the comprehension of terms is concerned, it seems plausible that the use of a word by another calls up the associated event representation, which in turn embeds the appropriate reference, without requiring that the referent be established independently of its context. In other cases a percept or a set of percepts (e.g., pictures and objects) may serve as the referent or the word may call on the child's own action (e.g., ''look,'' ''give,'' ''peekaboo''). The point is not that the child does not have available the makings of an interpretive system (involving perceptual representations and event knowledge) but that the conceptual basis for this system is not yet fully differentiated at 1 year.

The implication of the foregoing description is that children who begin to talk at different points in relation to their underlying conceptual development should proceed through the language-acquisition process in different ways. The fact that many children begin to talk early in the second year appears to reflect a desire to share experience with others rather than to exchange information or meaning. But if a child begins to talk late in the second year, that talk should reflect both functional and structural differences. In particular, the child should show much greater interest in using the language to comment on events and states rather than to simply name or exchange phatic comments. This is so because, regardless of individual interests, the possibility of constructing new conceptual relationships has been established, whereas earlier it had not been. In addition, children should proceed much more quickly through the various phases of talking, spending little or no time in the one-word stage. Both of these predictions seem to hold from the available data, but they await further systematic study for confirmation.

Let me summarize the developments envisioned here in terms of overlapping phases. It is important that these are not considered to be discrete or discontinuous stages. Rather, they are developments that take place over a long period of time (1½ to 2 years). In general, we can see a progression of the following sort: from the last quarter of the first year to the last quarter of the second year, the child moves through a prelexical phase in which vocal forms are used procedurally; to the emergence of lexical symbolic forms that are used to symbolize concepts; and thus to the formation of rules for combining words into combinations that can be used to communicate new meanings. The different types of words used in each phase are summarized in Table 3.1.

The protolexicon has been viewed in terms of three types: protorelations (formulas and action schemes), event referents, and names for pictures or objects. The protorelations appear to be similar to gestures in their employment and use. Like gestures, they occur commonly in the period between 12 and 18 months and tend to drop out as more adequate language is acquired (Bretherton *et al.*, 1981). It is suggested that event referents (e.g., "car" for watching cars go by) bear a developmental relation to later object concepts. However, early naming of

TABLE 3.1
Types of Words Used during Proposed Three Phases of Early Language

Types of uses	Phase 1 Prelexical 10–20 months	Phase 2 Lexical 16–24 months	Phase 3 Relational 19–30 months
Phonetically consistent forms	×		
Phrasal formulas	×	×	×
Picture naming	×	×	×
Names for object contexts (event representations)	×		
Names for object concepts		×	×
Words for action schemes	×	×	
Relational terms (verbs, adjectives, prepositions)			×

pictures and single objects is different. Picture-book naming may establish an important aspect of language for the child by stressing that things can be named, that is, referred to. Moreover, it may establish a communicative game that has its own importance (Ninio & Bruner, 1978). Nonetheless, evidence shows that pictures have a different "reality" for the young child than do experienced objects and that names do not transfer from one to the other in the same way. As indicated in Table 3.1, names for object contexts drop out as names for object concepts come in during Phase 2, while names for action schemes drop out with the appearance of true relational terms in Phase 3.

This scheme is based on an evaluation of data from numerous sources encompassing intensive longitudinal studies of single subjects (e.g., Bloom, 1973; Bowerman, 1976; Carter, 1979; Dore, 1974) as well as wider-based accounts (e.g., Benedict, 1976; Nelson, 1973b; Rescorla, 1980). No study has attempted to distinguish just these or all of these types, and many studies do not distinguish adequately among characteristics of word use at different ages. Thus, this description must be taken as an idealization inferred from a still inadequate base. Its developmental implications and their obvious relation to cognitive developments are important to recognize. Unfortunately, these developmental trends have not generally been taken into account when the conceptual and semantic issues addressed here have been discussed.

Semantic Domains and Superordinate Categories

A salient phenomenon observed in word use during this early period is that the extension of a term by the child to novel objects often seems to indicate an awareness of a superordinate (type-2 category) structure. It has been widely observed that children overgeneralize their early language terms along conventional category lines. For example, they may call a horse, but not a (four-legged) table, "doggie." Or they may call a banana but not a ball "apple" (see Anglin, 1977; Bowerman, 1976; E. V. Clark, 1973; Rescorla, 1980, 1981.) Does this indicate that they have established some sort of category boundary similar to "four-legged animal" or "fruit"?

The diversity of objects that are included under the child's labels as well as the fact that they usually obey category boundaries has led to the suggestion that children are using some notion of hierarchical categories in the formation of the lexicon. Yet the diversity of exemplars clearly also indicates that neither a simple notion of perceptual generalization nor an adult-defined category will account for the naming behavior. (For example, Rescorla's [1981] subject named clocks, watches, dishwasher dials, and dripping-water "clock," and Bowerman's daughter named grapefruit halves and a hangnail "moon.") While most of the things included under the term "doggie" or "car" bear an obvious relation to the adult's category "animal" or "vehicle," respectively, the examples of "clock" and "moon" do not all fall into a neat category. Rescorla explains some of these uses on the basis of different functional uses of words by the word-learning child. Some uses are relational or predictational—the child is attempting to say something about the object, as when the child says "daddy" upon spotting daddy's shoe (Example 2 in Chapter 1). Other uses derive from the child's assignment of close category members to the concept. Still others reflect the child's recognition of a similarity between the referent object and something else in the world, and thus are said to be uses of terms as analogies (see Winner, [1978] and Hudson & Nelson [1984] for confirming data). Although children frequently continue to overextend words along category boundaries past the time when they are constructing sentences, their use of looser "analogies" drops off. However, during the same time they make explicit analogies, following similar uses by parents, who frequently say "Yes, it's *like* a doggie, but. . . ." Thus, the supposition that children between 18 and 24 months use many words "inappropriately" to point out similarities between things seems to be reasonable. Bowerman's "moon" may be interpreted in this way.

Where does this leave the category question? Do 2-year-old children have lexical type-2 categories (in addition to or as opposed to naming concepts, percepts, or objects)? In the terminology employed here a lexical type-2 category is defined as a category that groups together several nameable concepts. The alternative to a lexical type-2 category is an overly broad concept, one that may be later differentiated.

The lexical-category explanation implies that the child who calls all four-legged animals "doggie" actually has several differentiated concepts (related to those of horse, cat, bear, etc.) that have not yet been named because of inattention to the names used by others or for some other reasons. However, the child, being cognizant of the similarities (functional and perceptual) between the related concepts, creates a superordinate category and gives it a label, "doggie." Thus, the child can economically refer to a large category of related things with a single name. In the small-child world, such economies are rarely ambiguous. When ambiguities become too great, the child might pick out one of the subordinate concepts and name it as well, still keeping the general term "doggie" for the superordinate class. Indeed, this is what a great deal of the data look like (see E. V. Clark, 1973; Leopold, 1939; Lewis,

1951; and Rescorla, 1976) and what many of these theorists have proposed. The alternative, the broad concept, accounts for the data by assuming that the concept itself is undifferentiated at first and that its subcomponents are not independently conceptualized but mutually exist under the "doggie" label.

There is now substantial evidence that children will often distinguish in comprehension between examples that they do not distinguish in production. Thus, they will reliably pick out "trucks" when asked to do so, although they will call the same object "car" (Benedict, 1976; Rescorla, 1980; Thomson & Chapman, 1977; but see Kay & Anglin [1982] for evidence that children overextend a new term in comprehension and *not* in production). On the face of it, this observation would seem to dictate in favor of the type-2 category notion. However, as speculated earlier, comprehension at this age may be based on different interpretive principles than productive language based on the conceptual system. In the present example, "truck" as used by another may evoke a particular percept or perceptual paradigm in the child that is associated with the same *concept* as that associated with the term "car." That is, more than one term may be associated nonhierarchically with a concept. However, this would be an unstable condition leading to differentiation.

What would be expected if children formed true lexical categories is that once the names for the individual concepts were learned, it would be easy to teach a name for the superordinate category itself, that is, to replace the earlier coordinate term "doggie" with the superordinate "animal." But this does not happen. Indeed, one of the intriguing observations from Macnamara's (1982) work (replicated by others as well) has been that many young children decline to state that a "dog" is an "animal," claiming instead that it is a "dog." (Markman [1981], explains this behavior in terms of the child's interpretation of categories as collections, to be discussed in Chapter 5. In either case, the point is that the child is not treating the term in the way expected of a superordinate category.) Moreover, superordinate category labels are rare in young children's vocabularies. Rescorla (1976) found only one example in her study. And children apparently continue to have difficulty with both the semantics and the logic of category terms throughout the preschool years (Inhelder & Piaget, 1964; Macnamara, 1982; Markman, 1981; Nelson, 1977a).

We would also expect, if the general term were acting as a category label, that there would be no need to provide explicit training for the differentiation of subordinate classes and their labeling (since the concepts are predifferentiated). However, what evidence we have (Gruendel, 1977; Mervis & Mervis, 1982) shows the reverse to be the case. Demonstrating a difference in the activity of an exemplar can lead to learning the name of the exemplar, as Gruendel's example of modeling an elephant's form and movements showed, whereas simply labeling without demonstration is not sufficient.

Figure 3.3 illustrates the difference between the hierarchical category model and the undifferentiated concept model as they apply to early word learning. As shown here, in the concept model the concepts underlying language terms are unitary at all stages and, as new concepts become differentiated from event representations and become named, they take on a unitary status as well. That is, the object concepts that are differentiated from the event representation (E) are not composed of subordinated instances but are conceptualized in terms of the actions (A) and relations in which they take part. These in turn may lead to subgroups such as *pet* or *farm animal* based on shared action or function, prior to being reformulated as inclusive semantic categories at T_4.

In the category model the originally posited category *doggie* breaks apart into its component members as these become identified and named. As all of the members are named, the dominating category node, originally given the name *doggie,* is no longer hierarchically connected to its subordinate members. These connections then have to be reestablished at T_4 in terms of the superordinate *animal.* This represents an inexplicable discontinuity in development in which the presumed natural base for conceptual categories appears, disappears, and reappears.

If over-general terms do not refer to type-2 categories of subordinate concepts waiting to be named, what gives the extension of these terms its frequent category *look* (Bowerman's "moon" and Rescorla's "clock" to the contrary)? This look, it is suggested here, is the result of category members occurring in the same real-world contexts. Animals appear together in zoos, in picture books, and on farms. Vehicles appear together on the street, in parking lots, and so on. Food items appear together on the table at mealtime, in the grocery store, and in the refrigerator. In other words, objects belonging to different basic concepts appear in the same *slot* in familiar *scripted* contexts, and are thereby assigned by the child to the same concept. (This thesis will be presented more completely in Chapter 7.) The child is not, of course, completely context-bound. Parents and others teach words that differentiate among the tokens that occur in similar slots, and the child can learn to differentiate concepts along both perceptual and functional bases from such tutorials. The point to be stressed here is that during the early period between 18 and 24 months the child is not spontaneously forming hierarchical

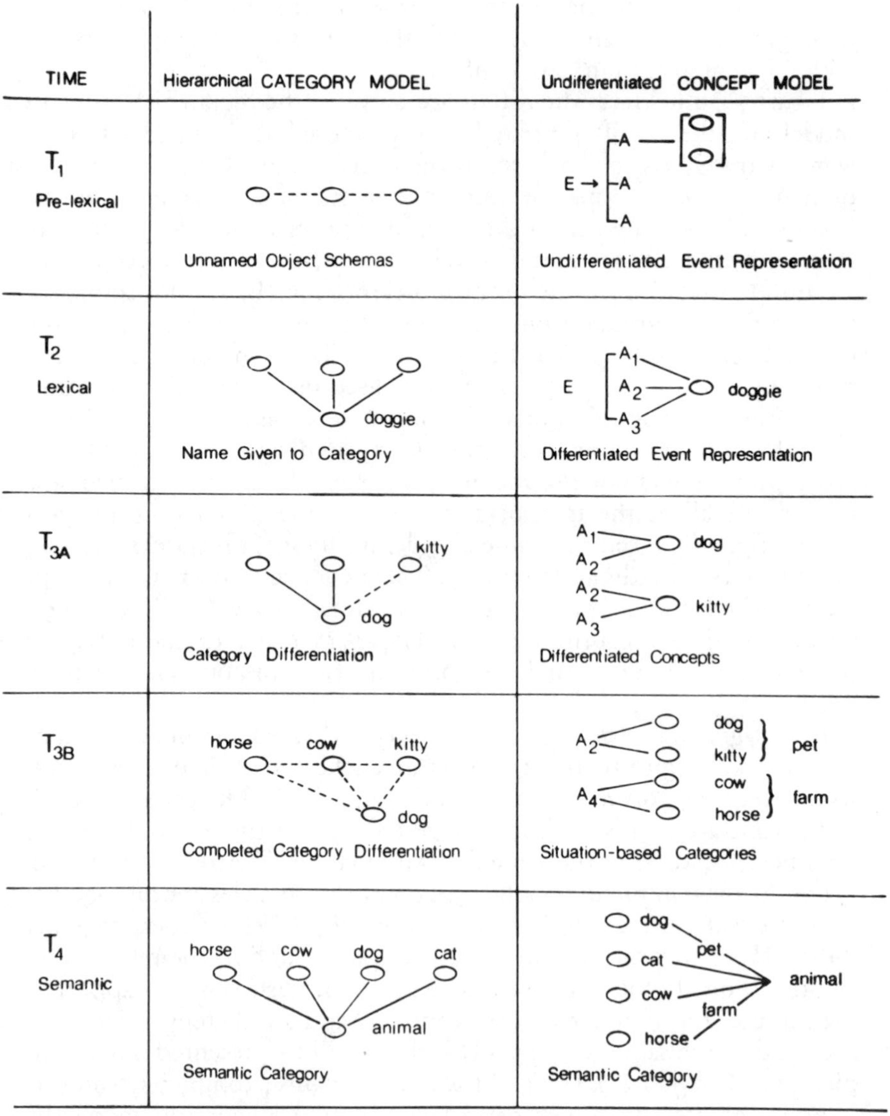

FIGURE 3.3   Hierarchical category and undifferentiated concept models of development within a semantic domain.

taxonomies. What makes it look that way are the contextual constraints in the world that are in turn reflected in the event-representational system that the child relies on as a source of concepts. The taxonomic system awaits the development of a true semantic system during the preschool years (see Chapters 7 and 8).

Lexical Acquisition and Lexical Development

The foregoing description of lexical acquisition during the second year has emphasized that significant developments take place that cannot be explained in terms of a single set of principles applicable at all points, whether these principles are taken from analysis of the adult language or of the child's own system at a given point. Moreover, our consideration of words in semantic domains suggests that significant developments in the lexical system remain to be tracked through the preschool years. A brief summary of what we have surveyed in cognitive and linguistic developments over the first 2 years can be given as follows.

Even young infants are disposed to categorize elements encountered in the world by treating distinguishable objects as the same. We call these types of categories perceptual, or type-1 categories. Between 12 and 18 months children begin to sort like objects together into a single group and by 18 months may label the group. Between 18 and 24 months they begin to relate two categories of things and attend to two dimensions at a time. Thus, important developments take place in categorizing abilities as evidenced in action during the second year.

Important developments also appear to take place in language-learning abilities over the same age range, including skills in categorization and relationships between categories. Prior to 16 months language use appears to be prelexical or "performative." Sometime around 17 to 20 months children usually begin to use language terms to indicate classes of discrete objects, demonstrating a conceptual basis for the term, and between 19 and 20 months they begin to relate words in primitive syntax. Although their comprehension of words long precedes their production of words, comprehension of grammatical relations does not. Thus, the development appears to proceed from words understood to refer, to words used in context, to words given an interpretation across contexts through their symbolic attachment to concepts.

A variety of different theories about the meaning of the child's first words were presented, and it is now time to evaluate their adequacy in light of the data. Referential–perceptual models were found to be inadequate to explain all the facts of word use and interpretation. However, the analysis of the types of words used in the prelexical period (first half of the second year) suggests that such models might be appropriate for development in this period. Children's use of words first appears to be activity-bound and can be seen as being part of the activity. However, the use of words to name pictures, objects, and whole events is a step toward the establishment of shared reference (as Bruner, 1983, has emphasized). Thus, children's first *meaning* system can be said to be in terms of reference. In this way children learn that words can be used to share experiences of objects and events in the real world. Once said, this seems obvious: Language meaning proceeds from the outside inward through reference to the real world. Language forms also proceed from the outside, where they are experienced, to the inside, where they may take on personal significance. There is little compelling evidence that a more complex theory of meaning is needed to explain the language acquired during the early months, although individual children may give evidence of a conceptually based lexicon, and some words may be used that have more conceptual content. Since development never takes place in discrete steps, these occasional *decalages* (Piaget, 1970) forecasting developments to come should be expected.

Conceptual–denotational models appear to be most appropriate for the symbolic period, including both the true lexical and the relational phases. It was argued that words are mapped directly onto concepts at this time. Thus, the suggestion is that concepts are identical to word meanings in the early stages of lexical development. As concepts change so do meanings and vice versa. How long this stage lasts will be considered in later chapters.

There is no compelling reason to suggest that a semantic-sense theory is needed to explain lexical developments during the second year. Indeed, it would appear that there is good reason to reject such theories. The differentiation of the lexicon within semantic domains can be as well explained in terms of conceptual differentiation as in terms of lexical features or contrasts. Moreover, the latter depend upon establishing systematic relations between words based on similarities and contrasts in their denotations. There is no evidence that children at 2 years of age utilize such relations. They reject the possibility of the superordinate relation. They do not understand opposition between terms (although they use "not" to negate). They are apparently indifferent to the use of a single term for more than one meaning at this time (as when the child uses "ba" to refer to both bath and bottle) and, although they may use terms synonymously, there is little indication that the overlap has any significance or is even noticed (there is little or no data on this point). In summary, whereas a lexical-contrast theory may be needed for describing later developments, its extension to the early stage of acquisition cannot be supported unless some evidence of the existence of lexical relations independent of the conceptual structure at this time is presented.

While a conceptual model is implicated to explain development in the second half of the second year, no particular model has been established as yet. The functional core model still appears to have heuristic value, but before defending or amending it further complexities of this developmental period need to be considered. In particular, variations in language development and their implications must be taken into account. Moreover, the way in which context and concept work together in the child's beginning interpretive meaning system needs to be explained in detail. These matters will be addressed in Chapter 4.

Notes

[1]It can be argued that [− polar] should indicate a lack of polarity in contrast to [+ polar], but this convention is not adhered to.

[2]Huttenlocher (pers. comm.) reports data showing that children as young as 15 months do use words to refer to specific objects independent of their context. This has also been observed by others (e.g., Bates, 1979) and is evident in my own data (Nelson, 1978b) for some children. However, the claim here is that the average child shows a shift in the basis of object naming in midyear and that prior to that time, with the probable exception of a few highly personal, meaningful objects, naming is based on perceptual paradigms or contextualized situations. It is also important to note that reference may be to an absent object (i.e., to a perceptual representation, an image) as well as to a present one. Thus, naming of things not in the immediate perceptual surroundings is not sufficient evidence of a context-independent concept.

[3]Bretherton et al. (1981) demonstrated that similar developments take place in terms of constructing combinations in both language and play during this period.

[4]It might be countered that the discrepancy between comprehension and production in vocabulary acquisition (Benedict, 1979) presents a contradiction to this hypothesis. Also, it appears that children learning manual signs (Bonvillian & Nelson 1982) acquire sign vocabularies as much as 6 months earlier than verbal vocabularies, that is, at about the same time that hearing children are responding to words but not producing them. However, careful studies of the contexts of signing are needed before concluding that signs have the same conceptual base as words learned during the latter part of the second year. Similar remarks apply to the basis for comprehension during this period.

4

Putting Context and Concept
Together in Language*

Variation in Language Acquisition

In Chapter 2 the ways in which language is embedded in contexts
were laid out and their effects on the child's understanding and use of
language in early verbal interactions were exemplified. In this chapter
the argument that variations among children in their styles of learning
and using language are at least partially attributable to the contexts in
which language is used will be set forth. Then, the relation of variation
in style or strategy to the development of meaning will be discussed
within an overall model of early meaning.

That children who are just beginning to use the language engage in
two or more different styles of talking that are related to the functions
that language serves for them is now well established through a number
of empirical studies. In particular, some children begin the language
game in a referential or analytic mode, using single words to refer to
objects and actions, while others rely to a large extent on an expressive
mode, using short phrases to communicate wants, needs, directives, or
affect. For these two groups of children language seems to serve different purposes. For other children different purposes are served by different types of language. These two different major purposes can be
referred to as *ideational* or *interpersonal,* in Halliday's (1975) terms. As
we shall see in the discussion to follow, many other terms have been

---

*Much of Chapter 4 is based on Nelson, 1981a; copyright © 1981 by the American
Psychological Association. Adapted by permission of the publisher.

used to refer to the two styles. A distinction that will be useful in relating the two approaches to the establishment of meaning is that of activity language versus reflective language. It will be argued that two different paths into language meaning can be taken by the child, one that uses language *in* activity and another that talks *about* activity (i.e., is reflective). It will be recalled that these uses were discussed in terms of the development of the conceptual basis for language in Chapter 3. Here we shall broaden the discussion to relate them to different developmental courses that may or may not eventuate in the same endpoint.

In the first sections of this chapter the evidence for two different approaches to language will be reviewed and some of the ways in which they have been characterized will be set forth. Explanations for the differences, including those both internally (child centered) and externally (adult centered) based will be considered. Data from studies of 2-year-olds and older preschoolers that reveal continued differences in active and reflective language will be reviewed as well. Later sections present a developmental hypothesis about the emergence of these differences and their general relation to the development of meaning, and the final section presents an overall summary of the development of meaning between 1 and 2 years of age in terms of development from reference to denotation.

Evidence for Individual Differences

Much of the recent work revealing differences in approach to language can be summarized in a set of polarities: word versus phrase, analytic versus gestalt, referential versus expressive, cognitive versus pragmatic, nominal versus pronominal. These dualities were first emphasized in a study I began in 1969 that focused on the presyntactic stage of learning to talk (Nelson, 1973b). In that study 18 children were followed longitudinally from approximately 1 year of age to $2\frac{1}{2}$ years. (The example of Christine in Chapter 2 came from one of these children.) The study used records of word use kept by mothers as well as tape recordings of language used by mother and child during monthly visits in the home and periodical probes of such developments as comprehension, imitation, categorization, and reference. A major outcome of that study was the identification of individual approaches to the tasks of learning the language. These approaches were reflected in several ways, first in the kinds of words and phrases children learned and used during the "single-word" period.

For most of the children (called referential), early vocabularies consisted of a large proportion of object names, that is, nouns, with some verbs, proper names, and adjectives. For a large minority (called expressive), however, vocabularies were more diverse, with a large number of social routines or formulas (such as "stop it," "I want it," and "don't do it") included among the nouns, verbs, and adjectives. These two primary characteristics representing content (vocabulary) and form (word or phrase) also appeared to be related to pragmatic factors of use, although the latter factor was not well demonstrated in this early study because of the nature of the data. It was also noted that expressive children tended more often to be second-born and to come from less highly educated families. A plausible case can be made that the conditions of language use are different in the environments associated with these factors (see the discussion below), although systematic observations of differences in function or context were not carried out with this sample.

Nominal versus Pronominal

The identification of a child as expressive or referential in my study was made at an average age of 19 months (or when a 50-word vocabulary had been acquired). Differences that persisted until at least 30 months were discovered in later analyses (Nelson, 1975a; 1975b). Although mean length of utterance (MLU) did not differ between the two groups of children at 2 or $2\frac{1}{2}$ years, size of vocabulary did, with the referential children using significantly greater numbers of different words than the expressive children. In addition, the expressive children used pronouns preferentially in sentences, while the referential children used primarily nouns in their early multiword utterances. This difference tended to disappear as the referential children began to use more pronouns in more complete sentences at the later age and MLU stage (over 2.5 words per utterance).

At about the same time that the first report from this study was published, Bloom (1973) described variations in the one-word period among the children who had been the subjects of her earlier grammatical analysis of multiword utterances (Bloom, 1970). On the basis of her observations, Bloom proposed that there were two routes to two-word speech and that these were associated with different characteristics of the children's two-word constructions as well as with differences in later usages and in the use of imitation. She observed that some children seemed to utilize relational terms (such as "all gone"), while others used more substantive terms (usually nominals such as "dog" or "flowers"). She also found that the "relational" children produced pivot–open[1] constructions and used more imitations and more pronouns (Bloom, Lightbown, & Hood, 1975). The substantive children used subject–verb–object sentence constructions (or reduced forms of such), used nouns rather than pronouns, and did not imitate.

The use of pronouns rather than nouns by expressive[2] children is especially interesting in terms of the expression of meaning. By using pronouns the child can refer to objects, people, and actions (using the proform ''do'') without specifying them. The semantics involved in the two uses is quite different. First, when pronouns are used the lexicon does not need to be as differentiated. ''It,'' to take the simplest case, may refer to any object, while ''ball'' must refer to objects specified by their appropriate properties. To use object terms the child must have built up perceptual or conceptual specifications for the words, but to use pronouns the child need only make general distinctions between people and things. The ''I–you'' distinction involves an ability to understand the deictic relationship (i.e., the shift in reference dependent upon speaker role), and ''he–she–they'' requires differentiation according to gender and number. However, these are very general distinctions in comparison to the fine-grained analysis required for distinguishing ''dog'' from ''cat,'' for example, or ''truck'' from ''car.'' The evidence indicates that at least for some children it is easy to learn nouns but less easy to learn pronouns, and for other children the opposite is true. The question is why this is so.

Analytic versus Gestalt

Since these 1973 accounts a number of studies have found related individual differences in early language. Many investigators have expressed surprise at the striking variations in characteristics of early speech, understandably so given the strong expectation from previous literature that the 15-month-old child may say ''doggie,'' ''bow-wow,'' or ''mommy'' but will not say ''I don't know where it is'' (Brannigan, 1979) or ''What do you want?'' (Nelson, 1973b) or ''I like read moon goodnight'' (Peters, 1977). Investigators who hear such expressions from 1-year-olds are likely to conclude that they are overinterpreting an unintelligible jargon sequence. It is only as these sequences are repeated in similarly appropriate situations that it becomes obvious that the child is using speech meaningfully. *Gestalts* such as these (to use Peters' [1977] term) have the characteristics of being wholistically produced without pauses between words, with reduced phonemic articulation and the effect of slurred or mumbled speech, but with a clear intonation pattern that enables the listener to construct the target utterance *in context*. An emphasis on intonation and form as opposed to clear phonemic realizations of content was also noted by Dore (1974) in differentiating two children he studied, whom he designated as *message* and *code* learners, respectively. Gestalt forms have also been referred to as "compressed sentences" (Brannigan, 1979), stereotyped units (Nelson, 1973b), or formulas and formulaic routines (e.g., L. W. Fillmore, 1979).

Thus far, then, we have noted three recurrent characteristics that frequently appear to go together. On the one hand, learning and use of nouns (object labels) in the first half of the second year, clear articulation of words of one or two syllables, and later two-word substantive combinations; and on the other hand, the learning and use of pronominals, whole phrases, and poor articulation but clear intonational patterns. There is at least one other characteristic of early language use that has been associated with these two styles. This is the use of "dummy" terms in early sentences. A much noted example of this was Bloom's (1973) Allison, who produced a form /WIDə/ that she combined with single words during the late one-word and early two-word period but for which there was no clear referent. The use of dummy terms (such as "uh uh" in combinations like "uh-uh down") by some nonreferential speakers was noted by Nelson (1973b) and has subsequently also been documented by Brannigan (1979), Peters (1977), Leonard (1976), and Ramer (1976). These terms seem to be serving the function for the child of "filling out" the sentence frame. They reinforce the notion, suggested by Peters and Brannigan, that some children are aiming at sentence targets rather than single-word targets from the beginning.[3]

Pragmatic versus Cognitive Functions

The different language styles just described have been attributed to the same child at different times and in different contexts as well as to different children. In my sample there appeared to be a continuum from highly referential to highly expressive, while many children employed aspects of both styles. Peters (1977) gave an excellent description of the way in which a single child used the two styles in different contexts. The gestalt style was used in social contexts when the child and another were engaged in free play and interactions or in speech contexts that Halliday (1975) would define as pragmatic, that is, instrumental, regulatory, and interpersonal; while the analytic style was used in specifically referential situations such as reading books with mother. The two styles were apparently well differentiated and highly context-specific. These findings strongly suggest that there are functional differences between the two types of early speech; that one type may be more appropriate in certain contexts than the other.

Explaining Individual Differences in Language Development

Peters (1983) cited four factors that may account for the style differences discussed above: individual makeup, type of input, type of speech expected by the environment, and perception of speech function. In considering these here it should be emphasized that, like Peters, we are not attempting to decide among them. Style or strategy differences may be multiply determined. Moreover, different patterns of acquisition-related factors may produce different styles. Although we have spoken of two seemingly coherent "packages" of early language characteristics, it has not yet been shown in any reliable empirical way that these are actually two distinct styles. What we may need to explain are a number of often correlated but logically independent variations. It can be noted that Peters' first and last factors derive from internal (child-centered) bases, while the second and third are external, environmentally determined. We shall consider the internal factors first.

Individual Makeup

Bates (1979) examined some of the data discussed above in terms of a hypothesized three-factor theory of symbolic development displayed phylogenetically as well as ontogenetically. The two cognitive factors were identified as *analytic*, which is related to the means–ends analysis of language and is also essential to tool using; and wholistic or *gestalt* processing, which is associated with imitation. The third factor was *communicative* intent. Bates notes that the first two factors may be related to competencies associated differentially with the two hemispheres of the brain, the analytic mode with the left and wholistic patterning with the right. Similar hemispheric function proposals have been put forth by Peters (1977) and Horgan (1981). Bates made the further suggestion that it is only when the three components become integrated that language—in the species or in the child—emerges. She noted that individual differences may result when there is an asymmetric development in the different components. A child who is relatively more advanced in analytic-type skills may rely on these in early language acquisition, while a child whose gestalt processing is relatively advanced may become a skilled user of whole phrases. This proposal is similar to one that I have set forth (Nelson, 1979b) and will discuss below.

A different hypothesis based on Geschwind's (1970) work would suggest that the different language areas in the left hemisphere may mature at different rates, leading to a word (Broca's area) or phrase (Wernicke's area) emphasis. Work by Marin, Saffran, and Schwartz (1976) with aphasics would support this hypothesis in that those with lesions at different sites appear to exhibit patterns of speech similar to those exhibited by referential and expressive speakers, respectively. Of course, any theory relying on the maturation of brain function must take into account the fact that neural development is interactive with experience; thus, no simple causal relationship can be invoked.

Wolf and Gardner (1979) described individual differences in all aspects of symbolic development that appear to implicate distinct cognitive styles associated with temperamental differences. They distinguish between *patterners* (similar to the referential–analytic groups described here), who consistently focus their attention on the object world, use other persons largely as means to ends, and use language to pick out physical properties; and *dramatists* (expressive–gestalt), who are socially oriented and use language to establish communication. These differences were displayed by the children they studied in symbolic play as well as language use, including metaphoric uses, throughout the preschool period.

The emphasis on a social versus object orientation as the basis for early language differences has been suggested in a number of reports, but the evidence that expressive speakers are more socially oriented is conflicting (e.g., Bretherton, *et al.*, 1973). The likelihood is that children who use expressive language are a varied group themselves. Probably some are socially oriented, while others are simply more involved in activity than in analysis of the object world. The case studies in Nelson (1973b) provide support for this supposition.

Another internal factor is the child's perception of speech function. Children who perceive speech to be primarily a social–communicative tool may readily acquire socially useful phrases, while those who perceive it to be a referential tool may more readily acquire descriptive labels. Such views are likely to be the outcome of early language exposure, thus to be the product of the interaction between the child's understanding and the parents' language use. This factor is discussed in the following section.

External Factors

An alternative to the internal factors just mentioned—neurological differential, maturation of skill, or cognitive style explanation of language style differences—is that style differences are determined by environmental conditions of learning. The suggestion that their appearance varies with educational status and sibling order (Nelson, 1973b) as well as related differences found by Allen (1977) in different social class groups points in this direction.

Research on the characteristics of mother–child interactions during the language-learning period has shown that infants hear adults speaking to them in playful interchanges (as in the "peekaboo" game), in caretaking situations (such as eating, dressing, and bathing), in behavioral control (such as "don't touch"), and in tutorials (such as book reading). Many studies have been carried out on the characteristics of adult talk to infants and children in the last 10 years, variously called the "baby-talk register" (Ferguson, 1977) and "Motherese" (Newport, Gleitman, & Gleitman, 1977). Catherine Snow's (1972, 1977) work was the first systematic investigation, and her findings have been replicated many times since. In general, it is found that mothers speak to their 1–2-year-old children in short, grammatically correct, highly intonated, high-pitched utterances, using many questions and repetitions. Recent research (Graves and Glick, 1978) has demonstrated that middle-class mothers increase their use of the baby-talk register when they are aware of being observed. Regardless of variations over time and situation, however, the formal characteristics described are quite pervasive across cultures, languages, conditions of observation, and even age of speaker. It seems likely that they accurately describe a great portion of the speech young children hear.

The specific characteristics of mother talk do vary according to the particular functions that the speech is serving, whether directive or conversational (McDonald & Pien, 1982), and according to the situation (Lucariello & Nelson, 1982b). Also, some mothers seem to employ some functions (e.g., directives) more than others do and to focus more on some types of content (child behavior or object characteristics) than others do (Lieven, 1978; Nelson, 1973b, 1981). The fact that mothers differ has made possible the examination of the question as to whether variation in the linguistic input is associated with variation in the characteristics of the language the child learns. For the most part, these studies have focused on aspects of child grammar rather than semantics. An exception was the Nelson (1973b) report that found a modest association between the mother's and child's focus on objects.

A later reanalysis of the speech used by mothers to their 2-year-old offspring identified as expressive or referential in the Nelson (1973b) study revealed a significant relationship between the mother's use of object terms and the child's noun–pronoun ratio, thus suggesting that there is consonancy between the language the child is exposed to and the language he or she learns along this dimension (Furrow and Nelson,

1984; see also Wells, 1980). Despite variations, however, it appears that the majority of parents in our society (working class as well as middle class according to the report from Miller, 1982) typically tend to provide children with single words to refer to things in their world, either through naming objects or looking at picture books. That is, they provide the child with a referential context and a referential language. In contrast, Schiefflin (1979) described a culture in which mothers try to teach children the appropriate formulas for dealing effectively with peers and older children. Although probably not many adults in our culture engage in similar teaching, no doubt many simply assume that the child will learn language without direct tuition and therefore by default provide the environmental conditions for the child to pick up socially useful phrases as well as single words, as Christine's mother did (Chapter 2). Another example is provided by Blake (1979), who described the close relationship between the pragmatic language used by a black mother–child pair, where the mother used speech primarily to transmit social information and supported the child's similar uses.

In contrast, Bruner and his colleagues (Bruner, 1975b; 1978; Ninio & Bruner, 1978; Ratner & Bruner, 1978) based their account of the development of language skills on the analysis of game-like formats that mothers (and presumably fathers and other adults) seem to engage in. These begin in such mundane contexts as the exchange of objects and playing "peekaboo." According to Bruner, through these formats mothers establish a structure that initially focuses joint attention on objects together with appropriate actions. In more advanced "games" such as book-reading (looking at pictures together and naming them), mothers provide a structured language routine in which the child gradually takes more of a role, progressing from pointing to naming, for example, in the appropriate *slot*. Thus, he has traced how, through the use of established routines, mothers gradually "up the ante," requiring more and more language contributions from their language-learning children.

This theoretical description places a great deal of weight on the role of the mother. To the extent that it is correct, one would expect to find style differences associated with mother's input. Lieven's (1978) analysis of the speech of two mothers whose children had quite different speech styles supports this expectation. Beth, a second-born, had speech that could be characterized as expressive, while Kate, a first-born, was more clearly referential. Both mothers adjusted their speech to their children along lines found to be generally characteristic of adult language to children, that is, shorter sentences and more imperatives and interrogatives than found in speech to adults. The interaction styles of the two mothers differed, however. While Kate's mother responded to her utterances 81% of the time, Beth's mother responded only 46% of the time. Kate's mother tended to respond more often with questions; there was more turn-taking in their conversation. Beth's mother responded more often, when she did, with a ready-made word or phrase, with a correction, or with a comment that ignored the child's utterance. In her summary of the two children's styles, Lieven says: "These two children appeared to be using language for different ends. Kate talked slowly and coherently about things happening around her and objects in her environment, while Beth devoted more time to using her speech to try and engage her mother's interest" (Lieven, 1978, p. 178). This description is consonant with the notion that children adopt different strategies and styles because they have different hypotheses about what language is used for. Obviously, such hypotheses must be based on their experience with language in use.

Note that the two children studied by Lieven differed in birth order. The likelihood that first- and second-born children may be exposed to different language environments supports the hypothesis that birth order may be related to style differences. Consider the differences in language uses that can be observed in different middle-class homes. For example, the mother who has a 3- or 4-year-old to cope with as well as a 1- or 2-year-old will characteristically use different language in interaction with both children than will the mother who has only one child of 1 or 2 years. A larger percentage of the function of language that the younger sibling hears is likely to be directive and centered around the child's own activities—to be, in effect, pragmatic and expressive. Thus, the child is likely to conclude that language is a pragmatic medium—useful for social control and social exchange—and this conclusion is likely to be shored up by exchanges with siblings. On the other hand, a child who is exposed to a mother who teaches through relevant questioning is likely to conclude that language is basically a cognitive or referential medium. Despite the plausibility of the sibling-order hypothesis, other studies (Bretherton *et al.*, 1983) have not found birth-order differences. This might be because such effects are evident at different ages and stages. Further evidence on this point is needed.

Tomasello and Todd (1983) provided a detailed analysis of mother–child interaction in the early word-learning period that supports the general interaction model. They found that the children of mothers who followed up the child's attention to objects with descriptions or other comments related to the child's interest were likely to acquire a large number of object terms, while the children of mothers who attempted to direct the child's activity acquired few general nominals.

As noted earlier, Peter (1983) also suggests that what others expect the child to learn affects what the child does learn about the language. For example, while mothers in our society "read" books to teach their beginning talkers object labels, children in Vietnam are expected to learn the honorific pronoun system first. In Schiefflin's (1979) study of the Kaluli, children are expected to learn how to deal with conflicts among peers using appropriate language forms.

In summary, despite the evidence that parents engage in a uniform "child-talk register" and that they provide "formats" within which children can take part linguistically, nonetheless there is considerable variability in the language forms and functions that different children are exposed to and in the responses that they get from others. Moreover, these variations are associated with differences in children's speech.

Language Function and the Language-Learning Task

Speech in different functional contexts displays different features. As various linquists and sociolinguists have pointed out (e.g., C. J. Fillmore, 1976; Gumperz and Tanner, 1979), an enormous amount of social speech is formulaic in character. Thus, the function of the language that the child is exposed to is reflected in its form. The mother who labels and responds to questions makes it easy for the child to break language into its component parts—to become a word user. Social-control language, on the other hand, is likely to be heard in clumps that are not easily broken up, for example, "D'ya wanna go out?," "I dunno where it is," or "Stop it." Segmentation of such sequences is difficult, but the tune, as Peters would say, is easy to learn.

Peters' (1983) analysis of the *units of language acquisition* and C. J. Fillmore's (1980) description of *preassembled parts* in the adult language are both relevant to this analysis. The language to be learned is traditionally thought of in terms of two basic units—the word and the sentence—words being learned as unanalyzed wholes, while sentences must be constructed from parts. Two problems arise with this description. First, words are not readily identifiable as separate parts in the speech stream; and second, many sentences are preassembled and can be used appropriately without further analysis or reconstruction in a new context. In other words, the difference between words and sentences—at least as they are displayed for the beginning language user—is not as great as traditional accounts have implied. The first problem for language learners is to isolate the parts that they will work with. They next need to learn what occasions of use the parts are appropriate to and, finally, how to construct new wholes out of old parts. While the traditional account has children first learning words and then constructing sentences, as we have seen, the process may proceed in a different fashion. There are, in fact, several accounts in the literature that suggest how children may proceed beyond the very early stages using preassembled parts (R. Clark, 1974; L. W. Fillmore, 1979; Snow & Goldfield, 1983).

The acquisition of preassembled phrases has an analogue in the representation of whole events. In both cases the whole is composed of parts that are not yet recognized as individuals by the person using them, although logical analysis shows that they are essential to its composition.

Language learning takes place within the framework of social interaction, and the nature of the particular kinds of interaction experienced determines not only the function and content of the language to be acquired but which segments will be learned first and how these segments will subsequently be put together or broken down for reassembly.

Because most children learning language learn to use it in a variety of contexts for a variety of purposes, most children will exhibit aspects of both formulaic and analytic approaches in their early language. The two approaches to the task both involve analytic and synthetic operations as well as pattern learning. As L. W. Fillmore (1979) suggests, the mastery of formulas provides the child with internalized sequences for applying analytic operations, comparing component parts, and reconstructing new wholes from old. For the word-learner the analysis comes first. It appears that children can master language in either way and probably also both at once. (The same, no doubt, applies to the representation of events and their parts.) Thus far, however, the general research tack has ignored the formulaic approach almost entirely in favor of the analytic (the favored scientific style of Western culture). It is important to recognize that both operations are possible for children and cannot be ignored in constructing a balanced account of the acquisition of meaning through language.

A causal chain has been implicated in this discussion. Let me make it explicit at this point. (1) Functional variation in context demands functionally appropriate speech, and such speech varies in form as well as function. (2) Exposure to primarily one type of functional context as the arena for mother–child speech during the early language-learning period disposes the child to (a) model this speech and (b) hypothesize that language is useful for this type of communication. *Or* (2') the child is disposed to attend to speech in a particular type of situation more than in others, and this leads to (a) and (b) as in (2). (3) Because of the association of form and function, a distinctive style of learning and use is displayed cross-situationally in speech by the child. It follows from these premises that these early dispositions or emphases can be fairly easily overridden if the case is as in (2) and the child is subsequently exposed to a wider variety of functional contexts of speech (e.g., book-reading for the expressive child). However, if the case is as in (2′), the child's disposition to engage in certain types of activities and their associated speech patterns may persist throughout early childhood and thus lead to further manifestations of a particular speech and cognitive style (Wolf & Gardner, 1979).

This causal chain is by no means established as fact, although all of the facts that we have appear to be consistent with it. What is clear is that early language, and later language, comes in two forms—clumplike gestalts and analyzed parts—and these forms are particularly appropriate to different contexts of use, where the emphasis is on the interpersonal or on the ideational, respectively.

Experimental Studies of Form-Function Relations

Additional evidence for the relation between form and function in early language use is available from several recent studies. An analysis of data from an experimental study of word learning (Ross *et al.*, in press) revealed a clear association of form and function. In this study 20-month-old children were taught nonsense labels for unfamiliar objects in a series of 4 learning sessions carried out in the laboratory in a standard manner. The sessions were videotaped for analysis, and the language used by the child was transcribed and coded by a trained assistant skilled in interpreting child language.

The mean MLU of the 20 children whose language use could be analyzed over 3 or 4 of the learning sessions was 1.43, with a range from 1.0 to 2.25. The relative use of nouns and pronouns (noun–pronoun ratio) was studied as an indicator of style differences in early multiword speech. Among this group there was a very balanced distribution of this variable, with 7 of the children using predominately pronouns [a (nouns)/(nouns + pronouns) ratio of .33 or less], 7 children using predominately nouns [a (nouns)/(nouns + pronouns) ratio of .67 or more], and 6 children falling in mid-range. (This outcome supports the suggestion that the difference reflected in this ratio is based on a continuum rather than a dichotomy.) Nominal–pronominal status was not related to MLU, amount of verbalization, or the receptive learning of object names.

Language functions in the third learning sessions were coded for the subjects who fell into the two extreme groups and who produced a sufficient number of utterances for analysis. There were five nominal (N) users and five pronominal (P) users who met the requirements. Language function was coded from the videotapes according to categories devised for this analysis, (based on Halliday's [1975] description of pragmatic and mathetic functions) roughly social and cognitive uses (definitions are given in Table 4.1). The reliability of coding into these categories by two coders reached 85% agreement.

Two categories were identified as primarily referential or object oriented (name–refer and comment–describe), two were identified as primarily personal–social in orientation (personal and interactive), and two combined social and object-oriented functions (instrumental–regulatory and show–give–take). The hypothesis based on previous research was that the pronominal speakers would use primarily personal–social functions, while the nominal speakers would use primarily referential functions. Mean scores for the two groups are shown in Table 4.1. As can be seen, there were large group differences in three of the four categories in question in the predicted direction, while there were no differences in the two categories that integrated social and object functions.

When the personal and interactive categories were combined, there was a nonoverlapping distribution between the two groups, with the pronominal speakers using these functions much more frequently on the whole than the nominal group (means of 27.5 and 11.7%, respec-

TABLE 4.1

Analysis of Speech Functions of Nominal and Pronominal Children in a Concept-Learning Session

	Percentage of total utterances	
Functional category	Nominal (N = 5)	Pronominal (N = 5)
Name–refer: Child names or refers to object (e.g., points and says "that")	24.6	13.02
Comment–describe object: Child names a property, action or state of the object	9.52	9.44
Instrumental–regulatory: Child attempts to regulate the action of another or use another to achieve an end	33.38	33.03
Show–give–take: Child engages other in showing or exchanging object	20.76	17.00
Personal: Child describes own action or state	11.00	21.81
Interactive: Child establishes or maintains contact with another	.74	5.70

tively). The outcome for the combined referential functions was less clear, although in the predicted direction.

The fact that there were not consistent differences between the groups in the use of the referential functions probably reflects situational constraints. That is, the context of the word-learning study was such that the child's attention was constantly directed to the objects to be learned. Thus, naming and referring were the expected or *framed* language uses. A child who might not ordinarily choose to talk about objects might feel constrained to do so in this situation. On the other hand, the personal and interactional uses were not specifically called out. The group difference in these latter functions, then, probably reflects a true difference associated with the language-form differences. It is also interesting to note that it was only the pronominal children who used negative utterances. For three of the pronominal children, 33% or more of their utterances were negatives (e.g., "no" and "I don't want it"), while only one of the nominal children used any negatives (4%). Negatives of the kind used here are clearly personal–social expressions.

Thus, under standard conditions of observation there is evidence that the nominal and pronominal styles are associated with functional preferences. Most children used all functions (although 4 N and 2 P children did not use the interactive function). The difference, then, was not one of what the child *could* talk about but of what the child *preferred* to talk about.

The nominal form difference was not, however, an artifact of the emphasis on personal–social speech by one group and not the other. Pronouns were used in all functions by pronominal speakers and vice versa, as the following examples from two children illustrate:

Nominal: Want mobol (P).[4] Mommy get mobol (I–R). I turn nutty (P). Put linky back (I–R).
Pronominal: I put back (P). Cover it (P). This (N–R). It's stuck (C–D).

Rather, the argument is that pronominal speakers customarily engage in personal–social speech and that pronoun use is particularly appropriate for such speech. Thus, pronouns are learned and used even in referential contexts. In contrast, nominal speakers use substantive terms in interpersonal as well as ideational speech contexts.

A partial replication of these results can be found in Furrow's (1980) study of the use of social and asocial speech among 2-year-olds studied in their homes during a free-play session. Using a similar functional analysis, he found that nominal-type speakers engaged in significantly more referential speech ($p < .05$), while pronominal children used more personal functions ($p < .01$). The referential-function difference held only for children at an early level of language mastery, however (MLU < 2.00). This is consistent with other evidence that shifts in the form–function relation take place late in the second year.

That many, perhaps most, children utilize both patterns of language use and that in some cases, such as Minh (Peters, 1977) and the Ross *et al.* study described above, language style is clearly distinguishable by functional context suggests that we may be able to distinguish style uses within children by studying situational variations, especially at around 2 years of age. If the gestalt or expressive approach is associated with social–interactive contexts and the analytic with more referential contexts, it should be possible to find within-child differences that are similar to those that have been found between children. A study by Lucariello and Nelson (1982b) allows the examination of this possibility.

In this study 10 mothers and their 2-year-old (2; 0 to 2; 5) children were videotaped in their homes under three conditions: a routine caretaking situation (defined as a socially scripted situation), free play with a varied selection of toys (defined as a familiar but nonscripted object-oriented situation), and play with a novel castle toy (defined as an unfamiliar object-oriented situation). We would expect both mother and child to produce more mathetic speech and more analytic language in the play situations than in the caretaking one, where pragmatic functions and gestalt speech would occur more often.

In this study language function was coded similarly to the Ross *et al.* study, based on Halliday's (1975) distinction between pragmatic and mathetic functions. As shown in Table 4.2, in the routine caretaking situation mathetic and pragmatic functions were equally frequent, while in the play context mathetic functions were used more frequently than pragmatic ones. Some of the specific functions were confined to specific contexts: the imaginary to the play situations and the informative to the routine.

Language form was examined by computing a noun–pronoun ratio [(nouns)/(nouns + pronouns)]. Nominal use was defined as a ratio greater than .5 and pronoun use as less than .5. As predicted by the context hypothesis, 7 of the 10 children showed shifts in noun usage across contexts. As shown in Table 4.2, there was an association between language form and language function in the routine and play situations. In the routine situation the nominal users concentrated on object-oriented functions (i.e., name–refer, comment–describe), while the pronominal users more frequently used the person-oriented mathetic function (personal) and the pragmatic social-oriented instrumental function. In the play situation the differences were less pronounced on

TABLE 4.2

Speech Functions of Nominal and Pronominal Children in Routine and Play
Situations

| | Percentage of total utterances | | | |
| | Routine | | Play | |
Functional category	Nominal	Pronominal	Nominal	Pronominal
Mathetic				
Name–refer	15.17	6.77	19.66	15.81
Comment–describe	16.51	10.52	18.82	11.28
Personal	5.8	13.55	15.87	16.17
Imaginary	—	—	9.66	6.87
Informative	7.39	6.61	—	—
Referential information requests	4.69	8.72	2.26	25.0
Total	49.56	46.17	66.27	75.13
Pragmatic				
Expressive	16.97	15.55	14.59	8.35
Interactive	4.32	2.88	—	—
Instrumental	8.44	13.1	—	—
Regulatory	7.47	6.7	4.19	6.08
Social information requests	4.52	7.86	1.48	2.66
Total	41.72	46.29	20.26	17.09

the whole, with the exception of information requests (primarily for
names of objects) by pronominal speakers. As in the Ross *et al.* study,
this is an indication that in an object-oriented situation children will
increase their use of object-oriented (mathetic) functions. These results
support the proposal that form and function are related and that both
are affected by situational context, in addition to whatever individual
differences in the disposition to use particular forms or functions may
exist.

Consistency and Inconsistency with Later Development

There is evidence from a number of studies that a shift in style of
use may take place developmentally. Brannigan (1979) traced such a
shift from phrases to single words for his subjects, and Horgan (1978)
reported a shift from an expressive to a referential strategy at 19 months
by her daughter. Such a shift also fits the pattern of results found in

the study of larger groups such as mine and that of Bloom *et al.* (1975). In my study (Nelson, 1973b, 1975a, 1975b) correlations of later language characteristics with early style tended on the whole to be low and nonsignificant at 24 and 30 months, with the exception of vocabulary size and the noun–pronoun use strategy.

In contrast to these apparent shifts, varying strategies have been observed at later periods that seem to be related to the early differences, such as the sentence reconstruction approach reported by R. Clark (1974) and the variations among toddlers and preschoolers reported by Horgan (1981). Moreover, there are indications in Wolf and Gardner's (1979) work and in Starr's (1975) report, both based on longitudinal studies, that similar stylistic differences persist beyond the second year. Peters' (1983) report clearly traces a relation between the early and later strategies that is not apparent in the correlational statistics.

Horgan (1981) reported on differences found among preschoolers that she identified as early "noun lovers" or "noun leavers" (i.e., referential or expressive) in the use of noun phrases in referential communication.[5] Horgan also described the longitudinal study of her own daughter Kelley, an expressive child (or noun leaver), whose use of language throughout the preschool years was unusual in several respects. She was highly sensitive to language patterns and used language in a playful, social–personal mode. Although she labeled objects, she did not ask for the names of things, preferring to assign her own nonsense names in the "Humpty Dumpty" mode of making words mean what you want them to. Her production of questions was similarly idiosyncratic. In other words, the specific characteristics that identified her as expressive at the outset did not themselves persist, but apparently related characteristics persisted throughout the language-learning period. As Horgan notes (in line with the observations of Peters, Brannigan, and Dore), Kelley was sensitive to the form, the tune, and the pattern of the language and was precocious with respect to manipulating these aspects. On the other hand, she appeared to be indifferent to its specific content; she did not view it as a particularly useful referential tool.

The evidence for the persistence of the specific style differences appearing in early speech is weak, suggesting that they are a product of specific learning characteristics. To the extent that the differences observed reflect differences in the approach to the initial learning task itself, we would expect them to disappear. To the extent that they reflect individual style differences, they would be expected to persist over time, or different style differences would be expected that were related to the earlier ones through their source but not in form. The latter appears to be the case based on the present evidence. Thus, part of the requirement here is to show how these specific early differences derive from the learning task itself.

Variation and the Acquisition of a Shared Meaning System

The variations in learning patterns outlined here seem to have a natural relationship to the types of language we observed as occurring in Phase 1 of the acquisition process in Chapter 3. Object and picture labels and relational terms referring to action schemes appear to be referential types, while social schemes and terms referring to or embedded in whole activities or scripts would appear to be more expressive or interpersonal. In order to account for the individual differences we have observed here, we need to have a general theory of development that encompasses both approaches.

Note to begin with that, as Halliday (1975) stressed, the mature language user coordinates the interpersonal and ideational in any language use. That is, any utterance incorporates both functions. In Lyons' (1977) terms again, they interpenetrate one another. However, before coordination can take place, the two major speech functions must be differentiated. A global meaning does not clearly encode either one. Recall Christine's ''Wait Johnny up'' from Chapter 2. Here the interpersonal and ideational are not coordinated but, rather, are undifferentiated. The phrase is part of an interactive activity but neither clearly encodes an idea nor expresses an interpersonal function. On the other hand, Halliday (1975) traced the development of communicative functions in his son Nigel through the protolanguage stage and claimed that at that point each utterance encodes only one of the two types of functions (the primitive ideational [mathetic] or the primitive interpersonal [pragmatic]).

The present proposal is that language is first understood and produced in conjunction with previously understood knowledge about the world, represented initially in terms of event scripts. These event representations, during the early part of the second year, do not appear to clearly differentiate the object and social realms; rather, they are unanalyzed and indissoluble. In terms of affectivity and action, however, differentiation of social and object domains seems to be achieved toward the end of the first year. This is evidenced in that during the last half of the first year, attachment to a primary caretaker and anxiety about strangers are established, as well as the exploration of space and objects and the beginnings of classification skills. This appears to be the period when the differentiation of the social and physical domains from a more global cognitive–affective milieu takes place (Bates, 1976; Sugarman, 1978).

The present proposal suggests that this differentiation of the social and object realms leads to an unstable adaptation to the world in which both intra- and interindividual differences can be expected. Some children may concentrate their attention on the social world, while others may concentrate on object relations; however, most children are likely to swing from one extreme to the other, depending upon the context of the situation. Thus, clinging to the mother or crying in distress appear in situations interpreted as posing a threat to social understanding (Ainsworth and Bell, 1974), whereas sustained exploration and manipulation of objects appear when the social equilibrium is not upset. After children are able to coordinate the two realms, they will be better able to use the mother as an interpreter of objective situations and to use exploratory and manipulative skills in mastering strange or threatening social situations. Thus, the last half of the first year is a period of the achievement of differentiation, but this very achievement leads to an instability that must be resolved through a higher-level coordination. The suggestion here is that the development of inclusive event representations, as exemplified in Chapter 2, provides this integration for the child. However, this very integration prevents, for a time, their use in symbolic manipulations as required by the language. Rather, the event representation supports the more global or unifunctional language uses observed during Phase 1. Thus, it appears that differentiation at the action level precedes differentiation at the representational level, which in turn precedes differentiation at the symbolic or linguistic level. Each process of differentiation proceeds from a more global to a more separated to a more integrated form, as illustrated in Figure 4.1.

The data on individual differences in early language bear on these suggestions. To the extent that the early part of the second year is one of imbalance, where the differentiated social and object domains are being reintegrated into inclusive event representations, we would expect that language forms and functions during this period would emphasize one or another of the domains. However, we would expect children who began productive language later on, in the latter half of the second year, to show a more balanced pattern, indicating that the social and object spheres were coordinated before language learning began. An analysis of the data from my sample of subjects studied longitudinally supported this hypothesis. Of the 6 children who reached a vocabulary level of 50 words prior to 18 months, 3 were highly expressive (using less than 40% object terms), 3 were highly referential (using more than 60% object

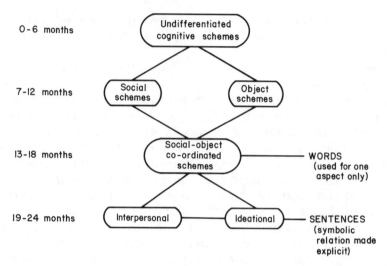

FIGURE 4.1   Differentiation and integration of social and object schemes and relation to early language. (From Nelson, 1979b.)

terms), and there were none in the middle range. Of the 6 who reached this vocabulary level at 19–20 months, 5 were in the middle range (40–60%) and one was referential. The 6 late talkers (those who began at 21–24 months) came from all three groups; many of these children had had exceptional difficulty in getting into the system.

Further support for the differentiation–integration hypothesis is provided by the data from the Ross *et al.* (in press) study reported earlier, showing that at midyear (20 months) all children used language for all functions (integration), but the pronominal speakers tended to use it for interpersonal functions more than the nominal speakers did. That is, the characteristics of the language forms predicted the language functions to some extent but did not at that age completely correlate with them. Differences attributable to the early differentiation emphasis persisted, but they were partially masked by the effects of the later integration of both form and function.

A very significant part of the learning process is the use of language by those around the child. Children need more than an interpretive system for understanding meaning; they need to exchange meanings with others in symbolic form. According to Bruner's (1983) account, mothers set up situations in which objects play a central part, suggesting that one of the functions of early verbal exchanges is to embed referring expressions in a social framework, thus coordinating the two. However, it appears that 1-year-old children do not, in general, take advantage of the entire framework offered in this way. Rather, some children pick up the social message offered and others pick up the object message. This suggests, as argued above, that while children may be exposed to similar types of interactions, they operate with different theories about what language is about. Some children seem to operate with a social (or expressive) theory, while others operate with an objective (or referential) theory. The former children translate into language forms the preverbal social messages (regulatory, instrumental, and interactive) that they have previously encoded in nonverbal signals and gestures. The others learn language that supplements their skills, that is, they learn words that refer to objects and actions and that can be used to stand for those objects and actions in their absence. It is apparent that the referential style of language has greater functional *potential* than does the expressive style, which is nearly as limited in function as the prelinguistic communication system.

In addition, the referential approach may enable the child to disembed concepts from their scripts by, in a sense, pointing out the parts. Thus, for these children language and representation work together, the one helping to differentiate the other, which in turn is necessary before the language itself can be used in an integrated way. That the referential approach is conducive to early language acquisition is apparent in the speedier growth of vocabulary and, according to some accounts (e.g., Ramer, 1976; Horgan, 1981), in generally faster language development by children identified as referential.

In the early stages of developments, language is learned and used in well-understood situations for purposes shared by the participants. Two-year-olds frequently need constant interpretation by a familiar person in order to make their statements clear to a stranger, and this is not simply because their articulation is faulty. Rather, language, at first, is an *addition* to the communicative situation. It refers to aspects of shared knowledge but does not spell them out; if knowledge is not, in fact, shared, the utterance is likely to be uninterpretable.

Usually, this condition has been interpreted in terms of the presumed facts that children talk about the "here and now" (Brown, 1973) and that their language is only interpretable in terms of the nonlinquistic context (Bloom, 1970). However, this is an inadequate description of the facts. Two-year-olds are not limited to thinking about or talking about the here and now. There are innumerable documented cases in which children of 2 years or younger refer explicitly to events that have happened days, weeks, or months earlier (see the Emily and Rachel examples in Chapter 2; see also Nelson, 1984b; Nelson & Ross, 1980; Lucariello & Nelson, 1982b; Sachs, 1982). The memories referred to could only be interpreted by mothers or others who had shared the event. In addition, we have informally observed children anticipating the next appropriate move in a situation on the basis of a single previous experience. For example, in the study of word learning previously referred to (Ross *et al.*, in press), we routinely handed out cookies at the end of a learning session. One 20-month-old on her first visit had asked for another and was told teasingly "Okay, one for the road." On the following visit, after consuming the first cookie she pleaded "One for the road?"

As discussed in Chapter 2, context is a very complex notion. Context is not only or always the immediate situation. Rather, context is the *representation of experience,* past, present, or future. A listener who participates in the experiences of a young speaker, for example, a mother, will be able to interpret the child's meaning because she shares a similar (although not identical) representation of those experiences.

The argument set forth here is that it is not that very young children cannot divorce themselves from the here and now, but rather that they cannot detach their language from the cognitive representation of reality. Moreover, they implicitly assume that others share that representation; they have not yet learned to use the language to *exchange* meanings, only to express them. That is, in addition to the differentiation and integration of different aspects of the representation (object and person), the language itself must be differentiated from the representation. This process is reflected in the building of vocabulary, its extension to novel contexts, and its recombinations to express new meanings in the latter part of the second year.

In order to advance to the place where language becomes a tool for negotiating the unknown as well as the known, with strangers as well as family members, the child needs to be able to make his or her implicit meaning structure available to various explicit operations of comparison and redefinition. Toward this end the language terms that the child uses need to be partially detached from the personal conceptual representation, and a new level representing the communal meaning of a term, that is, its lexical representation, needs to be established. This is a gradual accomplishment of the preschool years. When it is accomplished the child is able to modify, elaborate on, and add to lexical domains to bring them into closer conformity with the meanings of the linguistic community. At the same time, the establishment of such a level makes possible the organization of meanings and words independent of the experientially based conceptual level. Thus, word–word associations, the establishment of superordinate and subordinate terms, and so on become possible. In the next chapter we shall examine the extent to which some common findings in conceptual and semantic development can be explained in this framework.

Summary of Development of the Meaning System between 1 and 2 Years

In these first chapters the various components of the system by which meanings are established between individuals have been considered, and their early development has been described. In the picture that emerges I have tried to show how language first comes to be a meaningful symbolic-exchange system, the varied ways in which it begins, the conceptual base on which it builds, and the context on which it develops. Here I will attempt to summarize the important developments that take place up to the age of 2 years.

1. Prior to beginning to use any language forms, the infant–child enters into interactions with parents and others that are oriented around social purposes and object-centered activities. When the child begins to use identifiable forms, they are used in the context of these activities and are usually describable as *pure performatives*. Even when the parent and child are focused on an object, the protolanguage form seems to be *part* of the activity rather than *referring* to the object or the activity. Similarly, the child interprets the speech of others to indicate an activity. For example, the child crawls to the high chair in the kitchen when mother says "Do you want lunch?" The basic limitation on the child's entering into the meaning system at this point rests on the fact that neither perception alone nor action alone is sufficient to support word meaning. Both perception and action are ephemeral; the results of perception and action must be represented in a schema that preserves them as part of a meaningful whole in order that words can be given meaning across specific occasions of use. At this point, I have proposed, the child's representational system is largely organized around events that are undifferentiated, unanalyzed schemas without separable elements of concepts. Language terms, therefore, when they are understood or used, are confined to certain activity contexts and are embedded as part of these contexts. At the same time, the child may interact with objects outside of a well-understood event; thus, the object world becomes differentiated from the social activity world in action but only to a limited extent at this time in representation. At this point (termed prelexical in Chapter 3), the child's language, of whatever form, can be said to be *activity language,* not yet *reflective.*

2. Sometime in the first half of the second year the child begins to differentiate event representations into their parts. People and objects become conceptualized in terms of their functional roles, and these roles are no longer indissoluble from their specific event contexts. At this point the child may begin to use words to refer to objects in the world and build up a fairly extensive vocabulary for doing this. The word stands in a mediating position between the concept and the real-world object, but the connection between the former two may be rather weak. Words now refer, but what is referred to with the word may not match what is denoted by the concept to which the word is connected. The process of analyzing event representations into their parts may be hastened by the parents' use of words in connection with these events, that is, the discrete word forms may point out to the child the discrete, nameable parts of the event. For some children a similar process takes place as language gestalts originally used within a specific event are dissociated and transferred to be used in similar contexts in other events. Thus, the two types of early language forms both reflect a disembedding process. The initial effect of this disembedding is a loosening of words from the conceptual base; however, there is no other interpretive system available. The conceptual system is the denotative system. Thus, the connection between the two becomes firmer again with further development. At this point language is in a transitional state between activity and reflection on activity.

To put this point another way, children may enter language through using it in action contexts, but the action system is not available as a component of the meaning system. Action may support language use, but it cannot support meaning. Rather, meaning is based in a conceptual system that derives from the child's representation of experienced events. Taking part in social games may lead into language through its communicative functions, but these games must be cognitively represented before the language forms used within them become meaningful to the child. Thus, activity language must be transformed into reflective language through conceptual representation. This is *the* important transition of the second year.

3. Having disembedded words from their initial contexts and having differentiated elements from events, these words and conceptual elements can be recombined into new complexes. Children can now form propositions about the world; for the first time meanings can be freely exchanged. But while this new possibility opens up enormous potential, it also imposes a new constraint. For in order to understand one another without the shared context of an embedding event, people must share a denotational system that assigns common interpretations to the lan-

guage forms used. Thus, children must once again constrain their words to refer to things denoted by their concepts, and through exchanging meanings they can refine their concepts to fit the meanings conveyed by others. This third period, then, is one in which shared contexts give birth to shared concepts, and the interpretive system becomes conventionalized together with the grammatical system. When this is accomplished language can be used outside of activity to reflect back on it. Thus, by the end of the second year both reference and denotation are in place, and the stage is set for the development of a semantic system and the emergence of sense.

Notes

[1]Pivot–open constructions describe the type of sentences many children first produce where one word (the pivot) occurs in great frequency in fixed positions (first or last) in combination with a variety of other words (the open class). While this description was originally proposed as a first grammar, it was later abandoned as an explanation because it failed to fit much of the data, among other reasons (see Brown, 1973).

[2]The division of children into two groups is a descriptive convenience (see following discussion in text). Throughout the chapter expressive, pragmatic, pronominal, and gestalt will be considered roughly equivalent terms, in contrast to referential, mathetic, nominal, and analytic (see discussion in text).

[3]I suggested this explanation in an early unpublished paper titled "Word and Phrase Learning by Young Children" (Nelson, 1969b).

[4]"Mobol," "nutty," and "linky" are names for the object concepts to be learned. Letters in parentheses indicate the functional coding of the utterance.

[5]These differences are reminiscent of those reported by Bernstein (1970) among boys from different socioeconomic classes.

III

From Denotation to Sense

5

Development of Conceptual Structure in Early Childhood

The Problems of Conceptual Development

Section II of this book considered the beginnings of meaning and its development in the second year, the time when most children first begin to use and understand their native language. Three limitations on the child's meanings persist at the end of the second year. First, although words are linked to individual concepts (and thus denote), these concepts are not fully conventionalized, that is, they do not match the conventional concepts of the language community in all relevant ways. Second, they do not yet form a conceptual system that is distinguishable from the system of event representations from which they were partitioned. Thus, concepts have at this point syntagmatic links to other concepts, reflecting real-world conditions, but do not have links reflecting more abstract paradigmatic relations. Third, as shown here and in much other prior research, meaning during this period is to a large extent context-bound, although generalizations across familiar event contexts can be observed.

Development over the succeeding 3 to 5 years during early childhood involves interrelated changes in all three of these areas, with the result that at the end of the period a new level of representation—the semantic-sense level—has emerged that is conventional, based on paradigmatic relations, and relatively autonomous. This level does not emerge full-blown at one point, but results from a process of gradual differentiation of the conceptual and semantic systems. Prior to the completion of this process, the child's concepts and word meanings reflect to a greater or lesser degree the limitations noted above, resulting in performance on conceptual and semantic tasks that appears markedly deficient in comparison with that of older children. In this and the next three chapters, these deficiencies and their explanations according to different theories will be described and the functional approach to a developmental model will be outlined.

This chapter and the next present an overview of previous research and theory in both conceptual and semantic development during the preschool years. The claim here is that the two systems differentiate during this period, but that they begin as one system, and this is reflected in the fact that similar phenomena are found in both lexical and conceptual research with young children, for example, in the study of semantic and categorical hierarchies. Indeed, the majority of researchers have not distinguished between word meanings and concepts in their reports. On the other hand, only those issues in conceptual development that have direct bearing on semantic issues will be considered in this survey, in order to keep the discussion within reasonable bounds.

The aim is not to present a comprehensive review of cognitive development during the preschool years. Rather, the purpose of this review is to lay out the different problems that have been studied that are relevant to our concerns and to reveal what these studies have found. How these findings may be related to each other and accounted for in an integrated theoretical perspective is deferred to Chapters 7, 8, and 9. The present review does not attempt to build a case for this perspective, but rather to document its empirical foundations.

The development of a conceptual system implies several different processes, relevant to different system constituents. While these will be given more detailed consideration in Chapter 7, it is necessary to note them here in order to motivate the organization of the discussion to follow. First, a conceptual system consists of concepts and relations between concepts. Concepts are conceived of as wholes with internal structure (intension) that determines what aspects of the real world (or the conceived reality) the concept applies to (extension). How the internal structure is characterized, in terms of attributes, prototypes, or rules; whether a single structural characterization is applicable to all concepts; and whether the character of the internal structure changes with development are all relevant questions that have been addressed from different research perspectives. These will be referred to as structural questions and are considered in this chapter.

A system is constituted in terms of relations between elements, in this case concepts. Relations of various kinds (similarity, contrastive, hi-

erarchical) have been of much greater interest in descriptions of semantics and semantic development than conceptual development, where
internal structure has tended to dominate the discussion. There is, however, a vast literature on children's understanding of the relations between logical classes and their utilization of taxonomic relationships,
issues that are similar to those that enter into certain semantic domains.
Chapter 6 considers conceptual relationships of this kind, deferring to
the following chapters a full consideration of the types of relationships
that enter into both conceptual and semantic systems.

It may be noted here that these two aspects of the conceptual system,
which may be termed internal and external structure, are precisely analogous to the denotation–sense semantic distinction put forth by Lyons,
which provides the framework for the model of semantic development
laid out in Chapter 8. The relation between these two will be made
explicit in that chapter.

The present chapter will unfold in the following way. The first section
briefly considers the variety of types of conceptual structures and relations that need to be accounted for. Following this, research on the
development of internal conceptual structure is reviewed. Research on
system relations will be covered in Chapter 6.

Conceptual Types

Most theories of concepts and conceptual development treat all concepts as structurally similar, whatever this structure may be thought to
be (prototypic, criterial feature, or some other type). Nonetheless, it is
generally recognized that there may be typological differences among
conceptual structures, and some researchers have suggested that these
differences may have implications for development. For example, in the
Rosch et al. (1976) model, it is held that basic level categories are acquired earlier than superordinates; in Markman's (1981) model collections are cognitively simpler than categories; Mandler (1979)
distinguishes between schemas and categories; Huttenlocher and Lui
(1979) claim that action concepts (and verbs) are structurally different
from object concepts (and nouns). Still, the vast majority of concept
studies have focused on object concepts and the possible variations
among concept types, and their developmental implications have not
been given adequate analytic attention.

Throughout this book the discussion is similarly focused on objects,
in part because these have been the most commonly studied and are
the simplest to study experimentally and analyze theoretically. Even

within the category of object concepts, however, it is important to distinguish between different types, as the discussion in Chapter 3 emphasized. For one reason, children may find it easier to acquire some types of concepts before others, as the theories cited above suggest.

Among object concepts we can distinguish concepts of the single object, basic object class concepts, collections of objects, object schemas based on spatial–temporal relations, and hierarchical class concepts. Single objects (such as the sun) may give rise to concepts, and these may be formed very early, for example, in the child's concept of mother (see Nelson, 1977a). The characteristics of basic object concepts and hierarchical categories were discussed in Chapter 3 and will be considered again in Chapters 7 and 8. It is claimed here that hierarchical categories are a late achievement and depend upon the utilization of a symbol system. The distinction between collections and classes has been pointed out by Markman in a number of papers (e.g., Markman, 1981; Markman & Seibert, 1976; Markman, Horton & McLanahan, 1980) and will be discussed in detail in the following section. Object schemas may be based on functional relations between objects in a situation such as *lunch* and may reflect either syntagmatic or paradigmatic relationships. That such schemas enter into children's thinking at an earlier point than, and to some extent at least to the exclusion of, hierarchical concepts will be evident in the review of research to follow, particularly in those studies that include functional or thematic groups of objects. This type of conceptual structure is discussed in Chapter 7.

In addition to these types of object concepts, it is necessary to posit the conceptualization of relational concepts, such as actions, as well as to posit the existence of basic relations between concepts. It is generally assumed that the child has a concept of such actions as *run* and *play*, that is, these representations have informational content. Whether these concepts should be considered as having the same sort of structure as object concepts is a question that will be considered later in this chapter and in Chapter 6.

Objects can be analyzed in terms of their intrinsic attributes and their parts, and each of these can be considered as concepts in their own right. It is easy to see that parts can be conceptualized. For example, *button* is an object as well as a part of many pieces of clothing. *Red* and *round* are less obvious as concepts. Depending upon your ontological assumptions, these are either conceptual primitives (from which concepts are built) or they are derived on the basis of conceptual analysis. It is a fact that children do not name such attributes spontaneously prior to the third year, and usually these concepts require considerable explicit training. The reasons for this need to be considered in a developmental theory of conceptualization.

Finally, there are concepts that are not based directly on objects and object relations. For example, there are abstract concepts such as *justice* and *peace*. Although these concepts have not been subjected to developmental study in recent years, it is apparent that language is essential to understanding such abstractions. In addition, there are a large variety of concepts that depend upon implicit social knowledge such as social roles (e.g., *daughter, teacher,* and *policeman*) and norms (e.g., "big girls don't cry"). Although the present discussion will not be concerned with these types of concepts, because of its focus on the early years of childhood, the model to be constructed must be able to accomodate these as well as the more concrete concepts as the system develops.

Recent research has viewed the internal structure of concepts and word meanings from a variety of perspectives. Here we consider those that have the most potential significance for developmental issues.

Class Inclusion, Prototypes, and Part-Whole Structures

Category Structure. A topic of some current interest in cognitive psychology is the correct description of the internal structure of concepts and categories (see Smith & Medin, 1981, for an overview). The classical view of concepts proposes that they are composed of the logical combination of necessary and sufficient criterial attributes (e.g., *red* and *square* defining the class of red squares). The counterproposal by Rosch and Mervis (1975) (based in part on Wittgenstein's [1953] ideas) is that natural language concepts are organized around prototypes; that there are better and less good members that resemble to a better or lesser degree the prototype; and that members of a category may share family resemblances, that is, they may share features with the prototype, but two members of a category need not share any features with each other. This position denies that category membership is based on logical composition or that there are any necessary features that define natural language categories.

The notion of prototype in this and in other theories has been used in two ways: as a prime exemplar or specific image on the one hand and as a central tendency (e.g., Posner & Keele, 1968) or global representation on the other. Both have been used in developmental work; for example, Bowerman (1976) and Anglin (1977) seem to have in mind the notion of a specific exemplar (see later discussion), while Strauss (1979) demonstrated the abstraction of central tendency among stimuli by infants.

The aspects of Rosch's work that have had the greatest impact on developmental thinking have been the notions of family resemblances and the definition of levels of natural categorization. The former is associated as well with the proposal that human concepts have fuzzy boundaries (e.g., Labov, 1973) rather than being strictly defined according to logical definitions. The fuzziness of natural concepts and categories seems to fit much of the developmental data on word meanings in that, as discussed briefly in Chapter 3, children tend to apply their words broadly and somewhat inconsistently in the early years. In Piaget's (1962) view this tendency reflected the young child's inability to coordinate the logical intension and extension of concepts. Rather, he saw the child focusing on a single exemplar, or prototype, much as Rosch claims adults do. Of course, to the extent that adults' concepts are illogical in this sense, we would not want to fault the young child for the same characteristic.

The proposal that natural language categories can be distinguished as belonging to different levels complicates this picture somewhat. Rosch et al. (1976) claimed that there were three natural levels of human categorization: basic, subordinate, and superordinate. Basic level categories are those whose members share the greatest number of distinctive attributes, perceptual and motoric (that is, movements that people use with respect to them). On these grounds they suggest that at this level categories have the greatest cue validity. Subordinate category members within a basic category share as many attributes as the basic level but are distinguished from one another by only one or two attributes. On the other hand, members of superordinate categories share very few attributes with each other; the attributes they do share are largely functions. An example of such levels would be *chair* (basic), *rocking chair* (subordinate), and *furniture* (superordinate). Rosch et al. (1976) suggested that the correlation of attributes at the basic level would make it easiest to learn concepts and word meanings at that level, and their analysis of early vocabularies supported this view. Note that Rosch et al. do not make the distinction between concepts and categories that was made in Chapter 3. However, their basic level categories appear to fit the present notion of concept, while their superordinate categories are clearly type-2 categories, in which one member dominates or includes subordinate members. (The place of subordinates in this scheme has not yet been discussed).

Although the suggestion that categories are organized around prototypes has been applied to all levels in this theory, its most convincing application has been at the level of the superordinate category, where it can be shown that people naturally think of certain members as prototypical of the category and readily rank members according to their typicality. For example, most people think of robins as prototypical birds. It seems probable that the distinction between concept and category made here may relate to the two different types of prototypes, that is, concepts may be identified in terms of a central tendency, while categories are identified in terms of most typical members. In either case, however, the basis for identification need not determine the internal structure.

The Roschian position and related proposals seem to conflict with the classical descriptions of concept development and, in particular, the Piagetian and Vygotskian descriptions of young children's failings at logical classification tasks. In their major work on this topic, Inhelder and Piaget (1964) were concerned with young children's understanding of relations between parts and wholes of logically composed classes. They claimed that children prior to the stage of concrete operations (usually around 7 or 8 years) do not comprehend the inclusion relations between A and B when A and A' form a larger class B. Their primary test for this was the class-inclusion task in which the child is presented with, for example, a group of flowers consisting of 7 primroses and 3 daisies and is asked whether there are more primroses or more flowers. Their finding, which has been replicated many times, was that younger children would reply that there are more primroses. There have been many suggestions as to why the child responds in this way, including the suggestion that the child believes ''flowers'' to refer to the ''other flowers'' or that the verbal form of the question misleads in other ways. (See Trabasso *et al.*, 1978, for a review of these and some other proposals.)

One alternative explanation has been put forth by Markman (see Markman, 1981, for a review). In a series of studies she has shown that young children can solve the class-inclusion problem if the ''class'' is actually a collection. A collection in Markman's terms is a whole consisting of parts related in a particular configuration. For example, a *family*, a *forest*, and a *kindergarten class* are all collections, consisting respectively of family members, trees, and boys and girls. In contrast, *people, trees,* and *children* are classes organized hierarchically by the inclusion principle. The difference between the two can be revealed by testing the ''ISA'' relation; for example, a father *is a* person but is *part* of a family. Markman suggests that part–whole relations and logical set relations are two different types of classifying activities that people naturally engage in. Because of the part–whole composition of collections, they are analogous to concepts of objects, and Markman suggests that children treat them analogously to objects. If collections represent cognitive wholes for children, they may be operated on symbolically in the same way as concepts. Categories and classes (composed of groups of conceptualized objects) pose a different sort of cognitive problem, however, according to this analysis. The ease of operating on collections makes it possible for the child to solve the class-inclusion problems with them, but this success does not indicate that the child can operate on logical hierarchies.

In another test of children's classification abilities, Inhelder and Piaget (1964) (similar to Vygotsky, 1962) tested children in an object-sorting task and claimed that younger children could not use principles of logical classification to sort groups of objects consistently into exclusive and exhaustive classes. They found that 3- and 4-year-olds tend, instead, to put together things that are functionally complementary or to form complexes where each item is related to the next in turn but all are not related according to a single principle. As noted in Chapter 3, Sugarman (1983) found evidence in 2-year-olds for grouping according to classes based on perceptual similarity when the groups are small and distinctive. Recent analyses have tended to see the different kinds of constructions that young children sometimes make as reflecting alternative principles of composition, that is, categorical and relational. Moreover, the ambiguous instructions for the sorting task usually tend to encourage thematic grouping by asking the child to "put together those things that go together." In short, the results of object-sorting tasks do not provide a definitive evaluation of the child's ability to form classes of objects. As will be argued in Chapter 7, this task could not in any event provide evidence for an understanding of class-inclusion relationships.

Rosch et al. (1976) challenged the Piaget and Vygotsky characterization of children's classification abilities on the grounds that children were differentially able to manipulate categories at different levels of abstraction. Using a triads test with 3, 4, and 5-year-olds, they showed that even the youngest children were capable of correctly assigning items (i.e., naming the two out of three items that are alike) to *basic level* categories (such as *dog, car,* and *apple*), although the youngest children were not proficient on superordinate (e.g., *animal, vehicle,* and *fruit*) categories. On this basis, they claimed that young children are not deficient in categorizing ability when this ability is tested with basic rather than superordinate categories. The considerable body of work reviewed in Chapter 3 that shows that even infants categorize perceptually diverse objects and pictorial representations (Nelson, 1973a; Ricciuti, 1965;

Ross, 1980; Sugarman, 1981) and can learn names for such categories makes this conclusion unsurprising. That is, what Rosch *et al.* showed was that young (3-year-old) children could categorize objects according to a conceptual structure; they did not show that young children could construct higher-level categories that included lower-level ones. (However, 4- and 5-year-old children in their experiment did give evidence of higher-level categories such as *food* and *clothes*.) Although this experiment is another demonstration of basic categorizing ability, it still leaves the developmental discrepancy between basic concepts and hierarchical categories unexplained.

This work on category composition among children and adults, in particular the demonstration of the uses of prototypes and collections, indicates a natural focus on whole objects rather than on attribute or part analysis. Smith and Kemler (1977) brought out a related point based on their work with young children learning perceptual categories. They have found that younger (preschool) children focus on global properties rather than analyzing dimensions. That is, in forming equivalence classes children tend to treat dimensions such as size and brightness as integral, while adults treat them as separable.

The studies of collections, prototypes, and integral dimensions all suggest a similar developmental implication: *Young children focus on global wholes and their decomposable parts rather than on their analyzable dimensional or feature structures.* It should be stressed, however, that this focus is not confined to childhood; adults also focus on wholes for many purposes. Children, however, appear to be particularly bound to this aspect of structure and process.

Prototypes as Word Meanings

Bowerman (1978b) suggested that her daughters' first word meanings were organized as prototype structures (as noted in Chapter 3). Anglin (1977) extended this claim to the developmental period of early childhood. On the basis of interviews of children from 2 to 5 years of age about the meanings of selected words from different levels of noun hierarchies (e.g., "Volkswagen," "car," and "vehicle"), he concluded that the youngest children were using images of instances (i.e., perceptual prototypes) as the basis for their responses rather than an abstract definition, as he claimed adults do.[1] The major evidence for the instance claim comes from his analysis of responses to questions such as "What is food?," "What do you know about food?," and "Can you tell me some foods?" Even the youngest children were able to answer these questions to some extent. No formal quantitative analysis was carried out on the results, but Anglin emphasized that the youngest children gave more "concrete" instances, while the 5-year-olds were more general and abstract.

Table 5.1 shows a tabulation of all the reported responses given to questions about "food" by the children of different ages Anglin interviewed. Although there is some apparent difference in what these children think of as salient foods (the 2- and 3-year-olds concentrated on sweets, snacks, and cereals, while the 4- and 5-year-olds included fruits, meat, and "dairy", and all mentioned some vegetables), there is no evident difference in instance orientation or abstraction. The 2-year-old uses general terms (e.g., cereal and dessert), and all ages mention specific fruits, vegetables, or meats. To the extent that children do focus on specific instances, it seems likely that this only reflects a particular strategy of dealing with certain tasks rather than a general cognitive characteristic.

TABLE 5.1
Examples of "Food"[a]

	Age of child in years			
Example	2 (n = 2)	3 (n = 1)	4 n = 1)	5 (n = 1)
Cookies	X			
Crackers	X			
Dessert	X			
Chocolate				X
Fruit			X	X
Strawberries			X	
Potatoes	X			X
Carrots	X		X	
Beans			X	
Corn				X
Cereal	X			
Alphabits		X		
Wheaties		X		
Raisin bran		X		
Froot loops		X		
Meat			X	X
Steak				X
Eggs				X
Dairy				X
A bear				X

[a]Based on Anglin (1977, Figure 7.3, p. 222).

Ontological Constraints

Keil's (1979, 1983) work on ontological categories, that is, basic categories that organize experience, suggests a hierarchically organized constraint on what sorts of things can be conceptualized and at the same time a developmental progression of differentiation of categories. His basic paradigm has been to combine pairs of nouns and predicates and to inquire of children and adults whether the resulting sentence is sensible or not. For example, he may present the sentence: "The dream leaks out of boxes." This is obviously not sensible. It is neither true nor false; it combines concepts from two noncombinable categories (abstract objects and physical things). On the other hand, "Rabbits eat horses" is sensible although false, since eating is a predicate appropriate to the category animate objects. On the basis of his data Keil constructed a predicate tree, which in turn implicates a hierarchical category structure from the most all-inclusive to the general but restricted distinction between humans and all other animals. The tree structure cannot (it is claimed) be violated. Although children's tree structures are less differentiated than adults', they also respect the same constraints, according to Keil.

If Keil's claims are correct, this theory would have implications for our consideration of the development of a semantic system, although, like Anglin and many others, it conflates the conceptual and semantic and attempts to view the conceptual structure, as it were, through the one-way semantic mirror. However, other data (Gerard & Mandler, 1983) indicate that Keil's results are not replicable and that, like many other research paradigms, the particular findings are highly dependent upon the details of instructions given to subjects. Moreover, Carey (1983) demonstrated that the basic logic of the paradigm is flawed. That is, predicates that *should* apply to terms at a given level cannot be sensibly applied. It appears that, whatever the case may be for constraints on conceptual structures, people can and do manipulate predicates and their meanings in far more flexible ways then Keil's theory would allow (see also Bierwisch, 1981). At this point, then, it seems that we need not be too constrained by the particular claims of Keil's theory, although the possibility of constraints on basic categories cannot be discounted entirely.

Nominal Realism

Piaget (1976), Vygotsky (1962), Werner (1948), and Werner and Kaplan (1963) all subscribed to the theory that the young child believed that words inhere in things rather than being arbitrarily assigned by people. For the young child, according to this thesis, the word is as much a part of the thing as its color or form. This theory was supported by data gathered by Piaget in a series of clinical interviews. Piaget asked such questions as: "How did people know what was the sun's name? Why is the sun called the sun? Could the sun be called the moon?" An example of the first stage (5 to 7 years) is given as follows: "FERT (7) . . . said that the name of the Salève came *from the mountain.*— When the first men came, how did they know it was called Salève?— *Because it slopes.*—How did they know the sun's name?—*Because it's bright.*—But where does the name come from?—*By itself.*" Piaget (1929) comments:

> Although children may suppose they need only to look at a thing to know its name, it does not in the least follow that they regard the name as in some way written on the thing. It means rather that for these children the name is an essential part of the thing; the name Salève implies a sloping mountain, the name sun implies a yellow ball that shines and has rays, etc. But it must also be added that for these children the essence of the thing is not a concept but the thing itself. Complete confusion exists between thought and the things thought of. The name is therefore in the object, not as a label, attached to it but as an invisible quality of the object. To be accurate we should not therefore say that the name "sun" implies a yellow ball, etc. but that the yellow ball which is the sun really implies and contains the name "sun". (pp. 69–70)

Piaget comments further that this is analogous to the "intellectual realism" in children's drawings: "They draw what they know about an object at the expense of what they see, but they think they are drawing exactly what they see."

Markman (1976) investigated the nominal realism phenomenon with children in kindergarten, first, and second grades. She found that children at all three ages responded as though words were identical with the objects referred to when given standard questions about meaning and reference (e.g., "Suppose . . . all of the giraffes are gone, could we still have the word 'giraffe'?" [p. 744] or about the nonphysical nature of words (e.g., "Is the word rain wet?"). However, when an analogue task referring to pictures rather than words was used, children had little trouble with the questions. She therefore concluded that children had specific difficulty dealing with the intangibility of words, that is, while the task requires an objective, metalinguistic consideration of words, the ephemeral quality of words resists this type of reflection.

In addition, Markman found that while first graders improved on both tasks when given a choice of answers, second graders improved very little and, when asked the converse question (e.g., "Does *a* car start with 'kuh'?"), their performance actually declined. She speculated that second-graders had become sensitive to the metalinguistic properties of words (e.g., their phonetic compositions) and had begun to adopt a *referential theory* of word meaning, leading them to accept the necessity of existence of an object in order for a name to have meaning. This proposal is in contradiction to the theory developed here, which proposes that children abandon a simple referential theory early in life. It is apparent that the nominal realism phenomenon has not been exhaustively investigated, and further research might reveal further insights into it and its relation to semantic development in general.

There is a different interpretation of these data that conserves most of Piaget's argument and does not conflict with Markman's but comes out at a different point. Consider Piaget's point about intellectual realism in children's drawings in connection with his notion that ''complete confusion exists between thought and the things thought of.'' The correct implication seems to be that the child is unable to disentangle his thought, not from the world (the real sun, a mountain, etc.) but from itself, from the representation of these things in his head. As *mental representations* (concepts) the sun, a mountain, etc., are indissolubly linked to their labels and vice versa for the young child. The child is correctly reporting the subjective conceptual state but is unable to think about or report on (and indeed does not know about) the ''objective reality.'' This interpretation is in accord with the claim that the important context of any encounter between the child and the world is the cognitive context that the child brings to the situation (see Chapter 2).

This phenomenon has received only passing attention in recent decades, although it has been accepted as established by many authors. However, it deserves attention because it is obvious that, to the extent that the child believes that names inhere in things or that names are indissolubly attached to concepts, there is no semantic system per se, but only a system that represents objects and their inherent and indissociable labels. If names belong to things, they cannot be interchanged or used flexibly. The phenomenon therefore also has obvious consequences for theories of the development of metalinguistic abilities and metaphor.[2]

Function as a Conceptual Core

While psychology concentrated for many years on simple, well-defined perceptual concepts to the neglect of functionally defined concepts (Smith & Medin, 1981; but see Bruner, Goodnow, & Austin, 1956), recent scholars have emphasized that perceptual and functional features are not only correlated (Rosch *et al.*, 1976) but are essential to the definition of most natural language concepts (Labov, 1973; Miller & Johnson-Laird, 1976). Acceptance of this fact does not negate the possibility that children might preferentially rely on one or another of these domains in learning, defining, or identifying instances of concepts. Indeed, earlier theorists suggested that younger children were perceptually constrained to the neglect of function. More recently, the place of function in young children's conceptual development has been stressed (Anglin, 1977; Nelson 1973a, 1974a, 1978b, 1979a). The basic model that I proposed (Nelson, 1974) was outlined in Chapter 3. The propositions contained there have given rise to many experimental tests attempting to determine whether perception *or* function is crucial to children's concept formation and development. A brief review of the model and the research follows.

The functional core model (FCM) essentially proposed that the child came to language with a store of concepts of familiar people and objects that were organized around the child's experience with these things. Because the child's experience was active, the dynamic aspects would be the most potent part of what the child came to know about the things experienced. It could be expected that the child would organize knowledge around what he or she could do with things and what things could do. In other words, knowledge of the world would be functionally organized from the child's point of view. When the child began to learn language, the concepts attached to the words that were learned would be concepts reflecting this functional organization. Rather than abstracting a set of referents from those things that adults applied a particular name to and from there inferring an intension or set of features for the word meaning, the FCM proposed that children matched their concepts to the adult's use of a word in a particular context and then extended the use of that word to other items that fit the preformed concept.

The structure of the child's prelinguistic concept was proposed to consist of two primary parts: a functional core and identifying features. Other components of the situation or context were also assumed to be part of the concept, for example, actors and locations, but these were not deemed to be central. It was proposed that this ancillary knowledge dropped out except as it left slots to be filled in particular contexts. Under the assumption that the child formed concepts around salient functions of things, such functions were assumed to form the core of the concept, while the formal aspects of things would be used for identifying instances of the concept.

The structure of the concept was illustrated with the example of *ball* (see Figure 5.1).

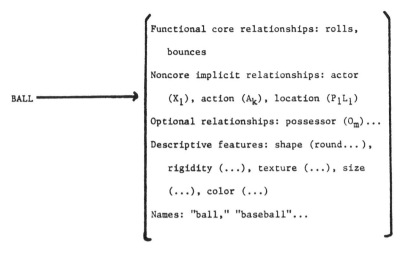

FIGURE 5.1   The FCM representation of the child's concept of *ball* (Nelson 1974a).

The most basic claim of the FCM was that all human concepts—as opposed to percepts—are formed in terms of their functional relationships within a system of real-world knowledge. Function means use; it implies action. Action implies intention as well as change. The functional core of an object concept is necessarily complex, involving relations to other people as well as to self, actions as well as temporal, spatial, and causal specifications.

Virtually all of the research designed to test this model has attempted to pit perception—specifically, form—against function to determine which is more compelling in assigning an object instance to a concept. The problems with this either–or approach are many:

1. Function is usually reflected in form (and vice versa). Indeed, the child may be expected to notice especially those aspects of form that are related to function (for example, the wheels on a car). Thus, separating function and form in most cases is not feasible.

2. Another problem is that objects in many, if not most, cases are multifunctional; thus, a single function may be changed or omitted without disturbing the child's assignment of an object instance to a concept.

3. Still a third problem is that function must be evaluated from the point of view of the child. One cannot expect a 15-month-old or even a 3- or 4-year-old to understand cultural conventions of function, for example, the uses of money. The child may, however, understand functions associated with eating, sleeping, toileting, and other daily routines

as well as the functions of playthings. The child's concept of *telephone* may differ from the adult's in many ways, but that is not to say that *telephone* will not be organized functionally, that is, according to the child's understanding of its function.

4. Further, it is difficult if not impossible to calibrate the dimensions of form and function such that they are equally salient to the child.

5. Finally, both function and form are essential to the object concept; thus, the either–or question is essentially meaningless.

The evidence for or against the functional basis of concepts must at the least be sensitive to differing definitions of functions, to relative salience, and to multifunctionality and must test core meaning rather than extension. Because this model is central to the more comprehensive theory outlined in Chapters 7 and 8, more detailed attention will be given here to a review of the research purportedly based on its claims.

Contrary to the assumption of some investigators, the FCM was not put forth as a developmental theory in the sense that it did not propose that children moved from concepts based on function to those based on form, but rather that function would form the core of the object concept at all ages.[3] Thus, evidence from older children and even adults is relevant to the theory. Of course, as will be shown later, there are developmental implications of this model, but these are not reflected in a function-to-form sequence.

As stressed in Chapters 2, 3, and 4, there is no one-to-one correspondence between what is named by the beginning language learner and what is conceptualized. Children can and do learn names for what can only be simple percepts, for example, the pictures of exotic animals that their parents name for them. Here it is relevant to emphasize that a basic assumption of the FCM is that the cognitive system is composed of subsystems at different levels, or layers, consisting at minimum of the perceptual, conceptual, and semantic, each resting on different principles of organization. The claim here is that the *conceptual* system is fundamentally functional in its organizing principles. This claim has only indirect implications for the perceptual and semantic systems.

Some evidence supporting the FCM was referred to in Chapter 3. For example, when children begin to name things, they are disposed to name those objects that have functional significance for them, suggesting that these things have been previously conceptualized (Nelson, 1973b). In support of this, Ross *et al.* (in press) found that objects that afforded a greater number of specific actions (that is, had more functional significance) were learned more readily than those with fewer. Moreover, when extending names analogically, children first utilize functional characteristics (Hudson & Nelson, 1984; Winner, 1978).

In a study of the differentiation of concepts by young children (based on a study by Labov [1973] of vague boundaries between terms), de Vos and Caramazzo (1977) reported that children between 3 and 6 years first differentiated the term "glass" from the more globally applied "cup" when required to name cup- or glasslike pictures in functional, in contrast to neutral, contexts. That is, perceptually ambiguous forms were assigned to the newly differentiated lexical category first in functionally appropriate contexts, thus indicating that function was a determining factor in assignment of objects to newly formed categories.

Verbal tasks support the importance of function for young children as well as older ones. Word associations by young children tend to be largely action or function based (e.g., Heidenheimer, 1978a; see discussion below). Similarly, studies of children's definitions have classically found that objects are defined in terms of their function (Al-Issa, 1969; Feifel & Lorge, 1950; Wolman & Barker, 1965). In Anglin's (1977) investigation of knowledge of word meanings by children from 2 to 5 years of age, he found they mentioned function or action characteristics more frequently than perceptual characteristics. A similar finding from my own research (Nelson, 1978b) is presented in Chapter 6.

In a direct test of the predictions of the FCM, Prawat and Cancelli (1977) used a semantic-retrieval task with 5- and 8-year-old children. They presented sentences encoding static, dynamic (presumed to be functional), or relational properties of animals to which the children had to respond as quickly as possible "Yes" (if the property applied) or "No" (if it did not). They found an interaction of age with type and salience of properties such that high-salient dynamic properties, but not other types, were responded to as quickly by the younger children as by the older. Thus, support for using this type of information in preschool as well as older children was provided.

There have been a number of studies that have failed to support the central role of function in the young child's developing conceptual and semantic system. The standard view of preschool children has long been that they are particularly oriented toward form and become sensitive to functional characteristics only later in development (see, e.g., Olver & Hornsby, 1966). The studies on which such conclusions have been based generally involved sorting, free classification of objects, or the verbal explanation of why some things go together. Such tasks (which involve the formation of supersets of already formed classes) call on different skills and bases for classification than does the formation of basic object concepts themselves (see Nelson, 1978b; Rosch *et al.*, 1976). While it is true that the formation of superordinate classes requires classification on the basis of function and that adults classify at this level according to function (Rosch *et al.*, 1976; Scribner, 1974), it is also true that young children define such classes in terms of function (Nelson, 1978b; see discussion below). However, when the perceptual characteristics of objects are made particularly salient, as in the free-sorting, match-to-sample, or picture tasks, and when instructions encourage perceptual responding, children may be led to rely on perceptual characteristics for their solutions. In fact, Olver and Hornsby (1966) reported an interaction between mode of presentation (visual and verbal) and type of response (perceptual and functional).

Potentially damaging evidence against the FCM has been presented in several recent experiments. In Gentner's (1978) study children and adults were required to learn nonsense names for two novel objects, each with a unique function. After learning, they were presented with an object in which the form and function conflicted, that is, the form first associated with function A was now presented with function B and vice versa. When asked what the object was, the preschool children based their choices on the object's perceptual characteristics, while the school-aged children based their choices on function. Adults, however, also based their choices primarily on perceptual properties. These results were interpreted in terms of a perceptual-to-functional progression, along the lines of the earlier Olver and Hornsby (1966) work, and were taken to contradict the functional core concept. However, other studies using similar paradigms (e.g., Casby, 1979) produced results conflicting with or at least less clear-cut then Gentner's.

Two other experiments (Prawat & Wildfong, 1980; Tomikawa & Dodd, 1980) concluded that perception is more important than function in concept formation among young children. Prawat and Wildfong (1980) essentially replicated a portion of Labov's (1973) experiment with adults, using pictures of cuplike forms in functional or nonfunctional contexts. They summarized their results across stimuli and grouped ages to conclude that function was stronger at older (school-age) than younger (preschool) ages. In contrast, de Vos and Caramazzo (1977), using a broader range of stimuli and age groups with a similar experimental paradigm, found a complex age and stimulus set interaction that was not examined by Prawat and Wildfong. In addition, Prawat and Wildfong used pictures to illustrate function, while deVos and Caramazzo required children to imagine functional contexts, as Labov (1973) had done, thus presumably calling on conceptual rather than perceptual processing. As noted above, an interaction of mode and dimension of this kind was reported by Olver and Hornsby (1966). In a follow-up study Anderson and Prawat (1983) compared pictorial and nonpictorial conditions and obtained conflicting results with this paradigm. The only clear outcome of this line of work seems to be that form and function interact in complex ways in the young child's application of these terms, and the particular results depend upon the task context (Nelson, 1983b).

Tomikawa and Dodd (1980) taught 2-year-olds names for objects that differed in function and were similar in perceptual characteristics or that differed in form and shared functions. They reported that the first category was far easier to learn than the second. While this result suggests limitations on the generalizations that can be made about the basis for learning names, the following reservations about its broader implications may be noted:

1. There was no independent assessment of the relative salience of the functional and perceptual characteristics, which were in any case extremely simple and one-dimensional. (Recall that the Ross *et al.* study found *number* of possible *specific* functions to be critical to learning.)

2. There was no attempt to make the objects functionally relevant to the child nor to put them into a meaningful functional context.

3. The shapes and functions (e.g., "open") were highly familiar to the children as characteristics belonging to a number of diverse object classes; thus, they would be unlikely to be seen as defining a new class on their own. Indeed, the learning task in this experiment is analogous to learning a superordinate class or category composed of all lower-order classes that share a single function (such as flying and walking), and such superordinate categories are difficult for the young child to learn, as much research has shown.

While this brief survey of studies of the functional core of concepts is no doubt incomplete, it is sufficient to indicate that the relation of function and perception in both concept formation and word meaning is complex. A preliminary summary may be ventured as follows: When a concept is being learned and generalized to new instances, learning is easier when functional properties are salient (Ross *et al.*, in press), while generalization is on the basis of perceptual features (although older children may generalize on the basis of functional characteristics [Gentner, 1978; Tomikawa & Dodd, 1980]). When a concept is being used in memory or in a verbal task, functional characteristics are most salient at all ages (Heidenheimer, 1978a; Nelson, 1978b; Prawat & Cancelli, 1977). When a concept is being defined or explained, functional characteristics are most important at younger ages but are replaced by class terms at older ages (Anglin, 1977; Nelson, 1978b; Watson, in press).

In concluding this review, it should be emphasized that, as originally suggested and as noted by Labov (1973), Miller (1978), and others, children do and must attend to both aspects of things in their effort to organize concepts of things. Therefore, the effort to disentangle the two is in large part misguided. Nonetheless, the central role of function in the child's concept structure has not been shown to be false by the work done to date.

Semantic Feature Theory

While the semantic feature theory was not put forth as a theory of conceptual structure, it has close ties with traditional abstraction theories and is often contrasted with the FCM. Thus, its treatment at this point is not out of order. Clark, in her comprehensive review of concepts and meanings (E. V. Clark, 1983), summarized and evaluated the semantic feature theory of word meaning, and it seems fair to quote her own description:

> The Semantic Feature Hypothesis began from the assumption that meanings break down into combinations of units—components or features—smaller than those represented by words, and that those smaller units, in turn, are based (ultimately) on perceptual and conceptual units common to all human beings (E. V. Clark, 1973). . . . When [children] first begin to use words, therefore, they do not know the full meanings, but have only parts of the adult meanings available. The acquisition of semantic knowledge consists of adding further components or features of meaning until the child meanings match adult meanings . . . As soon as children have some meaning attached to a word, they can use that information in trying to understand the word and in deciding when to produce it. But in production, their partial meanings should often make children's uses diverge from adult ones . . . I proposed that one could infer from the overextensions in the domain of any one word what the child considered its meaning to be . . . Another set of predictions . . . concerned the acquisition of words related in meaning and their relative order of acquisition. If two words shared meaning components or features in common, then children who had not acquired their full meanings might well confuse the words in production and comprehension . . . The theory also predicted that when children were learning semantic components or features, they should learn the more general ones first, where these were the features held in common by several words. Moreover, if word meanings consisted of features related to each other hierarchically, then the order of acquisition for features should be top-down, from the most general feature first, with the others acquired in order of hierarchical dependence. (pp. 816–817)

An additional condition was later added: that children have to work out the meaning components of each word, and therefore words that are related in meaning might not be recognized as such.

These predictions have not always held up (see discussion below; Carey, 1982; Richards, 1979). E. V. Clark herself (1983) noted four areas where problems with the theory have appeared: the status of semantic features, the addition of features during acquisition, the general-to-specific direction of acquisition for features, and the differences between production and comprehension. The status of features in this theory was questioned by Nelson (1974a) in that simple perceptual features like *furry* or even *round* do not seem to have the same status as abstract contrastive features in the adult lexicon such as ± *polar*. As Clark more recently noted, the features attributed to children's meanings rarely map onto adult ones. Another problem noted by Nelson (1974a) was the constraint implied in the proposal that features were added to the original meanings. This essentially ruled out other changes in children's word meanings such as broadening or realigning an original hypothesis. However, such changes, reflected in initial underextensions and overlaps rather than overextensions, are commonly observed. Moreover, subsequent research has not substantiated the general-to-specific feature-acquisition claim even where this can be reliably established (e.g., Bartlett, 1976; Brewer & Stone, 1975). Finally, the SFM could not account for apparent differences in feature structure in the comprehension and production of words.

In the light of these problems, E. V. Clark (1983) proposed a new but related theory, the *lexical contrast theory* (LCT). This theory (similar to that proposed by Barrett, 1978) proposes that "children work off two basic principles of language and lexical organization, namely *contrast* and *conventionality*" (p. 820). These principles are stated as follows:

> *Principle of Contrast:* The conventional meaning of every pair of words (or word-formation devices) contrast.
> *Principle of Conventionality:* For certain meanings, there is a conventional word or word-formation device that should be used in the language community. (p. 820)

These principles assume that children assume that a new lexical item contrasts with old ones and that "the word-learner's goal is to *fill lexical gaps* in finding words for whatever conceptual categories he wants to talk about" (p. 821, italics in original).

Clark uses these principles to reinterpret the data the SFM was meant to explain but failed to and to extend the LCT to new domains. She finds that the theory is more adequate to the task than was the SFM for a variety of reasons.

While it is too early to assess this new proposal completely, and it would be inappropriate to evaluate it on conceptual grounds in any event, it does not appear adequate to the developmental problems of concern here. Where it succeeds in explaining the data it seems to do so because of its extreme generality and lack of specificity with respect to what meaning contrasts may be involved. As Carey (1982) notes, "A theory of semantic development will provide limits on incorrect lexical entries," but this one does not.

One advantage and two problems can immediately be discerned. First, it is a relational theory of the sort demanded from a Sausserian view and thus may handle sense relations that are apparent later in childhood. Thus, it is likely to form at least part of a successful theory of semantic development (see Chapter 8). On the other hand, while the appropriate tests have not yet been carried out, it seems unlikely that the claim that children assume contrasts from the outset will hold up. There are examples of synonymous use in early language, such as the use of "cellar" and "basement" by my 2-year-old subject (Nelson, 1984b). While there is no evidence that some contrast is not implied in such uses, we have no reason to believe that it is. More seriously, the notion of contrast implies a prior identification of a lexical domain within which contrasts are made (Barrett, 1978), and no basis for such an identification has been suggested. It seems likely, rather, that notions of both domain and contrast must be achieved before they can be applied.

Relatedly on a more general level, the LCT does not explain developmental shifts such as those noted in the early phases of word learning (see Chapter 3 and 4) and in the development of hierarchical terms, or those involved in developmental shifts in meaning such as that for "big" (see Chapter 7; Maratsos, 1973b). A theory of semantic development must be more than a theory of lexical acquisition: it must explain changes in the patterns of acquisition at different ages. Moreover, Clark seems inadvertently to violate her own stricture against conflating conceptual and lexical knowledge in this statement of the theory, incorporating the notions that lexical items "pick out conceptual categories" and that contrasts inhere in categories. Exactly how to draw the distinction between a lexical contrast and a cognitive category contrast has not been clarified. Thus, a preliminary assessment suggests that the LCT is more satisfactory than the SFM in accounting for more of the data and in being more sensitive to the conceptual status, cognitive abilities, and strategies of the child, but it is not likely to be wholly successful as a theory of semantic development and it explicitly denies applicability to conceptual development.

Concept Types and Concept Structures

The theoretical approaches covered in this chapter have concentrated on the internal structure of concepts and categories of objects to the neglect of concepts of attributes, relations, and abstractions. The proposal that either criterial attributes or perceptual prototypes constitute internal conceptual structure can only be appropriately posited as applying to object concepts. These notions are less appropriate and frequently inapplicable to concepts of perceptual attributes, such as *color* and *size*, to actions such as *throwing*, to relations such as *up* or *down*, or to abstractions even as simple as *play*. What could be the prototype for *big* or the criterial attributes of *play*? The notion of fuzzy concepts or family resemblances is of only minor help to us in deciding on the content and structure of concepts of these latter types.

Before examining this issue—which will be considered in Chapter 7— further, it is necessary to review the research relevant to the development of conceptual systems; this will be undertaken in the next chapter. Because issues of internal and external structure are closely related in development, conclusions based on the research reviewed here will be deferred until the end of Chapter 6.

Notes

[1]Anglin's basis for the latter claim was the responses from two Harvard students; whether they can be considered representative of the general adult population seems questionable.

[2]After completing this review, I came across the article by Rosenblum and Pinker (1983) comparing "word magic" (nominal realism) among bilingual and monolingual children. They claimed that neither group displayed the phenomenon. However, their subjects were from professional families and averaged 5 years old, beyond the age where this phenomenon is usually observed. This illustrates the fallacy of considering the preschool period to be a unitary one, ignoring the substantial cognitive developments that take place within it. Nonetheless, they found an interesting difference between the two groups, with monolingual children basing their rationale for the possibility that an object may have more than one name on the existence of its various properties, while bilingual children cite different social contexts in which the name is used.

[3]This was stated explicitly in Nelson (1974a) in the following terms:

> It is important to bear in mind that this process is not proposed as a stage theory of development. Although language development may depend on the acquisition and elaboration of concepts, as shown above, there is no "functional stage" or "attributive stage." Rather all concept acquisition is assumed to involve both of these processes, whether the concepts are formed in infancy or in adulthood. (p. 284)

6

Development of Conceptual Relations: Research Findings

Relations between Concepts

In this chapter evidence for the existence of relations between concepts of various kinds, derived from different research traditions, is examined. In these studies much of the research is atheoretical (in contrast to that reviewed in Chapter 5 on internal structure). Therefore, the problem is to discern what these research paradigms have revealed about young children's conceptual systems rather than to determine the value of a particular theory in accounting for data. We begin with the venerable tradition of viewing conceptual structure in terms of associations between words.

Word Associations

The psychological study of the relations between words has a century-long tradition in the free-word association test (FWA or simply WA), in which the subject in an experiment is presented with a word and must respond with the first word that comes to mind. As noted earlier, since the first experiments with children (Woodward & Lowell, 1916), a developmental progression or shift in responding from syntagmatic to paradigmatic has been reported. Briefly, the syntagmatic–paradigmatic shift refers to the observation that younger children tend to give associations that could occur later than the stimulus word in a sentence frame (or syntagm) and older children give associations that could occupy the same position in a sentence as the stimulus word. However, the data do not all fit this conception neatly. Although there tends to be a shift between 7 and 10 years from giving words of a different form class (noun–adjective, for example) to giving words of the same form class (noun–noun), these are not all appropriately described as syntagmatic or paradigmatic, respectively[1] (see Brown and Berko, 1960; Entwisle, 1966; Ervin, 1961). Furthermore, the shift is strongest for adjectives, with nouns tending to elicit nouns at all ages over 6 and verbs tending to elicit syntagmatic associates, even among adults (see Deese, 1967; Entwisle, 1966).

An alternative conception of the shift evident in the grade-school years characterizes it according to the logical (inclusion) relations between the stimulus word and its associate (see Riegel, 1970). In this light, it appears that younger children (6- and 7-year-olds) use many different relations—superordinates, coordinates, subordinates, and properties—while older children and adults produce primarily coordinates (see Nelson, 1977b, for a fuller description). Thus, the word-association data have suggested a semantic memory that becomes more conventionally organized within a hierarchical system with increasing development. However, there are few data available for children under age 5, and thus development prior to this point is an open question. Moran's (1974) report on preschool-aged Japanese, Taiwanese, and American children, however, found enactive responses to dominate, implying a syntagmatic stage for nouns. Moreover, unpublished data collected by Halperin (reported in Nelson, 1977a) from 3- and 4-year-old children found that nouns elicited syntagmatic responses at this age period; about 85% of the noun responses were syntagmatic.

This early syntagmatic stage may indicate a significant conceptual development. The kinds of logical relationships that nouns enter into with other nouns are primarily paradigmatic (i.e., superordinates, coordinates, and part–wholes). But situational relations (actions, functions, and locations) are likely to be syntagmatic. In Halperin's study over half of the high-frequency responses were actions or functions of the stimulus word, whereas only 18% were noun responses and 5% were attributes. Thus, these young children seemed to be primarily set to give responses that reflected how things were used, or their relations in the real world rather than in logic or language. The implication is that their words at this point are not organized semantically but according to conceptual relationships derived from active experiences and represented in terms of events and actions. Petrey's (1977) analysis of Entwisle's (1966) data for 4- and 5-year-olds supports this assumption. He claims that the youngest children responded with words that were related in terms of real-world *situations,* such as "dark–moon." These are contrasted with linguistically related pairs such as "dark–night" (syntagmatic) or "dark–light" (paradigmatic).

By school age, children reflect logical relations at least some of the time, and these begin to appear in early childhood. Superordinate as well as coordinate associations are found in the data, exemplifying predications of the type *"X* has a *Y"* (part–whole) or *"X* is a *Y"* and necessary inferences such as *"X* and *Y* are both *Z"* or *"X* is in the same class as *Y."* In the later preschool period, adjectives as responses to nouns increase (Entwisle, 1966), indicating an interest in the properties of objects, perhaps the shared properties of objects from the same class.

Evidence accumulated by Moran (1974), Penk (1971), and Cramer (1974) in regard to the kinds of relations reflected in children's word-association data is relevant to the hypothesis that children are developing an appreciation of hierarchical relations through the analysis of object properties during early childhood. Properties, functions, and relations of instances of *single* concepts named by the lexical stimulus item appear in the preschool data. Relations, synonyms, coordinates, and contrasts based on relations between *two* concepts or words appear later; superordinates and parts relating a concept at one level to its dominating category or to a part of the thing named, itself a lexicalized concept, appear at an intermediate stage. Thus, on the one hand, there seems to be a progression from responses related to *single* concepts (their properties, qualities, and functions); to *vertical* relations *between* concepts, relating them to superordinates, subordinates, parts, and wholes; to *horizontal* relations between concepts, in which concepts that are both included in the same superordinate category will be related to each other. Note that this implies building relations between coordinates *through* the superordinate relation, contrary to the usual "bottom-up" theories of classification on which such tasks as sorting implicitly rest (see Figure 6.1).

On the basis of these observations, the course of development being reflected in the word-association data can be described as follows: From the earliest stage of word learning, words become associated with concepts that incorporate possible functional relations and perceptual attributes on the basis of the child's episodic experience (Nelson, 1974a). If word-association data could be obtained at age 2 years, they would be likely to reflect actions, locations, possessors, and objects in their experienced spatial or temporal contiguity with the object–concept in question. Responses from preschool children represent real-world situational information associated with the single concept represented by

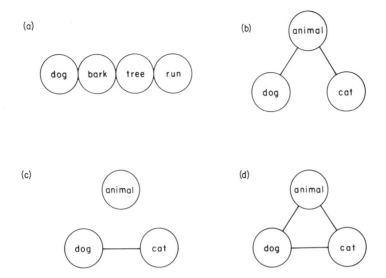

FIGURE 6.1   Types of relations found in children's word-association responses: (a) nonhierarchical (e.g., contextual), (b) vertical relations only, (c) horizontal relations only, (d) all relations available. (From Nelson, 1977a.)

the word. However, some use of vertical hierarchical relations is reflected in the early appearance of superordinates in word-association data.

Young children seem to have difficulty, however, coordinating group members, that is, operating on more than one member of a category at the same hierarchical level at the same time. Consider the response given in Lippman's (1971) study in which the young child is asked to say why dogs and cats are alike: ''Dogs bark and cats meow.'' The child in this case has not found a single attribute that is common to both; rather he has hit on a dimension along which they *differ*. Both *dog* and *cat* are subsumed under the category *animal* through the animal–sound function, but the child cannot yet coordinate them; he is not able to consider their relation to each other through the animal category explicitly, although he can make the connection implicitly. This is consistent with the finding that coordinates appear later in word-association data than do superordinates.

In summary, the word-association data suggest the emergence of a new facility for relating words and concepts to one another paradigmatically at around 5 to 7 years, while prior to that time words are related directly to concepts and both word–word and concept–concept relations are syntagmatic in character.

Hierarchical Categories

On the basis of the above discussion, it is clear that the word-association data are relevant to the question of the establishment of hierarchical categories in the young child's conceptual and semantic systems. Many other research paradigms have also addressed this question, which is central to so many theories of the development of the young child's thought.

There is a long history of research on the development of understanding of taxonomic categorical structures, most of it undertaken within a cognitive rather than a linguistic framework. A taxonomic structure is best portrayed as a tree structure (see Figure 6.2), where a term (or a concept) at the top dominates and includes terms lower down. Thus, *clothes* includes *pants, shirt, dress,* etc. Even though preschool children tend not to employ these taxonomies in verbal tasks (such as free recall and false recognition), they clearly know something about them. When asked to indicate which of a set of pictures are food, clothes, or animals, they readily do so; and when asked to produce the names of different foods, clothes, animals, etc., they have no problem in complying (Nelson, 1974b, 1978).

Children's difficulties with the structure of taxonomic categories have been attributed to logical deficiencies or to the lack of abstract ability. As discussed in Chapter 5, the classic work of Inhelder and Piaget (1964), Vygotsky (1962), and Goldstein and Sheerer (1941) all supported the notion that young children were not capable of sorting groups of objects into classes according to logical principles and thus did not possess classification or categorization ability. Younger children, faced with a group of assorted objects, tend to put together things that are complementary or have functional relationships to each other, or they form complexes

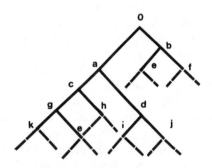

FIGURE 6.2   Tree structure of taxonomic categories. (Based on Lyons, 1977.)

in which each item is related to the next in turn but all are not related according to a single principle. This has led to the notion of "complexive" rather than "classificatory" thinking on the part of the younger child.

As noted in Chapter 3, very young children often name groups within categorical fields, such as animals and vehicles, that seem identical to the taxonomies that are later established as subordinate–superordinate relationships. However, these children seldom learn that superordinate terms "animal," "food," and "vehicle," and if they do, they resist applying the terms to members of the class that have their own names, such as "dog" or "tiger" (Macnamara, 1982).

Anglin (1977) carried out a series of investigations based on the hypothesis that the level at which children learned to name objects—basic level, superordinate, or subordinate—would be determined by adult naming practices, which in turn would be determined by adult perceptions of which term had the greatest discriminative utility for the child.[2] While his data supported this model (derived from Brown, 1958), it did not speak specifically to the difficulty that children might have in learning superordinate terms. In contrast, Horton and Markman (1980) attempted to demonstrate that preschoolers could easily learn a new term for a basic-level set of objects although they had difficulty learning new words for a superordinate set. There are problems in defining a novel superordinate set, however, that this study did not address. If superordination or hyponomy is defined in terms of dominance relations rather than in terms of perceptual diversity, the set used by Horton and Markman could not be considered a superordinate one. This point is important to the consideration of the status of hierarchical structures in young children's thinking.

In research using the free-recall paradigm, studies have found that when items from familiar taxonomic categories such as *food, clothes,* and *animals* are included in a list of words to be recalled in any order by children and adults, items from the same category tend to be recalled together. However, most studies of preschool children using the free recall and other paradigms, such as false recognition and release from proactive inhibition, have failed to find evidence for categorical organization similar to that displayed by older children (Hagen, Jongeward, & Kail, 1975). Several factors other than a lack of categorical organization in semantic memory have been proposed to explain the relative "deficiency" in category use among younger children. The possibility that young children do have "categorical" organization but that their categories differ from the adult's—for example, that they contain different dominant members—was tested by Nelson (1969a) and Tenney

(1975) with negative results. In contrast, when thematic organization was compared to taxonomic organization in lists used with 6-year-olds, Denney and Zibrowski (1972) found greater clustering with thematic materials. Smiley and Brown (1979) used a triads test and training to explore the proposal that younger children *prefer* thematic (functional) relations but can *use* taxonomic ones as well. Their results confirmed the hypothesis for children as young as 5 years. Others (Bjorklund & Zaken-Greenberg, 1981; Lucariello & Nelson, in press), however, have not found thematic clustering to be superior. In the latter study, 3- and 4-year-old children were found to cluster "slot-filler categories" (i.e., items filling the same slot in a script) but not context-free categories or thematically related items. The relevance of these findings to conceptual development will be considered in Chapter 7.

Perhaps the most straightforward assessment of category knowledge is to ask children to produce category members in response to their category label or to identify pictures belonging to a category. In an early study (Nelson, 1969a, 1974b) children (5 and 8 years) were asked to name members of categories such as *animals, clothes,* and *furniture.* The younger children named fewer instances of the categories but, with few exceptions, their responses were otherwise similar to those of the older children and to adult norms. Saltz, Soller, and Sigel (1972) and Neimark (1974) each used a picture-recognition technique in which the child was asked to pick out all the food items or clothing items or things to eat or wear. Although Saltz *et al.* claimed that the younger children's categories were more fragmented and restricted than the older children's, there was no evidence that they were formed according to different principles. While these studies do not show that kindergarten children have categorically organized semantic memories, they indicate that they can *mentally sort* according to categories when this is required, that is, the category information must be somehow available to them. These findings contrast with the WA and recall tasks. The latter tasks call on implicit organization, the former on explicit knowledge. This difference may then represent an important developmental distinction, one that marks a transition from the precategorical state of the preschool years to the taxonomic organization evident at later ages.

In addition, other studies have shown that even very young children often utilize categorical relationships between objects in *nonverbal* tasks. Discrimination tasks (Daehler, Perlmutter, & Myers, 1976), habituation of attention (Faulkender, Wright, & Waldron, 1974), and priming tasks (Higgins, McGarry, & Huttenlocher, 1975) have all shown such evidence for 2- to 4-year-olds, although Steinberg (1974) and Daehler, Lonardo and Bubatko (1979) failed to find any category advantage for 2-year-olds. Moreover, the stimuli used in these tasks often reveal other bases for relations in addition to the categorical one, such as appearance in a common situation.

In summary, the original finding appears to hold: Young children often fail to utilize categorical relationships among words in recall and other verbal tasks, even when they are familiar with the categories and when they may use them in nonverbal tasks. The conclusion that they do not *naturally* rely on such principles in long-term semantic memory seems appropriate. The implication for conceptual development remains to be explained.

Huttenlocher and Lui (1979) challenged the conclusions from the word-association data and related research that there is a general developmental shift in semantic organization of the syntagmatic to paradigmatic type that affects categorical organization. Using both release from proactive inhibition and free-recall paradigms with 3-, 4-, and 5-year-olds, they presented pairs of concrete nouns related taxonomically and concrete verbs related in terms of movement, state, or "saying." They found that nouns showed significant effects of categorical relatedness, although verbs did not. Huttenlocher and Lui argue that verbs are organized differently from nouns for both adults and children and that verbs are related first to their noun arguments (e.g., *eat: apple, boy,* etc.). While it seems clear that verbs *are* organized according to different semantic relations than are nouns for adults (e.g., see Miller & Johnson-Laird, 1976), this in itself does not explain the many differences on verbal tasks, including word associations, between children's and adults' responses. Although Huttenlocher and Lui dismiss the WA task as a barometer of semantic organization, they also claim that a sample of 4-year-olds gave 74% paradigmatic responses to nouns and 23% to verbs. These results for nouns conflict with those of Halperin and Moran. Moreover, as the above discussion has shown, paradigmatic responses may reflect a number of different types of relations, from "primitive noun responses," to "situational" or "contextual," to the hierarchical that Huttenlocher and Lui believe to be central. Indeed, the noun pairs that they used in their main experiment are not consistently hierarchical, for example, their paradigmatic lists pair *desk* with *house* and *chair* with *wall,* which do not reflect categorical relations.

Despite the interest that has been shown in this area from a cognitive perspective, and despite the clear findings that, in general, children learn basic-level terms in a semantic domain first, there is little work to support a theoretical account of why superordinate terms should present particular difficulty to the young child. As Rescorla (1980) and others have shown, children learn words from the beginning in what appear to be broad categories (see Chapter 3). Moreover, they sometimes learn, as one of the words that refer to members of these domains, the superordinate term itself. For example, Emily (Chapter 2) at 22-months said: "I like milk and toast and food." Yet, it seems clear that these terms do not *organize* the semantic field; they do not occupy a dominating node in a tree structure but rather are wastebasket or umbrella terms. When asked to say what a *dog* is, children below the age of 6 or 7 virtually never say that it is an animal (Anglin, 1977; Nelson, 1978b; Watson, in press). When asked to provide word associations to a term like *dog* they will give attributes (*barks, fur*) but not coordinates (*cat*) or superordinates (*animal*). On the other hand, young children can tell you what an animal is: "It eats and runs," for example, and "Tigers and elephants are animals" (Anglin, 1977; Nelson, 1978b). Markman's (1981) research on collections suggests that the problem is that children have part–whole relations but not "ISA" relations[3] between words (or object collections). However, this leaves open the question of how the ISA relation becomes established.

An alternative explanation, to be explored in more detail in the following chapters, is that the categorical or collective structures available to the young child are in fact rooted in the spatiotemporal structures derived from representations of the real world and have not yet become established as semantic structures, and that it is *only* as semantic structures that hierarchical relations between words are established.

This proposal is consonant with the claim that superordinate terms are linguistically defined, although conceptually based. That is, a superordinate term dominates a set of hyponyms (subordinate terms) or lexemes for related classes or types. The hyponyms, in turn, may refer only to unnamed tokens or may dominate a set of hyponyms at a lower level. For example, *fruit* dominates *banana* as well as *apple*. For many adults in our culture, *apple* in turn dominates *Granny Smith, McIntosh,* and so on, while *banana* refers to undistinguished tokens (despite the best efforts of the Dole and United Fruit companies to establish differentiated subclasses by such devices as sticking labels on the skin). Whether or not a possible conceptual class is named by a language at any level is a matter of cultural convention (Deese, 1967; Rosch, 1975). That a child may consider that books and magazines form a natural group of objects based on similarity of form and function does not alter the fact that there is no natural single lexeme in the language that can refer to this group. Thus, the use of superordinate terms and categories requires the ability to categorize into higher-level relationships, but the actual categories that are named in the language and thus the hierarchical meaning structures to be acquired are somewhat arbitrary.

Almost nothing is known at this point about what general knowledge preschool children may have with respect to superordinate categories and relations or what the basis for their knowledge may be. Virtually all studies have focused on categories such as *animals, toys, clothes,* and *food,* which are readily exemplified in the child's world. Much of the discussion of the child's understanding of categories and classes treats these categories as groups of things. The standard test of classification, of course, is whether the child can form appropriate groups of dissimilar objects. However, a category or class does not depend on grouping but rather on establishing an abstract inclusion (ISA) relation. *Animals* include *cats, dogs, lions, tigers, aardvarks, slugs,* and so on. A relevant research question is whether the child uses natural groups as the basis for understanding hierarchical categories, and if so, whether that helps the child in forming more abstract categories. However, this question should not be confused with the logical basis for taxonomic categorization.

Semantic Fields: Time, Quantity, Cause, Size, Color, and Action

Hierarchical relations reflect one kind of semantic relation. Another type is reflected in those relating terms within domains such as time, size, and color. Here we find concepts that are related because they lie along a single dimension or in a multidimensional space. Much of the research on semantic development in early childhood has been concerned with these domains, most of it considered within the semantic feature framework.

The cognitive significance of temporal terms (e.g., "before," "after," "first," "last") derives from Piaget's (1971) claims that the young child is unable to construct a temporal sequence or to reverse an order mentally. The implication of these claims, based on the young child's presumed egocentrism, is that the child should have difficulty marking a temporal order of events correctly. The child should, for example, use terms like "before" and "after" somewhat interchangeably in describing a sequence of events. In terms of causal relationships, Piaget's (1969) claim was that young children did not differentiate between a cause and its effect. He presented data to indicate that before the age of 7 years children would complete a sentence such as "The man fell off the bicycle because . . ." with "because he got hurt." That is, the child appeared to confuse the cause and the effect, or perhaps to interpret the term "because" to mean "so."

The linguistic significance of the acquisition of these terms was originally laid out by E. V. Clark (1971) in a study of "before" and "after." Briefly, she claimed that children learned "before" before "after;" and that "after" was first interpreted as meaning the same as "before." This was explained by proposing the acquisition of the features + time, − simultaneity, + prior, and − prior, in that order. This proposal was supported by a series of studies in which children had to act out two clauses in the appropriate order, for example, "Mary Ann kisses the dog before she pats the bunny." Like many other claims from the early version of the semantic feature theory, this one immediately generated numerous attempts at replication and refutation.

Most have failed to replicate Clark's results (see the review by Richards, 1979). In particular, children do not uniformly comprehend the term "after" later than "before," nor do they confuse "after" with "before." The data that have accumulated (e.g., Amidon & Carey, 1972; Coker, 1978; Coker & Legum, 1975), in fact, indicate no clear pattern. Rather, they appear to indicate that preschoolers have some knowledge of the terms, but that their performance is greatly influenced by the context of particular task demands (Carni, 1982).

Some hints as to the basis for children's knowledge of these relations have emerged from studies based on the analysis of children's script knowledge (French & Nelson, 1982, in press). When children are asked to tell what they know about "what happens" in a familiar event, such as eating lunch or going to a birthday party, even the youngest (3-year-olds) order the component actions in a correct temporal sequence. When they make a mistake, they reverse and repair, using temporal markers to indicate the correct order (e.g., "but first" and "before"). In one sample of protocols from 43 children, there were 14 uses of "before," 33 uses of "after," and 63 uses of "first," all of them used appropriately in context. Moreover, comprehension of "after" when used by the experimenter in probes was correct 74% of the time. The implication of this finding is that when children have a well-organized representation to support the temporal term, it will be used correctly, in contrast to its uncertain use in experimental situations where the experimenter presents the child with arbitrary sequences to relate to one another.

An experimental test of this interpretation using a series of picture sequences was undertaken (Carni & French, 1984). Half of the sequences were familiar but arbitrary (such as taking a walk in the park) and half were familiar and well structured (such as going to the grocery store, where events such as getting a cart, buying food, paying, and bagging have an invariant order). Children were required to indicate what happened *before* the third (of five) pictured events or what happened *after* by pointing to the appropriate picture. Three-year-olds employed a "next event in time" strategy on the arbitrary sequences, but on the structured sequences they were correct at above-chance levels (73%) on both terms. Four-year-olds were near the ceiling on both tasks, although they performed better on the structured task. This study demonstrates that when children understand the situational structure, they can interpret temporal-order terms correctly. But note that both forms of the task provided pictorial support for a *familiar* context. What was present in the nonarbitrary sequences was a *preestablished, cognitively structured context* over and beyond the pictured sequences. That is, the helpful interpretive context was in the child's head and not simply in the experimental task.

These conclusions gain support from further analyses of the script narratives by 3- to 5-year-olds, which reveal that these young children use logical connectors ("or," "but") and causal terms ("because," "so," "if . . . then") correctly when they are reporting on these well-known events.[4] Earlier research claimed that young children did not grasp the meanings of these terms, but Hood and Bloom (1979) showed that even $2\frac{1}{2}$-year-olds used causal terms correctly in the course of everyday activities. The script narrative data are unique, however, in that the context that supports the use of these terms is conceptual and not perceptual; the child must rely on a conceptual representation of the event being reported. The evidence therefore suggests that these events are mentally represented in temporal and causal form and that the appropriate terms are available for their verbalization in these forms. Taken together, these results would seem to indicate the need for a reevaluation of the role of context in semantic development and, indeed, for a redefinition of context itself, along the lines suggested here and in Chapter 2.

Size and color terms have long been staples of early childhood education and assessment. Size terms, as well as temporal terms, figured in E. V. Clark's (1973) semantic feature account. A prediction was generated as to the order of acquisition of these terms on the basis of their purported complexity of feature structure. "Big" and "little" would be learned first because they contained only the feature "extent" in addition to ± polarity. "Long" and "short" would be learned next, containing the feature + vertical, and "wide" and "narrow" (or "skinny") later because they contained the feature + horizontal. Again, E. V. Clark (1973) reported data that appeared to support this order of acquisition, and subsequent tests also supported the claim (e.g., Brewer and Stone, 1975). However, as Carey (1982) pointed out, there is no within-child consistency in the treatment of these terms when their comprehension is compared across tasks. This replicates the similar finding for "before" and "after." A different but equally contradictory proposal was put forth by Maratsos (1973b), whose data showed that "big" is first used correctly for general extent and then applied only to a single (vertical) dimension and finally correctly applied to three-dimensional (integrated) space, with "tall" taking over the previously delimited vertical space.

Size terms are primary examples of terms that must be interpreted in context. "Big" has meaning only in reference to particular items to be compared or to categories of objects (cf. Katz, 1972). Just as with temporal terms, size terms can only be employed if the child has an appropriate cognitive representation of the particular structure applicable to the comparison at issue. General knowledge of the concept is essential but insufficient.

On the other hand, color terms appear to represent, not a feature space, but a closed perceptual space. Berlin and Kay (1969) and later Rosch (1973) showed that, although different cultures divided up the color field in different ways (see also Brown and Lenneberg, 1954), there was a predictable structure to any given division. If a culture had only three colors, they would be black, white, and red; if four, blue would be added. Moreover, each nameable color had an identifiable focal point within the color spectrum, so that one could predict just where the boundaries would fall as the field became more differentiated in each language. Rosch (1973) furthermore showed that both young children and members of a culture in which there were no color terms at all would sort color chips and learn color names in terms of the focal (or prototypical) colors. Thus, there was reason to believe that there was a sound theoretical basis for predicting how children would begin to define the color space and how color terms would be learned and generalized.

Unfortunately, the data do not support the theoretical expectation (Carey, 1982). Bartlett (1977) found that nonfocal colors such as "pink" and "orange" were among the first to be learned by some children. Moreover, Carey and Bartlett (1978) taught a new color word, "chromium," to children whose color lexicons varied in size and found no differences in the acquisition of this nonfocal color term attributable to the already available lexical domain. That is, children apparently learned color words as individual, not related items.

Bowerman's (1982) analyses of her children's verb uses and errors reveals an important phenomenon that is related to this observation. First, children use noncausal verbs such as "fall" and "walk" correctly. Between 3 and 5 years, however, they begin to produce errors that, when analyzed, are quite systematic. For example, they will use "fall" in a causal (intentional, transitive) sense, as in "I falled it." Bowerman claims that such errors are the result of a new level of componential analysis that establishes previously nonexisting relations between verbs and extends a feature such as "cause" inappropriately to verbs that are in other ways close in meaning (e.g., drop–fall). The important point here is that such errors reflect a delayed analysis into featural components of previously established unrelated wholes.[5]

The most general conclusion that can be drawn from the results of these studies in several different relational domains is that children between 3 and 4 years of age are highly competent at using relational terms appropriately in context, but that in arbitrary experimental tasks they fail to reveal knowledge of the abstract meaning of these terms and of their relation to one another. One characterization of this finding is in terms of partial knowledge (E. V. Clark, 1975). A more revealing explanation is that these terms, like object terms, are mapped onto a *conceptual* representation of their conditions of use, but that they have not been established within a *semantic* system where the relations between the terms (rather than the relations of the terms to real-world conditions) may determine their meaning. The former relational structure seems to begin to appear gradually as the terms themselves become established in the child's lexicon, and their internal structure is subjected to analysis.

The Free Elements Model

Ehrlich (1979) described the development of semantic memory[6] in terms of a *free elements* system. In the mature system, elements (which Ehrlich assumes to be equivalent to words) are free to enter into different kinds of organizations, depending upon momentary or permanent cognitive needs. Having entered into an organization, they do not thereby become frozen, however, but remain free and flexible and capable of being organized into a different system when needed (see Posner & Warren, 1972, for a similar view). Thus, the question is not, What is *the* structure of semantic memory?, but rather, What are some of the organizing principles and relatively permanent organizations within semantic memory? Ehrlich also sees developmental implications, which will be considered here.

Ehrlich made a basic distinction between the relational and informative functions of elements. He does not consider these to be different classes of elements, but rather different aspects of all elements. Thus, the word "apple," for example, denotes a particular type of edible object. This is its informative function. "Apple" also relates to an eater and the action of eating. "Eat," in turn, relates both to someone who eats and the object eaten.

Ehrlich outlines a course of development that bears a strong resemblance to that set forth in Nelson and Nelson (1978) in terms of a cognitive pendulum model. In the beginning, according to this account, the child's concepts and their relations are global and undifferentiated.

> When these representations are able to be verbalized explicitly, that is, during the child's second year, they form the first structures of semantic memory. These structures are global and poor. They correspond at first to general situations within which different referents are not distinguished. For example, when the child says *gone,* he does not differentiate among a departure, a disappearance, the cessation of a stimulation . . . Later, when the different referents of a situation begin to be individualized, it is in a global form: a *bird,* for example, is first represented in the form of a dark mobile state; it does not have *wings.* (Ehrlich, 1979, p. 204; compare with Chapters 2 and 3.)

This state is followed by one of differentiation in which the global structures of the first stage are analyzed at the perceptual and the semantic levels, so that in the case of objects, for example, spatial and temporal locations are differentiated, as well as constitutive parts, physical and psychological qualities, and function and use. The important characteristic of this stage is that the various elements are impervious to one another; they cannot be connected or composed. Each representation exists as a unit. This characteristic is consistent with the literature reviewed above suggesting the imperviousness of relational structures to other structures of a similar (paradigmatic) type.

Ehrlich cites evidence from an experiment by du Boucheron and Cotillon (1978) in which 4-year-old children were asked whether certain things were alike or different. They responded almost entirely in terms of difference, even when the objects were very similar. For example, although they would affirm that pancakes and brioche could both be eaten, they noted that they were different because "A pancake is flat. A brioche is not flat." These responses are similar to those given by children in the experiment by Lippman (1971), who affirmed that dogs and cats were alike because "Dogs bark and cats meow." Both results indicate that children are sensitive to similarities as well as differences (otherwise they would be unable to pick out just the dimension on which the difference lies), but they are still attuned to separability rather than to a potential combinability within a more general hierarchical frame.

The next stage described by Ehrlich requires that "referential properties detach themselves from the semantic structures to which they belong and become functionally autonomous," and thus become recombinable. In this stage,

> Semantic memory has become a system of free and connectable elements. The subject's activities are no longer connected to the contingent aspects of the primitive (concrete) semantic representations [resulting in] a large set of possible optional structures. All of this indicates a great mobility and a great adaptive flexibility of memory, conditions of creativity. (p. 208)

Ehrlich supports this description with an experiment in which children of 6 to 8 years were given three types of sentences: possible ("I mash the banana with a fork"), impossible ("I mash the rock with a fork"), and "eventually possible" ("I mash the banana with a ladle"). The youngest children labeled the last type impossible, while the 8-year-olds agreed it was possible. There were no age differences on the other types. Ehrlich comments:

> Among the youngest children, the instrument of action cannot be detached from its most common use: *the ladle is used to serve soup.* Not being detachable from this situation, the *ladle* cannot be inserted in another construction . . . in the second stage . . . the element *ladle* is already differentiated but . . . it remains attached to one particular situation (SERVING SOUP) and cannot be utilized in any other. (p. 208)

While much of this theoretical description is compatible with the data under review, there are two aspects that require further comment. First, Ehrlich does not distinguish between the conceptual and semantic levels, but only between the perceptual and semantic. Second, and this is related to the first point, the free elements of the third stage seem different in kind from the elements differentiated at the second stage. While the inflexibility at the second stage is important to note, the openness of the system at earlier points in development also needs to be recognized and dealt with. Initially, concepts enter into relations with each other in both temporary and more or less permanent structures in a manner similar to that which Ehrlich has described in terms of the organization of free elements. In order to reconcile these developments, it is necessary to conceive of two different systems—the conceptual and the semantic—evolving at different times.

As has been emphasized throughout, this distinction between conceptual and semantic organization is not an empty one. It distinguishes between shared and idiosyncratic knowledge, between meaning and knowing. Moreover, as the present analysis reveals, this is a developmental achievement of considerable importance.

Definitions, Categories, and Conceptual Structures

Data from an experiment partially reported in Nelson (1978b) can help to illuminate some of these relational developments further. The purpose of this experiment was to explore the distinction between the conceptual and the semantic systems in the preschool years and to determine the principles of organization of each system. Based on the results from word association tests, it was hypothesized that young preschool children would not have differentiated between the conceptual and semantic systems. Further, the study aimed to examine responses to different types of words (i.e., verbs and adjectives as well as nouns) that had been largely ignored in previous studies but that represent important types of concepts, as outlined earlier. Controlled interviews focusing on definitions and knowledge of concepts were used rather than word associations (see Nelson, 1978b, for details).

Children between 3 and 4 years participated. Each child was asked to respond to words in one of four ways, designed to contrast definitions with real-world knowledge and also to elicit verbal responses analogous to responses to sorting instructions used for evaluating classification behavior. In condition 1 the interviewer asked the child to "tell me what X is" (or what X means). In condition 2 (world knowledge) the child was asked to "tell me what you know about X." In condition 3 (grouping) the question was "What goes with X?" and in condition 4 (thematic), "What belongs with X?" The latter two conditions were designed to be analogous to instructions used in classification tasks.

The basic word list was composed of 5 object words (nouns, e.g., "tiger"), their related superordinates (nouns, e.g., "animal"), possible salient properties of the objects (adjectives, e.g., "striped"), functions or actions associated with the objects (verbs or adjectives, e.g., "run"), and spatial–temporal organizers (STOs) specifying a time or place in which the objects might appear (nouns or adverbs, e.g., "zoo"). Note that there is no one-to-one correspondence between word-form class and conceptual type.

The first questions asked were whether preschool children respond appropriately to verbal probes for semantic knowledge and whether they are sensitive to differences between probe questions and between types of words. The answer to both questions was affirmative.

The answers were coded in terms of quantity of information contained in the meaningful responses. For this purpose, every specific element mentioned by the child—property, action, object, or category—was given a value of one. For example, in response to "animal," "A duck went swimming" was given a value of two, counting both duck (subordinate member) and swimming (action) as separate responses, while "animals goes in the zoo" was valued at one, because "animals" is the stimulus word and "goes in" is a nonspecific locative relation of animal to zoo.

The first analysis compared the "what is" or lexical (L) and "know about" or world-knowledge (WK) questions. Figure 6.3 displays the mean numbers of responses by word type and question type. As can be seen, different questions elicited consistently different numbers of responses. "What is X?" produced fewer responses than "What do you know about X?"—the contrast that was expected to illuminate the difference between lexical knowledge and knowledge about the world. It is also apparent that the difference varied across the terms, however. Property terms showed the least differentiation by question type. Regardless of the questions asked, these terms tended to elicit lists of ex-

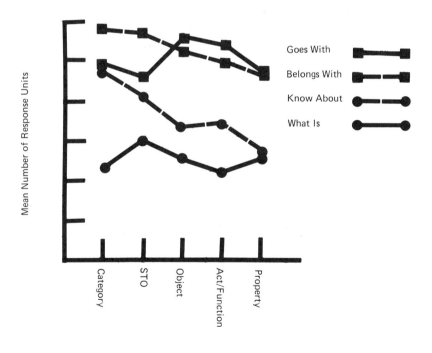

Word Type

FIGURE 6.3   Mean number of responses by word type and question type in word-meaning interviews with preschool children.

emplars, whereas action–function terms elicited high proportions of contextual and unscorable responses.

If the semantic system is originally undifferentiated from the general knowledge system, one would expect that the L and WK questions would elicit similar amounts and similar types of information for younger children, but that both the amount and type of information would become increasingly differentiated as the child's semantic system contracted (that is, as it became confined to conventional meanings) and the knowledge system expanded. In order to subject this hypothesis to test, the sample was divided into older (4- and 5-year-old) and younger (3-year-old) groups and the data were examined for age differences. The overall pattern of results for the noun types (objects, categories, and STOs) was in accord with this expectation. The mean response rate for L questions was almost as high for the younger subjects (1.19) as for the older (1.41), and the difference between the two questions was greater for the older children (2.22 to 1.31) than for the younger ones (1.56 to 1.29).

However, there were differences by word type in this overall pattern. While object words showed little increase in response quantity with age, general knowledge increased significantly for category terms, and the STO terms showed an actual decrease in responses for older children compared to younger for "what is" questions and an increase for "know about" questions. For example, younger children gave about one item of information in response to object terms (e.g., "What is an apple?," "You eat it"); older children added a bit more (e.g., "red," "round," or "has seeds"). Both younger and older children gave more responses when asked "know about" questions (e.g., "grows on trees"). Lexical responses were generally noncontingent, while WK responses were more wide ranging. Responses to category terms were terse for L questions but elaborate for WK questions, primarily because these terms elicit examples. STO responses seemed to be mixed and uncertain, probably because the situations themselves are more complex and less easily defined. No doubt similar patterns would be found with adults for these terms.

A more detailed qualitative analysis of responses supported these suppositions. Here the responses were classified in terms similar to stimulus words (i.e., category, STO, example, function–action, property–part, context, and unclassified). When the responses to the L and WK questions were compared across types for all children, the rank orders revealed that about the same number of function responses was given to both questions and that function responses ranked first overall for both. However, when the question was "What do you know about X" (where

X is a noun), there were almost as many examples given as functions, and properties and parts became common, ranking third as compared to fifth when the question was "What is X?" Of equal interest is that when the question was phrased as "What is it?," category responses, although of low frequency, appeared often enough to rank fourth, while they were last in rank and appeared at a rate of only 1% when the "know about" question was asked. This appears to indicate an early sensitivity by young children to the appropriateness of category information for the definition of nouns, although it does not, apparently, become a dominant response for several years more. Category responses did not increase with age in this study; they were uncommon in both age groups.

The general trend for the different types of stimulus words can be summarized as follows. When the question asked was "What is it?," category terms elicited primarily function responses followed by STOs and a scattering of examples, contextual, and unclassifieds. When the question was "What do you know about?," function responses dropped, while examples increased sharply, STOs and contextual responses increased, and properties appeared at a moderate level. Thus, categories (e.g., *animals, clothes, furniture,* and *fruit*) seem to be basically defined in terms of function ("you wear it," "you eat it," "they run"), together with some coding of where and when to find them ("in the zoo," "in the home," "at lunch") and a reserve knowledge of what instances belong to the category and how to identify it by intrinsic properties.

For object terms, when the question was "What is it?," function also dominated, followed by STOs, with a few categories, properties, and associated objects. Responses to "What do you know?" were little different for object terms, primarily because there was not the same opportunity to list examples. Both function and property responses increased. Object words, like category words, appeared to be basically defined in terms of function, with some tagging of where and when to find them, and reserve knowledge in terms of parts and properties, that is, how to identify them.

In response to STOs younger children gave examples of items that belong with the STO term, while older children produced functional responses. For the older children, function appears to be the core of the definition of these words, with reserve knowledge of contextual information and associations. Children of both ages had difficulty handling these terms, however.

Property terms tended to elicit examples, regardless of the question. Action–function terms, on the other hand, were distributed across a number of different response categories, with examples predominating only for the "What is X?" question. Responses to function terms were those that fit the questions who, what, when, and where. For example, "drive" elicited "you drive" (who) and "car" (what), as well as "drive means be careful." "Warm" elicited "blankets" (what), "in the bathtub" (where), "like a fire" (what), "summer and spring" (when). Thus, when the term to be defined is an action or function, it elicits people, places, and things that are related through that action or function to the self. When the term to be defined, however, is an object or object category, the functional aspect of the relation is central and the people, places, and things are peripheral. To put this in semantic terms, the relational term elicits its main arguments, while the nouns, in turn, elicit a major relation and through that relation its further arguments.

"Belongs with" and "goes with" questions elicited more responses than either "what is" or "what do you know about" questions (see Figure 6.3). On the whole, the response categories were more like WK responses than L responses. In other words, these questions differed from definitional questions in the amount of information they elicited and in the type. Rather than attempting to denote a concept, children responded with contextually associated items, examples, locations, times, and so on. In contrast, when asked "What is X?," they responded primarily with actions and functions, or in the case of property and function terms, with examples.

The responses to the "belongs" and "goes with" questions indicate that these phrases do not elicit well-defined categories. If they do not do so in a verbal task, there is no reason to expect that they would do so in a sorting task. The important methodological point is that sorting tasks using these instructions should not be relied on as measures of categorical knowledge structures. In contrast, the L and WK questions clearly indicated that children can give conceptually based definitions when the question is appropriately phrased.

A comparison of children's definitions with those given for the same terms in the dictionary showed that the children included many of the same elements in their responses as did the dictionary (Nelson, 1978b). While the children's responses to object terms included more functions and fewer features and superordinates, the dictionary definitions of category terms are defined primarily in terms of function, just as the children's category terms are. For example, "clothes" are defined as "articles, usually of cloth, designed to cover, protect, or adorn the body; wearing apparel," while furniture is "the things, usually moveable, in a room, apartment, etc. which equip it for living." That is, the superordinate category definitions are basically functional, and the children's definitions reflect the same basis. It may be speculated that what happens with increasing age is that this functional information is referred to in the definition of object terms, not directly, but through the use of the superordinate term, for example, ''A tiger is an animal [and an animal moves, eats, etc.] with stripes.'' From this point of view, the superordinate term is not simply a *grouping* term that dominates a list of more specific instances. Rather, the superordinate term is defined according to a broader functional definition and, as we have seen in the children's responses, this is so from the beginning of their use of such terms.

To summarize the findings of this study, children relate basic object and object category words to their functions and properties but not to other objects or categories; they relate functions to a variety of relations or arguments; and they relate properties to those objects that display them. In other words, children can produce a large number of appropriate syntagmatic relationships, different types for different types of words. What they do not do is produce paradigmatic relations, even when the question form might be expected to elicit them (e.g., ''goes with'' or ''belongs with'').

Dimensions of Development

The review of the literature relevant to concept development in early childhood in the last two chapters reveals both the strengths and weaknesses of young children's conceptual structures. At this point we might note some of the dimensions of change that have been posited as explanatory mechanisms for the development that takes place in the conceptual system from early childhood to later childhood and adulthood. Some of these mechanisms will prove to be more helpful than others in building a conceptual and semantic developmental model in the following chapters. A brief consideration of their usefulness will help to set the stage for what follows.

Global to Differentiated

According to Werner and Kaplan (1963), word meanings (in common with all other aspects of cognitive development) develop from global, diffuse meanings to differentiated, precise meanings. Anglin's (1977) description of development also incorporates the notion of globality of meaning followed by differentiation, as does Keil's (1979) ontological theory. Similarly, Smith and Kemler (1977) proposed that children progress from global to analytic processing. Differentiation is a very attractive developmental concept, but with a few exceptions it has been used very loosely and therefore has lacked explanatory power. In too many cases (such as Keil's) the exceptions to the differentiation proposal have been too easy to find.

An opposing view has, in fact, been advanced by Saltz and his colleagues (Saltz, 1971; Saltz, Soller, & Sigel, 1972). They argue that young children's concepts are overdifferentiated, that is, that they exclude members that older children include in categories such as *food, furniture,* or *clothes.* Both over- and underdifferentiation need to be explained, and thus the dimension of differentiation cannot, it appears, be utilized as a single explanatory mechanism.

Simple to Complex

Implied in the semantic feature theory, as well as in many other theories, is the proposition that semantic and conceptual development take place primarily in terms of a move from simple structures to more complex ones. As we have seen with respect to semantic features, the simple addition of features is not adequate to explain the data; thus, other mechanisms need to be posited, including the subtraction of features, if the theory is to work at all (although, as noted above, current thinking rejects the theory). It is possible to define complexity in many ways, however. As an explanatory principle its power depends upon the precise nature of that definition and its domain of application.

Concrete to Abstract

The proposal that word meanings and concepts develop from concrete to abstract is one of the oldest and most commonly accepted theses. Children are thought to begin with concepts about the concrete physical world and not about abstractions not evident in the here and now. Evidence in favor of this view is available from a number of sources, for example, in the fact that children learn basic object words prior to superordinate category terms or terms such as "justice," "nation," and "peace."

Yet, in an important sense, all words are abstract since they denote, not physical entities, but mental structures. The word "car" is an abstraction across all potential members of the set denoted by "car." Worse, many of the words learned and used by very young children are far more abstract than this. "Because" and "so" are abstract causal terms that are known by 3-year-olds; the morpheme "ed" denotes pastness, " 's" possession, and so on, and these are acquired even earlier.

Thus, the concrete-to-abstract dimension needs re-thinking in its application to language. As it stands, it lacks explanatory power.

Intuitive to Logical

Piaget suggested that the young child's thought was intuitive rather than logical and that word meanings were based on transductive rather than inductive or deductive reasoning (Piaget, 1962). Intuitive meanings are organized around examples or prototypes rather than around logical class membership. To Piaget this implied that children's meanings are fuzzy and changeable, not fixed and conventional like adults'. However, the more recent proposals that adult concepts are organized around prototypes and have fuzzy boundaries rob this claim of its force. Although it seems unlikely that any theorist would accept the proposal that the child becomes *less* logical with age, there is a growing tendency to argue that the young child is equally as logical as the older (e.g., Fodor, 1975; Macnamara, 1982).

Personal to Social

A related notion is that children's concepts are at first egocentrically based, personal, and idiosyncratic, becoming with time more conventional and social. This thesis, too, derives from Piagetian theorizing and has received support from Anglin's (1977) analysis of young children's word usage and definitions. In illustration of this notion, Chukovsky (1968) provided many charming examples of preschool children's inventions of novel words to fill a personal need. For example, he cited children who talk of a bald man having a "barefoot head," a mint candy making a "draft in the mouth," and the husband of a grasshopper as a "daddyhopper." While apparently delighting in these and numerous other examples of children's creativity with words, he warned that adults have the obligation to train the child to speak correctly. "No matter how much we admire the child's word creations, we must tell him: 'we don't say it this way. You should say thus and so' " (1968, p. 16).

And yet, from a different view, that of a social interactionist such as Vygotsky (1962), word meanings are inherently social and with development become personalized as the child comes to "possess" them as his or her own. In recent years the construct of egocentrism has come under increasing attack. Still, although words may be inherently social, the child's concepts do not need to be so conceived. The usefulness of this dimension remains to be further examined.

Context-bound to Context-free

A frequent proposal is that word meanings progress from being bound to particular contexts of use to being context-free in the sense of being autonomous and not situationally constrained. Many studies of young children's language uses showing dependence upon the perceptual array for the interpretation of the meaning of an utterance have been interpreted in this way. In these decriptions the child is thought first to interpret the meaning of the situation and then to assign a meaning to the language term, and only later to interpret the term and apply it in the absence of a supportive array. While a type of decontextualization plays a role in the theory to be developed here, the important context is considered to be that provided by the child's model of reality, as was discussed in connection with the development of the understanding of temporal terms. The most important puzzle in this respect is how the child utilizes experience of words in context to construct a systematic meaning that can be applied in all other contexts.

Extension and Intension

It is a premise of logic that the extension of a term is determined by its intension. Piaget (1962) proposed that young children had not co-ordinated the intension and extension of their concepts and this explained their confusions in the application of class terms. Anglin (1977) believed that he had found evidence for this position in that the young children he interviewed did not always include as members of a class those things that shared all of the characteristics that they had mentioned in defining the class; and, on the other hand, they might name as a member a thing that did not share all of the defining characteristics. Thus, he claimed that development took place primarily through the increasing coordination of the intension and extension of the concept. This proposal rests on a number of questionable methodological and theoretical assumptions, and as we examine more closely the development of children's conceptual systems it will be found to be irrelevant to the model put forth here.

In summary, none of these dimensions stands by itself as an adequate explanatory mechanism for conceptual and semantic development. Nonetheless, several of them remain useful. In particular, the concepts of differentiation, decontextualization, conventionalization, and systematization will be reconceptualized and will serve as useful constructs in the description to follow.

Conclusion

The overview of research on young children's concept development in this and the preceding chapter yields the following conclusions:

1. When considered in terms of structure and content, children's concepts of objects appear to be similar to those of adults, incorporating knowledge about function and perceptual attributes. There is no evidence that the structure of children's concepts is less logical than adults; suggestions to the contrary appear to be based on the misconception that adult concepts are logically organized.

2. Although children as young as 3 display knowledge of some common superordinate categories and can name category members and provide relevant functional information about them, there is little or no evidence that categorical organization of objects plays a significant role in these children's conceptual or semantic representations. Evidence from a variety of verbal tasks suggests that they do not.

3. Evidence from several different research paradigms indicates that relational concepts (e.g., *time, size,* and *action*) are based on situational conditions of use and are therefore in significant ways context-bound.

4. Acquisition of concepts of objects and actions is followed by analysis of their components, which subsequently may be independently conceptualized and may be used to form relations between concepts based on similar components. There is no evidence that concepts are built up component by component; rather, componential analysis follows conceptualization.

5. Words appear to be firmly attached to concepts in early childhood; there is no independent level of semantic representation.

6. Relations between concepts in early childhood are dominantly syntagmatic. Little evidence of paradigmatic organization of any kind is found during this period.

7. When categorical relations are established, they tend to be based on shared roles in situations, and the vertical relation is established before the horizontal one. When horizontal paradigmatic relations begin to be established, they are first based on dimensions along which concepts differ rather than on shared features.

Taken together, these findings suggest a course of development involving an increasingly organized relational structure based on componential analysis emerging from an initially open system of single concepts loosely related in syntagmatic structures. These developments will be traced in the following two chapters.

Notes

[1]This is because they cannot occur together in sequential sequences or occupy the same slot in a syntactic frame.

[2]Anglin, however, did not classify terms as "basic level" in his study.

[3]As in "A daisy ISA flower."

[4]Many of these terms were also used appropriately in the presleep monologues of Emily (Chapter 2) at 22 months (Nelson, 1984b).

[5]See Bickerton (1981) for an alternative explanation.

[6]*Semantic memory* as it is used here is essentially equivalent to knowledge system or conceptual representation system. (See Nelson, 1978b; Miller & Johnson-Laird, 1976; Tulving, 1972).

7

Development of Concepts and Conceptual Systems

The Conceptual System Problem

The significant conceptual developments that take place during the preschool years were summarized at the end of the previous chapter. In the course of the discussion of research findings, considerable complexity and contradiction were uncovered both in the descriptions of phenomena and in the explanations that have been advanced to account for such development, and no explanation was found to be wholly adequate. In the present chapter I propose an integrated description of conceptual development between the ages of 1 and 6 years that accounts for the child's interpretation of meaning during this period and that provides the basis for the development of an autonomous lexical system, which will be described in the following chapter. This model incorporates the child's knowledge of the social world and of conditions of language use as important components of meaning. The problem as I see it concerns *how this knowledge is used to construct a system of conventionalized concepts reflecting relations within the semantic system of the language being learned.* While the present chapter lays the groundwork for such an explanation, the full account is deferred to Chapter 8.

Let us reformulate the problems addressed here. Consider the child who says "I have to do X because Y" or "we do X before we do Y" or "I went to see the *animals* in the zoo." Now all of these concepts (cause, sequence, temporal relation, object class) have been shown in standard experimental tests to be, at the least, inadequately grasped by young children (see Chapters 5 and 6). Yet, in the course of natural conversations, children verbalize these concepts using appropriate terms in appropriate relationships (French & Nelson, in press). This poses a problem for theories of semantic development that has not generally been addressed. Most theories have viewed such development in terms of the partial-linguistic-knowledge state of the young child in comparison to the full-knowledge state of the older child or adult (see E. V. Clark, 1983). The partial-knowledge explanation rests on the assumption that the child's word meanings are componential representations that may be incomplete in comparison with the full adult meaning and thus may lead to incorrect uses. As a familiar example, "before" may be represented in terms of − simultaneity and + polarity but lack the component + prior. The most complete statement of this position is in terms of the semantic feature theory (see E. V. Clark, 1973, 1983). Yet, as Carey (1982) pointed out and as discussed in Chapter 5, componential theories have not been able to account adequately for the experimental data. More seriously, they cannot account for the discrepancies between language in natural use and in experimental contexts. A different approach to the problem is needed, one that takes context to be part of meaning.

Not only do children use terms such as "because," "before," and "animal" in appropriate ways but, equally important, children seldom use such lexical terms incorrectly (French & Nelson, in press) except in experiments, although they would be expected to do so if the partial-knowledge explanation were correct. That is, lacking the component + prior a child might be expected to say "Before I eat breakfast I go to school," but children do not make such errors in natural discourse contexts. Thus, it appears that the child's representational system generally constrains use of language terms to those conditions where they are appropriate, although these conditions may not cover all of the potential uses of the term as understood by the adult. The problem, as it is viewed here, is to describe how young children integrate knowledge from their experience with the language and the world to produce representational structures that enable them to use language terms meaningfully in discourse and to avoid frequent errors in natural discourse contexts. It is proposed that the correct explanation for these facts lies initially in the support provided by the development of the conceptual system and only subsequently by the lexical system. That is, the proposal is not that the child's lexical entry expands, as the partial-knowledge position would have it, but that the child becomes less dependent on particular representational contexts to support word use. The specific developments involved and their implications are described in this chapter.

The basis for the discussion in this chapter and the next is the developing relationship between the conceptual system and the lexical system.[1] The complexities of the structural relationships that lie behind the use of language are what need to be explained. No theory has provided an adequate account of these relations, and no developmental theory has even been broached. Thus, the present discussion should be viewed as a beginning attempt in this direction.

The Syntagmatic–Paradigmatic Conceptual Model

Syntagmatic and paradigmatic relationships and their interaction are central to this discussion of the development of the conceptual system. Thus, it is important to have in mind the nature of these relations and their implications. As noted previously, de Saussure (1959) based his structural linguistics system in part on this distinction, in the following terms:

> In a language-state everything is based on relations . . . relations and differences between linguistic terms fall into two distinct groups, each of which generates a certain class of values . . . They correspond to two forms of our mental activity, both indispensable to the life of language.
>
> In discourse, on the one hand, words acquire relations based on the linear nature of language because they are chained together . . . The elements are arranged in sequence in the chain of speaking. Combinations supported by linearity are syntagms . . . in the syntagm a term acquires its value only because it stands in opposition to everything that precedes or follows it, or to both.
>
> Outside discourse . . . words acquire relations of a different kind. Those that have something in common are associated in the memory, resulting in groups marked by diverse relations . . . co-ordinates formed outside discourse . . . are not supported by linearity. Their seat is in the brain; they are a part of the inner storehouse that makes up the language of each speaker. They are *associative relations*. (de Saussure, 1959 [original 1915], pp. 122–123)

Several points contained in this description should be emphasized. First, Saussure states that these two basic types of relations in the language correspond to two forms of "mental activity." The syntagmatic–paradigmatic model (SPM) takes this correspondence seriously and proposes that the syntagmatic–paradigmatic distinction can be found in conceptual organization prior to and independently of the linguistic system.

Second, it is important to note the attribution of linearity and sequentiality to syntagmatic relations. The use of language necessarily imposes a linear structure on its elements. It is not necessarily the case, however, that either events in the real world[2] or conceptualizations are linearly composed. This raises a question about the source of sequentiality that must remain open at present.

Third, note that nonlinear coordinations are asserted by Saussure to be formed outside of discourse "in the brain." These associative or paradigmatic relations must therefore be internally constructed: they are not transparent in the language as spoken. Note that these relations are based on similarity ("those that have something in common"), but similarity is a derivative relation, one based on comparison processes. Note also that this process yields "diverse relations"—similarity can be based on many different types of comparison, for example, acoustic features, position in a sentence, and reference to similar objects. Because of the generality of the comparison process, paradigmatic organization in the conceptual system may reflect different kinds of relations than those of the linguistic system.

Note further that although Saussure speaks of these as "associative" relations, it is necessary to assume more complex processes and organization than simple association in order to derive paradigmatic structures such as *noun, superordinate, synonym,* and so on. What processes of conceptual analysis may underlie structures of this type will be given some consideration later in this chapter.

The paradigmatic–syntagmatic structural framework has often been ignored in discussions of semantic development or, if recognized, syntagmatic organization is attributed to syntax and paradigmatic organization to semantics. Thus, the shift in word associations from primarily syntagmatic to primarily paradigmatic was seen by McNeill (1970) as indicating the late development of a semantic system. Or, as in Huttenlocher and Lui (1979), the two different types of organization were attributed to different parts of speech (i.e., paradigmatic to nouns, syntagmatic to verbs).

However,

> the structure of the language-system depends *at every level* upon the complementary principles of selection and combination . . . We identify units by virtue of their potentiality of occurrence in certain syntagms; and the selection of one element rather than another produces a different resultant syntagm . . . languages can be seen, *at each level of analysis,* as having two dimensions, or axes, of structure; and every unit has its place at one or more points in the two-dimensional structure. (Lyons, 1977, p. 241, emphasis added)

It is not that some types of lexemes are organized in one way and other types in another; the two are complementary and every lexeme enters into both types of organization at least once. For example, the term "before" enters into a contrastive paradigmatic relation with "after," but as a conjunction it enters into syntagmatic relations with clause structures. A similar claim applies to all parts of speech, verbs and adjectives as well as nouns. The import of this claim is that the syntagmatic and paradigmatic relations work together to form a system. Insofar as they are basic structural relations, they both play a crucial role in the development of the child's conceptual and semantic systems.

These statements apply to *langue* in Saussure's terms, that is, to the language system as a whole, and also to the fully developed system for each individual. What we are concerned with here is how concepts and not just language *become* systematized within the developing child's cognitive system. For this consideration we do not need to assume that both types of organization play their roles at all points in development. Rather, it is possible that they may develop asymmetrically. Indeed, Saussure's statement that paradigmatic relations are acquired "outside discourse," "in the memory," "in the brain," and in "the inner storehouse of each speaker" suggests that these relations are more abstract and developmentally later than are syntagmatic "linear" relations displayed in discourse or in direct experience. Moreover, how these relations may be applied in the conceptual system may differ from their application in the semantic system.

Event Representations as the Basis for the Syntagmatic-Paradigmatic Model

The notion of the event representation as a basic conceptual structure was introduced in Chapters 2, 3, and 4. At this point, the description will be elaborated to show: (1) how this conception leads to an analysis in terms of paradigmatic and syntagmatic relations that are similar to those of the language system, (2) how these relations form the basis for both a system and the internal structure of concepts, and (3) how this system supports the child's use of language in context (see also Nelson, 1982; 1983b; 1983c).

We begin with the proposal introduced in Chapter 3 that the basic unit of conceptual representation is the *event*. Events come in many shapes and sizes and embed people (or other active agents), objects, and change of some kind, usually action. *Event representations* (ERs) are organized as a sequence of actions or changes of state. Because of their sequentiality it can be said that they are organized syntagmatically. That is, the actors and objects in the event are related to actions and to each other syntagmatically. Conversely, different objects (and people) that play the *same role* within an event are related to each other paradigmatically. As with language, the paradigmatic relationship depends upon the syntagmatic one. For example, balls are things that can play a specific functional role in a certain type of event. Something that looks like a ball but cannot fit into a "ball event" is not a proper member of the paradigmatic set of balls.

This statement assumes that events are conceptualized as linear structures, that sequence itself is constitutive of the event. However, this assumption can be questioned, as noted above. It might seem that without the imposition of language structure on the representation of the event, the ER would not be characterized by a linear sequence. Indeed, there may be some truth to this claim. Becoming a language user in the second year may be instrumental in both partitioning and sequencing one's ERs. Nevertheless, although scenes and events in the world may display more simultaneity than allowable in our language structures, individual experience has an important sequential component as well. I would like to propose that even prior to language, actions are organized as sequences and perceptions of events integrate the actions of others into sequences that may be coordinated with one's own. The 1-year-old who enters into the bath and breakfast routine displays knowledge of sequence as well as scene (see Chapter 3). It would be difficult at this point to sort out how much is contributed *to* language from prior conceptualization. The working assumption here is that children understand their own roles in events in terms of sequential structure, however other contextual factors that may enter into the ER may be organized. (Note that outside of language, syntagmatic structures may be nonlinear, that is, schematic structures—such as scenes—may be considered syntagmatic even though they are not sequentially organized. The essential characteristic of syntagmatic structures is not linearity but relations between unlike elements. However, for the most part, the discussion here will concentrate on sequential structures because of their potential relation to the language.)

To return to the basic framework of the SPM, it is assumed, based on the results of our script research (Nelson, 1978a), that event representations order sequences of actions and states through temporal, causal, and spatial links and relate actors and objects to these actions and states. Further, the ER specifies for any given situation those actions, objects, and actors that are required and those that are optional.

The general form of an ER can be schematized as shown in Figure 7.1. In this framework an event is represented in terms of a sequence of acts that are linked together through temporal or causal links, one act resulting in a state and leading in sequence to the next. Each act requires an actor and may also require objects acted upon. This structure

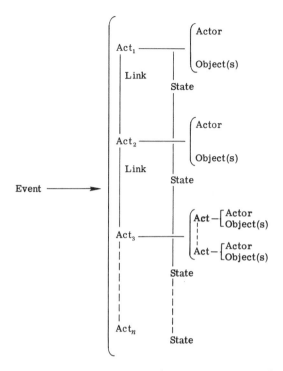

FIGURE 7.1   General schema of the event representation.

is recursive, so that an act at one level may be respecified in terms of a sequence of lower-level acts. For example, *eating* may involve both using a spoon to eat soup and drinking milk from a cup. In general, an ER may be represented in terms of subscripts or scenes (see the lunch example presented in Chapter 2). The links between acts may also involve spatial relations, for example, getting ready for lunch may involve a spatial change from the playground to the lunchroom.

The model does not assume that the child's prelinguistic representations will fit neatly into a propositional framework such as actor–action–object or that these particular elements are ordered in any specific way. The order inherent in the ER is a sequence of *acts*. It does not necessitate any particular order between participants in the acts. Moreover, there are no assumptions about the *size* of the child's representational structures. Event representations can be ball-rolling small or meal-eating large. Thus, this model avoids unwarranted assumptions about any sort of ''natural fit'' between early representations and language structures.[3]

Relations within the ER are syntagmatic. That is, the relation of the object to the actor and the act is a syntagmatic, not a paradigmatic, one. Paradigmatic relations emerge from the ER structure on the basis of substitutability within slots. This process is described below in the consideration of the development of a system.

The SPM and the FCM

At this point we can outline in a preliminary way how the functional core model (FCM) is related to the syntagmatic–paradigmatic model through the event representation structure. The SPM is a system model, while the FCM was a model of the internal structure of a concept, where concepts are units that enter into relations within the system. It happens, however, that the place of an object in the ER may determine the structure of the object concept, which can be seen to be the reverse view of the structure shown in Figure 7.1. That is, the object concept can be formulated in terms of actions, actors, and resultant states within events, as the concept of ball was formulated in the example shown in Chapter 5 (Figure 5.1). The FCM applied primarily to object concepts. However, as a system model, the SPM accounts for many more conceptual types, such as certain relations, syntagmatic structures, and relational hierarchies. It does not account for all of the relations expressed in language, however. This problem will be considered later.

Development of the Syntagmatic–Paradigmatic Conceptual System

In this section the emergence of concepts and categories from the ER to form a system of concepts and conceptual relations is described. For this description we view the developing conceptual system through the child's use of language terms, as described in Chapters 2, 3, and 4.

The First Phase: Establishment of Event Representations

If event representations are basic and are based on syntagmatic relations, we should be able to see evidence for this in the child's initial types of language use. Moreover, we should be able to find evidence for the emergence of paradigmatically based concepts in the language used during the second year. As suggested earlier, the beginning language learner has been attributed with concepts of single objects (e.g., *mommy*), object classes (e.g., *ball*) and simple (one-place) relations (e.g., *up*) on the basis of the learning of such terms. However, as the review of early language in Chapter 3 showed, most of the words used before about 18 months, or prior to the typical "word explosion" in the middle of the second year, can be given a different nonconceptual interpretation that appears to fit the data more successfully.

Indeed, the proposal that the child is working with and within event representations can help solve many puzzles of early language use. Recall the phases presented in Chapter 3 in terms of the following descriptions.

In Phase 1 wordlike forms are used as or to accompany action schemes (e.g., "Hi," "there," and "thank you") or to name whole events ("car" for watching cars out the window) or to participate in social games such as looking at picture books or naming familiar objects. There is scant evidence in any of these uses that the child has *parts* of activities (objects, actors, or actions) differentiated from the whole. During this phase language comprehension seems to rush ahead of production for most children. The words children comprehend at this time generally include words used in social games (e.g., "pattycake") and directives for actions ("give me") as well as object terms. Although there is ample evidence that object terms are generalized to novel instances by young children, when such terms are acquired during the first phase they are usually applied to a single instance or are restricted in use to a single context (see Chapters 2 and 3; Nelson *et al.*, 1978; Nelson *et al.*, in press). The only class of terms that appears to be applied in a wider range of activity types in this first phase is that involving action schemes, that is, the child's own already generalized actions. These words are analogous to the more general schemes (e.g., *mouthing, banging*) that the child applies to objects in the first year before acquiring specific schemes appropriate to specific classes of objects (e.g., *drink from cup, hold telephone to ear*). Thus, these relational terms appear to exhibit a primitive type of generality, that is, they are generally applicable to all objects. Action terms must first become more specific with respect to the objects to which they apply before they are truly generalizable. For example, a child needs to learn that throwing applies to balls and not to all objects before learning that disparate classes of things can be thrown *like balls* (for example, apples or candy), a generalization that follows the original differentiation. Similarly, the term "throw" may be learned in specific application to balls and may not be applied to other objects or object concepts for some time (see the examples of Billy's restricted interpretations in Chapter 2).

In Chapter 3 it was suggested that early object words were either part of a social script (e.g., picture naming) or referred to a script (e.g., ball playing). In either case the child learns to produce words within a familiar routine. The basis for such use is the child's understanding of his part in an event, based both on others' expectations and on his own event representation. Such production does not reflect an object concept denoting a class of objects. The proposal here, rather, is that denotation of words is an achievement of the second year based on the partitioning of the original whole event representation.

The proposal that reality is first represented in terms of whole events whose parts must be subsequently differentiated appears to pose severe problems. How can the constituent units (objects, actors, etc.) be represented if they are not already recognized as individuated? That is, how can a mental whole be composed of units that cannot be decomposed and that have no independent existence? These problems with respect to representation of events are no more nettlesome than those of any other theory that proposes a holistic phase of representation followed by a subsequent phase of differentiation, whether it be of objects, language, or whatever. Only those theories that view representation as built up from sensory primitives can escape these problems.

Moreover, these problems evaporate if the initial event representation is viewed as a *perceptual* representation subject to subsequent analysis and reconstruction on a conceptual level. That is, the units (objects, actors, etc.) are cognitive constructions. The general principle here is that the perceptual system may present more than the conceptual system can immediately use. Put this way, the representational paradox disappears.[4]

To elucidate this proposal more completely, it is necessary to view the child's cognitive system as consisting of a series of representations subject to internal analysis. The initial representation of an experience will be some sort of perceptual image. This percept, which is an interpretation in terms of the child's current understanding of the world, will persist as a perceptual representation. As Kosslyn (1980) demonstrated, such representations do contain more than the conceptual system "knows." For example, it is only through accessing an image that many people can say whether or not a German Shepherd has sharp ears. However, once the image is analyzed, such knowledge can be stored in a propositional format that is available independently of the image itself. Of course, the image is not a specific percept, but instead some sort of generalized perceptual prototype of the object class in question.

Analogously, we can assume that prelinguistic children have generalized prototype representations of events they are familiar with. Through a process of conceptual analysis, these event prototypes may be partitioned and *reconstructed* on a conceptual level. In this way, the units and the relations between them become individuated on a new level in which they can be mentally manipulated independently of the whole.

It may be objected that the claim that event representations are basic is unmotivated since so much of the work on infant perception and cognition has clearly shown an understanding of and preoccupation with objects and object characteristics by 1-year-old children. Surely the traditional view that objects and object relationships are the building blocks of cognition and language must have some truth to it.

There is no question that infants are fascinated by certain objects and enjoy exploring their possibilities. Nonetheless, the discussion in Chapter 2 set forth the crucial role of the broader social and cultural context within which the child's activity is set and proposed that events embed objects and not the reverse. Of course, the child who spends a great deal of time (alone or with others) interacting with objects may come to partition them from their embedding events more readily than a child who spends little time in object play. That, however, is an outcome of activity, not a prerequisite for its representation. Moreover, it may be conceded that many of the child's first ERs are centered around particular objects, for example, the ball-rolling game. However, others contain substitutable objects (e.g., *give and take*) or a variety of different objects in particular roles (e.g., *lunch* and *bath*).

Three further points need to be made about this early period. They depend upon the distinction between the perceptual and the conceptual levels, the claim that things may be recognized at the perceptual level but they are only "knowable" at the conceptual level, and that only knowable things can be said to have meaning at the lexical or semantic level. First, the general position taken here does not deny the ontologically primitive status of objects at the perceptual level. That is, this position is perfectly consistent with the claim that objects are viewed as whole and substantial by the infant (rather than constructed from perceptual attributes or one's own actions). Second, the process of disembedding objects by partitioning events may begin early and proceed slowly to establish certain important figures (e.g., mother and father) and objects (e.g., a favorite toy or blanket) as independent knowables long before most events are partitioned. Thus, some things may be nameable much earlier than most other things in a child's world. The process may then accelerate early in the second year until it results in the naming explosion that confers names on all the known parts of an activity.

Finally, it should be stressed also that because ERs serve as the basis for action and participation, they guarantee at least a minimum of *shared* interpretation with other people. Although the child's representation of the activity may differ in many ways from the parent's, their expectations for each other in well-practiced routines constitute *shared knowledge* and thus form the basis for the establishment of *shared meaning*.

The point here is that, although a conceptual basis for meaning must be established if the child is to participate in the full ideational potential of the language system, a basis of intersubjectivity must be established in order to ensure that meanings can be shared. Participation in situations where each person understands both his own and the other's role enables the child to establish the representational basis that makes mutual understanding possible. Thus, the event representation serves at once both as the foundation for intersubjectivity and as the source of conceptualization, the two essentials of the development of shared meaning.

The Second Phase: Concepts within Event Representations

In Phase 2 of the language-acquisition sequence outlined in Chapter 3, names of objects, people, and actions are learned and applied to event components that have been differentiated from the original event representation. This phase may begin early in the second year, for example, as the child learns to name or request different food. Often the acceleration of productive vocabulary around 17 to 19 months signals the onset of Phase 2, although there may have been particular objects, people, and so on who were identified and named earlier. The recognition that a single object plays a role in different relationships within a given situation can lead the child to form a concept of that object that will include a number of different actions and relations and, perhaps, different actors. In this way the ER can lead to a *situationally specific concept* of an object. As noted earlier, turning the ER structure around and respecifying it in terms of the object, we then get something that looks very much like the functional core model. To restate some of the claims of the FCM, the concept of *ball* will be formed because it is a focal object in a dynamic situation of some interest to the child. It is the situation or event that determines *what* objects will be conceptualized. In turn, these objects will be perceptually analyzed for their identifying characteristics and will therefore be identifiable by the child outside the original situation. Participation in more than one action or relationship is assumed to be necessary to begin the detachment of the object from its syntagmatic and therefore context-defined relationships, at least in the early stage of conceptual development. Later, concepts may be set up on minimal bases.

With the assumption that the event structure, not the object structure, is primary, it becomes clear why function or action should be important to the child's formation of concepts and thus to early word meanings. It is not simply because the child's own actions are fundamentally defining (as one reading of Piaget would suggest), but because conceptual representation is in the first instance the representation of event structures and objects are known in their relation to the events of which they are a part. That is, the actions of others or the event the object enters into are as important to the establishment of the object concept as are the child's own actions, so long as they are viewed as essential to the ER.

The conceptual development of this phase involves the first establishment of paradigmatically based concepts, in contrast to the syntagmatic relations between the components of the event representation itself. It will be noted that the paradigmatic concept depends upon the existence of the syntagmatic structure. Note also that paradigmatic relationships of even the simplest type require more abstracting from context than syntagmatic relationships.

Again, the discussion here is in terms of conceptual representation, not perception. A child may know what a ball looks like, for example, before she knows what it does. This level of knowledge enables object recognition but not knowledge at a deeper conceptual level. If all the child were presented with was the pattern of the word and the pattern of the object, it is unlikely that much language learning would take place. The place of the object in the pattern of activity represented by the child's ERs needs to be established for the child to establish the object within the conceptual system. The object is represented in terms of a system of conceptual relationships. The concept of an object may then be seen as an achievement through the abstraction of the consistent appearance of the representation of a particular object or set of objects within a system of relationships. Formation of the object concept involves the creation of a unit abstracted from the relationally contexted particulars. Thus, when *ball* is conceptualized on the basis of its place in the ER, it may be, as it were, removed from that context and considered on its own, in other contexts, and in novel combinations insofar as these contexts and combinations are consistent with its context-based concept.

In many situations objects that are perceptually quite diverse and therefore clearly distinguishable as different objects recur in the same *slot* in an ER over different occurrences of the event. For example, mother may offer chopped liver and spinach for dinner on one day and fried chicken and peas on another. The child may hate liver and spinach and love chicken and peas; thus, the two are distinguishable, but both occupy similar slots in the dinner sequence. This presents an ideal situation for the child to form a simple equivalence class, namely, *food*, although it may not be given this label.

There is evidence that very young children do recognize categories of this kind, as the review in Chapter 6 showed. Preschool children report that they "eat food" or "have dessert" when asked about what happens at lunch, and even the 2-year-old often uses some terms for items that recur in the same slot in an event sequence, occasionally a category term such as "fruit," but more often the name of a particular fruit such as "apple" (Rescorla, 1981). This kind of "error" in the application of a term appears to verify the psychological reality of *slot filling*. When children apply a term incorrectly to all instances that fill the same slot, or that appear to be able to fill that slot, it indicates that they are forming concepts on the basis of their places in the event. Many examples of apparent perceptually based overextensions may reflect this process. For example, the chlid's use of "ball" in pointing to the moon (Example 1 in Chapter 1) may actually reflect the child's expectations that the moon can fill the ball *slot*. What the child must do in order to learn the more appropriate specific lexical terms for the different objects that fit into the slot is to disentangle, on the basis of perceptual characteristics, those objects that were identified as equivalent on the basis of their similar place in an ER. In this way the adult's use of words can enable the child to form concepts of objects that are perceptually distinct from one another and to note conceptual distinctions that may have been overlooked previously. Later, children will be faced with the task of relearning essentially the same general conceptual categories on essentially the same basis as they started with, that is, they must learn that the items included in the category serve similar functions. This process is considered below.

Note that this type of category formation on the basis of inclusion in slots within ERs is based on *substitutability* rather than grouping items on the basis of either similarity or contiguity, the classical bases for association. Category formation on the basis of substitutability requires recognition on the part of the child that different elements occupy the same position in a given structure at different times. Whereas similarity and contiguity require consideration of elements simultaneously present (in the environment or in the cognitive representation), substitutability requires a more abstract process of noting possibilities and of integrating information about potential members of a category that appear at different times.

The most basic object category, then, is of objects that can fill the same slot in an ER. If these object types are recognized as having perceptual features that are relevant to their similar functions within the event frame, they will be categorized as the same by the child. It may happen that they are also given the same name by the language community as, for example, in the hypothetical cases of "dog," "car," or "ball." However, in other cases objects that fit into the same slot in an event frame do not look alike and are not given the same names in the language, for example, food items such as apples and bananas. In such cases the child may learn a general category word to fit the slot as well as the distinct names that differentiate the members that can fill the slot. Thus, category names such as "food," "fruit," "toys," and "games" are sometimes learned early and are used by the child in script-appropriate situations. Usually they are used as alternates to the more specific terms rather than in hierarchical dominance relations (Macnamara, 1982). Thus, the child may talk readily about animals, and if you ask him what some of the animals are he may be able to tell you, but he will resist telling you that, for example, a dog *is* an animal (see Chapter 6). Hierarchical classification of this kind has not been established at this point. On the other hand, if the adult tells the young child that a wombat is a kind of animal, the child can interpret this information on the basis of ER knowledge structures and attribute appropriate functional relationships to *wombat* on this basis.

It is clear that syntagmatic relations are essential to the development of all these basic types of paradigmatic categories. Different types of conceptual categories are built up depending upon which relationships they share in the ER structure. Note that none of the conceptual and categorical operations outlined thus far necessarily involve any analysis of the similarity of objects independent of their functional relations within the event. Rather, the present analysis assumes that the child operates for some time with a conceptual system based on relations between concepts of different types and not on relations between concepts that have similar internal qualities. Similarity relations are assumed to rest on a more advanced analytic cognitive operation that becomes activated only after basic concepts have been formed. This statement applies to general categories as well as basic object concepts. That is, the similarity of objects included within categories such as *furniture* or *food* is not necessarily noted by the child prior to the formation of the category, although it may become apparent after the category is formed. This problem is considered in later sections of this chapter and in Chapter 8.

In this first phase of conceptual development, words are attached directly to the disembedded concept. Words are no longer embedded in particular event contexts, but they are not free of conceptual context. Rather, they share all of the relationships of the concepts to which they are attached. As will be discussed in more detail below, this means that a child may be able to use words appropriately whenever he is able to apply a concept, but he will be unable to interpret meanings that are not already established within his conceptual system.

The Third Phase: First Syntagmatic Structures

When the child has disembedded a number of concepts—that is, when the ER has become differentiated into its parts—the parts can be reintegrated into new combinatory structures, that is, syntagms. The ability to use words to express the concepts the child has achieved makes it possible to construct primitive sentences. At first, these sentences state the obvious, general, expected, or usual case: "Daddy shoe," for example, or "Mommy eat." Similar structures based on familiar situations are found in the child's play, as she feeds her doll or pushes a truck.

But the conceptual differentiation not only makes possible the externalization of the obvious, it also makes it possible to construct propositions expressing reports of past events and anticipations of the future, false as well as true. For example, in our study of 2-year-olds' conversations with their mothers (Lucariello & Nelson, 1982b, in press), we found children talking about what happened at their play group or anticipating a walk to the park. In the latter case the child asked "Joan coming?," thus formulating a question about a possible, but never previously experienced, variation on a familiar event. The proposal here is that knowledge of the *park* script provided the support for this question about a possible new slot filler. At the same time, the concept *coming* fits into the familiar ER. The child does not ask about implausible things, for example, "Is Joan going to take me to see the elephants?," presumably because these are not part of the park event. If the mother suggests something novel, for example, that they are going to buy a boat to sail in the park, the child might have great difficulty interpreting this statement, even though all of the component concepts are in some sense familiar, because he lacks the preexisting ER structure for doing so. In other words, so long as words remain tied to conceptual structures and those structures rest on event representations, experience must lead language rather than the reverse.

On the other hand, consider Christine's "Johnny did it" in Chapter 2, a palpable lie according to her mother. Evidence of false statements of this kind indicate that the child has considerable flexibility to make jokes and statements that are contrary to reality.[5]

Thus, the early differentiation of ERs into paradigmatic concepts also makes possible the construction of new syntagmatic relations that can be realized in language as well as in thought and action. The constraint remains on constructing new relations on the basis of language alone without the support of conceptualizations based in experience.

Building a System of Concepts and Relations

The developments just described rested on the establishment of relationships within ERs as the basis for concepts. Subsequent development involves making connections between concepts in different ERs, based on comparisons and contrasts.

Paradigmatic Analysis and Synthesis

There are two possible bases for extending paradigmatic analysis across different ERs. First, analysis of intrinsic perceptual features of objects, established along with the differentiation of the ER into separable concepts, can lead to identification of objects in different ERs. Thus, if an object (e.g., *apple*) or a category of objects (e.g., *food*) occurs in more than one event representation, it may come to be recognized by the child as the same even though the situation is different. Recognition of sameness may be easier if the same object also serves similar functions in the different ERs. For example, *breakfast, lunch,* and *dinner* all provide slots for *cups* and *spoons*. It is likely to be more difficult to recognize as "same" an object that serves different functions in different scripts, for example, a cup that is used to hold pencils as well as milk. In the latter case, the cup might not, in fact, be recognized as the same object in the new functional context. Recognition of the same object in different ERs can lead to an expansion of and integration of conceptual relationships.

Another basis for making new conceptual connections is to see that different objects play the same functional roles in different events. Thus, a child may readily call a park bench "chair" because of its seating function in the *park* script despite its different intrinsic perceptual features from the chairs he is familiar with at home, for example, its concrete construction, solid base, and rectangular configuration. When both intrinsic perceptual features and functional roles are similar to objects already conceptualized, recognition should be maximized and conceptual relations integrated, and a new ER can be formed incorporating these relations when necessary.

That a child might have greater difficulty extending slot-filler categories than basic object concepts across ERs is apparent in this analysis. Whereas the basic object concept has identifying perceptual characteristics that enable the child to recognize an object in novel circumstances, higher-level object categories by definition are diverse perceptually, without consistent and reliable perceptual characteristics. Although categories such as *animals, money,* and *fruit* are functionally similar, they are not usually perceptually similar enough to provide for context-free identification of perceptually novel instances. Thus, some mechanism beyond private experience is usually needed to ensure that the child who sees animals at the zoo and feeds turtles and gerbils at the preschool classifies both as "animals." Even when adults make the connection for the child by calling instances in both contexts "animals," the child may resist this classification, deny that some animals are animals, or give them distinctive labels such as "wild animals" and "pets."[6] If there is overlap in the membership of the categories in the two ERs, the child may be able to make these connections. However, when this is not the case or when the category is very diverse, its construction will be dependent entirely upon instruction through the language, and using language to build new cognitive structures appears to be beyond the capability of the young preschooler. Its development is considered in the next chapter.

Categories that are extracted across ERs are more general and less tied to spatiotemporal context than categories based on a single ER, since the ER, while general, is essentially spatially and temporally context-bound. The formation of higher-level categories then represents a powerful conceptual move in which paradigmatic relations among concepts are extracted from syntagmatic ones, not within a single ER or context, but across contexts. Note that when a basic object concept is found in two or more ERs, its syntagmatic relations may become more complex; however, when a slot-filler category is found in more than one ER, its paradigmatic relations (i.e., potential membership) become more complex. In the case of the basic object concept, perceptual similarity may be sufficient for its extension. However, recognizing similarity between functions, often of quite an abstract kind, is necessary for establishing the basis for a category drawing on two different contexts. Even when the adult, in effect, picks out or defines the context-free category as, for example, when the adult tells the child that both gerbils and elephants are animals, the category may lack psychological reality for the child.

Moreover, it is not enough for the child to note that "animal" can be used to fill a slot in an event frame as an alternative to a particular instance. The child must somehow master the relation of "animal" as a term that subsumes all the members of the sets that fit into the various frames in which "animal" is the general term. This move is the equivalent of establishing the ISA relation. The argument here is that this move is dependent upon language; it would not take place conceptually without language. It becomes possible only because of the possible abstract manipulation of symbols. It results from a process of conceptual analysis and synthesis that is only made possible by language. This argument is developed further in relation to the analysis of semantic development in Chapter 8.

As the word-meaning study described in Chapter 6 demonstrated, preschoolers have some well-founded conceptions about superordinates such as *food, clothes, animals,* and *furniture,* including knowledge of their instances. Thus, the conceptual structure appears to be able to support some forms of categorical relations, but these are far from fixed and complete and do not appear to operate automatically at the semantic level, as they will eventually.

Macnamara (1982) also argued that the difficulty with terms such as "animal" and "toy" is lexical, not conceptual, but his argument is somewhat different from mine. He found that, although in a sorting task 2-year-old children will sort animals and machines into different groups, they will not agree that a dog is an animal. He suggests that they treat "animals" at first as a collective term that cannot be used for individuals or for tokens of the same type. For example, he found that children will call a set of cows, horses, and pigs "animals," but not a set of only pigs. By 3 years, however, they seem to have come to the appropriate superordinate understanding of the term, at least insofar as its application to a group of diverse types is concerned. However, Macnamara goes further to claim that they have the superordinate *concept* all along, as evidenced by their sorting behavior. Many studies have now been undertaken of children's sorting, and it is clear that from very early on they will put perceptually similar things together (sometimes). Animals (of the kind used by Macnamara—pigs, cows, horses, dogs) are clearly more perceptually similar to each other than to machines such as trucks and boats. (Indeed, these animals are sometimes all called "dog" at first.) The grouping behavior of these children in the sorting task cannot, then, be used as evidence that 2-year-olds have a superordinate concept *animal* that includes different types. Even the verbal evidence from the 3-year-olds may indicate a different categorical relationship than the superordinate, the hierarchical structure of which differs from that of concepts like *dog,* as Macnamara is also aware.

The argument here is that this different conceptual structure is the result of conceptual analysis that is evoked by linguistic usage and that takes place after the initial acquisition of both the subordinate (e.g., "dog") and superordinate (e.g., "animal") terms. The assumption that concepts and word meanings are subject to analysis subsequent to their representation is important to the present model, and some evidence in support of it from other research was presented in Chapter 6 (see especially in this regard, Bowerman, 1976; 1982; Karmiloff-Smith, 1979; Maratsos, Kuczaj, Fox, & Chalkley, 1979). The fact that unanalyzed terms (including terms like "animal") may enter the lexicon is reason to be cautious about the ready acceptance of a child's correct use of a term as indicating a full understanding of its meaning. Contrary to Macnamara's assertion, meanings are not the same at all times and to all people.[7] In particular, meanings develop—both conceptually and in terms of lexical relations—as children gain experience with the language and with conceptual complexity.

In summary, the argument with regard to the conceptual status of hierarchical categories is that their formation takes place gradually over several years and has its basis in the analysis of syntagmatic relations in event structures, but that ultimately it depends upon the establishment of an autonomous context-independent lexical system. This proposal is considered in more detail in Chapter 8.

What Is a Concept? Another Look at Internal Structure

The development of concepts and categories from event representations implies an organization of representational structures of different types existing simultaneously in different layers or levels. That is, the evolution of the system progresses in terms of its increasing complexity. The complexity of the system has implications for the structure of concepts. In Chapter 3 concepts were defined as cognitive units that could be manipulated and named. By now, conceptual structures appear to be vastly more complicated, incorporating relations to other concepts of different kinds and at different levels of abstraction. It might appear that the concept as a unit has been replaced by a relational network in which issues of internal structure are no longer relevant. Yet, without postulating internal structure, there is no way of accounting for analysis of similarity and contrast within and between concepts, which are essential to advanced levels of conceptual and lexical systematization. The "empty concept," whose concept is defined only in terms of relationships to other concepts, leaves too many problems unresolved.

In order to be clear about how the child's conceptual and semantic systems develop, it is necessary to have some working model of both how concepts are structured and how they enter into systems on the basis of this structure. The requirements for such systems include (1) a specification of the information included within the concept and its relational structure, (2) a specification of how concepts are related to one another, (3) a mechanism whereby concepts can enter into more than one structure, and (4) a mechanism whereby concepts can evolve and structures can change.

For all the attention given to concepts and categories (e.g., Smith & Medin, 1981), these requirements have not been met in current models. In particular, requirements (3) and (4) have been neglected.

Replicability

To the extent that a single concept enters into more than one structure or system simultaneously—on a temporary or permanent basis—the concept must be *replicable*. For example, the concept of *apple* may be represented in the child's mind as a concept in a *lunch* script as well as in a collection of *fruits* derived from that script, and perhaps in a story involving a poisoned apple. Is it the same concept in each of these contexts? How can the concept maintain its integrity in different conceptual structures? If the child is to process the poisoned apple story effectively, the *apple* concept that enters into that story should not drag along all of the conceptual baggage of the *lunch* script, much less all of the incidental knowledge that the child has garnered about apples, although it is also the case that some of this knowledge may be relevant to the story and should be available to be called upon in its interpretation. The concept, then, must be replicable in a pared-down version and at the same time maintain its links to other representational structures. That is, there must be some invariant element that can enter into temporary relationships while the concept itself maintains its integrity and its connections with other concepts. The conceptual system must be at the same time stable and dynamic.

One obvious proposal for maintaining invariance is through words, since words are endlessly replicable. The word "apple" can enter into any number of representational structures simultaneously without risk of destruction of any of its copies. Another possibility is that an image of an object, something like a photographic negative, can be used to reproduce an indefinite number of positive copies. Both of these standard proposals rest on the use of symbolic forms to stand for the concept itself. However, neither will serve the present purpose.

The concept must be represented in a replicable form that is not dependent upon language, not only because it is assumed here that concepts precede the learning of words in developmental sequence, but also because concepts are continuously formed, differentiated, and reconstituted independently of the language forms used to communicate them. Conceptualizing is a dynamic process that cannot be tied too rigidly to the words used to express it (although, as we noted earlier, the young child does appear to consider this relation to be a rigid one). The problem with the image is even more straightforward: not all concepts are imageable, as the Wurtzburg School discovered almost a century ago in the study of "imageless thought."

It is necessary, then, to postulate a concept that is replicable in different structures independent of language or image. The tentative solution proposed here is a non-information-bearing concept nucleus within a larger conceptual structure. In this conception the nuclear concept itself is capable of replication and enters into other conceptual structures at nonnuclear locations. The nuclear replicas represent the concept; they do not themselves contain any content or structure. This information is recoverable, though, through links to the concept "mother." Each mother concept has only one nucleus, and only one mother concept contains a given nucleus. The conceptual structure includes, in addition, locations to be filled in by linguistic representations, perceptual paradigms (where relevant), and replicas of related concepts that form the core of the concept. An example of such a concept is shown in Figure 7.2.

In this figure the central area within the concept is the nucleus, the part that is replicable. Other locations within the concept structure are labeled by those functions that may be filled, although they do not need to be for every concept. In the case of object concepts they include concept names, perceptual representations, functions, actions, locations, actors, possessors, and other objects closely aligned with the object conceptualized (for example, cup as a container for milk). This conception is illustrated in Figure 7.3, where three concepts that relate in different ways are depicted. In each case the nucleus is represented only once, while the replicas enter into other concepts at nonnuclear locations.

The proposals that different locations within the concept are allotted

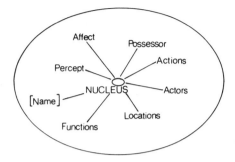

FIGURE 7.2   Representation of the nuclear concept.

to different functions or relations, that the nucleus is replicable, and that the concept is bounded have certain representational advantages in relating concepts within a larger network or in different types of structures. For example, locations within the concept serve to define the relations between concepts. That is, *high chair* is a location in the concept of both *eating* and *apple*. Thus, the internal structure and the relational system are clearly interdependent. At this point the replica notion has been applied to only a small part of the structure, but it is useful to the consideration of growth of the system as well.

Evolution and Change

It should be emphasized that even at the beginning of conceptual formation and differentiation concepts do not exist in isolation. Initially, they are embedded in event representations; thus, conceptual

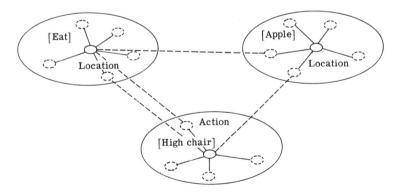

FIGURE 7.3   Different types of relations established between three concepts through replication.

links to other concepts within the parent ER need to be specified as well. The ER is one of many possible organizations of concepts. Like the concept itself, ERs are organized within boundaries. The basic concept incorporates a small network of syntagmatic relations and is related to larger networks of different kinds through the relations formed by the individual concepts in different contexts. This notion can best be illustrated through considering the different ways in which concepts formed in a particular event frame may evolve within different representations as the system develops. Such a scheme is shown in Figures 7.4 through 7.8.

In this scheme six levels of representation are outlined, corresponding, in part, to the phases of development discussed above. In Level 1 (Figure 7.4), perceptual representation, a specific experience is represented at the perceptual (not the conceptual) level, in this case an experience of eating lunch. No assumptions are made here about the characteristics of representation at this level or its veridicality. It is as-

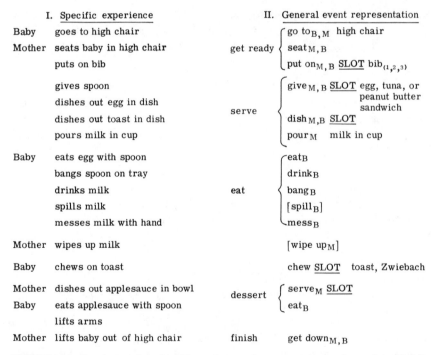

FIGURE 7.4   Levels 1 and 2. Specific and general event representations of the child's lunch experience.

sumed, however, that what is represented at this level has implications for what can be conceptualized at further levels. In this particular case specific foods and other slot-fillers are connected with specific actions involved in eating lunch. The representation is presented as having temporal order in accordance with its order in the real world, although again this is not a necessary assumption. Not shown here is the representation of the discourse that takes place in this situation, although, as will be made clear later, this is an important factor in determining other parts of the representation as well as setting up conditions for language use.

At Level 2 (also shown in Figure 7.4), there is a general representation of the event *eating lunch*. Here slots represent possible foods, bibs, and so on, and actions can be grouped into larger scenes or subscripts (e.g., *get ready, eat,* and *finish*). It is assumed that the proclivity for forming general conceptual representations of this kind is basic to human cognitive functioning (see Nelson & Gruendel, 1981; see also Chapter 2). The processing mechanisms that produce general structures from specific experiences must involve pattern analysis and perceptual categorization, but the extent to which particular general categories (such as action, actor or agent, instrument, etc.) are innately specified is unknown and not germane to the present argument. The language used in the event (e.g., "Let's get ready for lunch" or "Are you finished?") may aid the child in structuring the event into components. The running commentary provided by mothers on the activity (e.g., "Eat your spinach" or "Do you want your juice?") may provide not only the words and the forms for talking about it but also the units that may be used in setting up the representation.

It is worth noting that in this structure two types of slot-fillers are found. One, *bib (1, 2, 3)* results in a basic object concept that is called by one label, *bib,* although the child may discriminate finely between the three possible members. The second type, different foods in different slots (e.g., egg, tuna, and peanut butter), contains more than one basic object concept that are each called by different labels. These two types relate differently to the concepts at the next level. Some events contain collections as well. For example, *laundry* may be an early collective structure for the child. (The individual pieces that make up *laundry* may be identifiable on their own in other contexts [e.g., getting dressed], but in the collective they merge as parts in the whole.)

Level 3 (Figure 7.5), consists of the concepts formed on the basis of the relations represented at Level 2. It should be emphasized that these two levels are interdependent, in that the syntagmatic structure of Level 2 relates the paradigmatic concepts of Level 3 to one another; in turn, the concepts of Level 3 are formed on the basis of the relations at Level

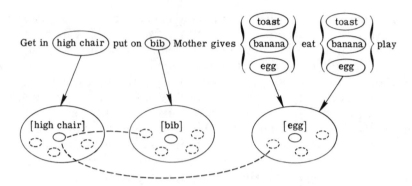

FIGURE 7.5   Level 3. Paradigmatic concepts derived from the syntagmatic relations of the event representation.

2. It is at Level 3 that substitutability as a principle of categorization enters. Concepts at this level are structured as in Figure 7.2. Concepts of different types (e.g., actions and objects) may have different potential internal specifications (perceptual representations, functions, agents, etc.) All object concepts contain locations for both perceptual representations and labels, although these need not be filled in particular cases. Any given concept may contain any number of unfilled locations. At least one location must be filled for the concept to be represented, but no particular specification is necessary. Other locations may be filled in later or may remain unfilled. Thus, a concept may be set up simply because a name is learned, but it will not be related to any other concept until some of its other locations are filled. (This suggestion implies that concepts may be formed outside of event representations. This implication is only partially acceptable. The child who hears a word hears it in some context, and therefore it is related to some event. The relation of the conceptual context to the context of word use is discussed later.)

Concepts at Level 3 are arranged into interlocking networks through concept replication, that is, the mechanism by which concept replicas enter into the internal relational structure of other concepts. Since each replica is linked to its original in the mother concept, a system of syntagmatic linkages is set up. Since the relations in the internal structure are based on ERs, the resulting network also reflects the event context.

At Level 4 (Figure 7.6), previously established concepts are subjected to further analysis and compared for similarity and contrast. In this analysis any component of the concept may serve as the basis for comparison, including but not limited to perceptual representation. On this basis concepts of attributes and parts may be formed and new concep-

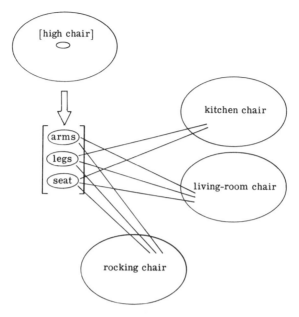

FIGURE 7.6   Level 4. Analysis and relating of paradigmatic concepts on the basis of similarity and contrast of componential structure.

tual structures may be formed that are not related directly through events. Operating within this level, children may engage in analogizing quite diverse things ("Bandaids are like spiders," "The grapefruit is like the moon") and make temporary connections that have no functional utility (and thus do not persist). However, some of the connections made will persist as more or less permanent conceptual structures (round things, things that are "naughty," things with eyes, and so on, ad infinitum). It is also possible that internal analysis can be carried further through referring back to the mother concept whose replica is a component of the conceptual structure under analysis.

For example, the concept *chair* can be analyzed in terms of *sit* and related to other concepts in which *sit* is a component, such as *sofa* and *bench*. In turn, *sit* can lead back to its mother concept, where it contains component actions or action routines as well as locations for sitting. This recursiveness makes deep analysis and recombination within the system possible without requiring that each concept consist of an exhaustive set of primitive features. The system can then act like a network but has the advantages of a feature system and the flexibility required of a dynamic system.

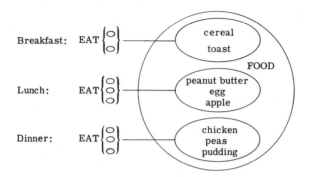

FIGURE 7.7   Level 5. Formation of general slot-filler categories.

At Level 5 (Figure 7.7), concepts from lower levels are combined through synthesis into general structures on the basis of containing similar membership. As with Levels 2 and 3, Levels 4 and 5 are interdependent. One important result of the event-based system is the emergence of slot-filler categories as they were described earlier, that is, categories of independently defined concepts, each of which may be a possible alternative within a particular position in an event. The psychological reality of these categories for young children has been demonstrated in an experiment by Lucariello & Nelson (in press) in which slot-filler categories were shown to be powerful organizers of recall of word lists in contrast to larger taxonomic categories or thematically based lists. Internal analysis of concepts, then, makes it possible to combine slot-filler categories from different events by uncovering similar functions in different events. Those concepts that share the same function may then all be grouped together into one larger concept that contains only a function and member concept replicas. Evidence for the existence of general categories of this kind is provided by the word–concept experiment reported in Chapter 6 (Nelson, 1978a). This larger concept group will be bounded, like the basic concept, the ER, and the simple slot-filler category. However, positing a boundary does not imply that it is inviolable; continuous expansion, contraction, and differentiation are considered to be basic characteristics of the system.

This conception appears to conflict with that of Rosch and Mervis (1975) in positing boundaries. However, the following considerations indicate that the two are not irreconcilable. First, the basic concept derived from the ER at Level 3 is the equivalent of their basic category. In the present model these concepts do not contain *instances* but characteristics, one of which may be a perceptual prototype; thus, the prototype inclusion proposal may be applied here as well. The notion of family resemblances applies at this level, but only in reference to the extension of the concept to instances in the world; it is assumed here that such extension is not determined for the child by a requirement that all instances display all characteristics included in the concept. Moreover, such characteristics are subject to continuous modification as development proceeds. At the collective level (Level 5), concept instances are included in the grouping, and again this grouping structure is not inviolable. Concepts belong to more than one group (e.g., *breakfast* and *food*), and the Roschian notions of typicality and fuzzy boundaries may apply quite well at this level. Because of the fluidity of structures at all levels of the conceptual system, the characteristics implicated in Rosch's description are quite compatible with the system proposed here.

As a final move, at Level 6 (Figure 7.8) conceptual symbols are utilized to form hierarchical semantic structures. Although dependent upon the previously established conceptual structures, this move is dependent as well upon cultural representations in the language. The claim here is that there is no way that the child can get to Level 6 simply through analysis of an experientially derived conceptual system. Such a hierarchical scheme is not based on analysis of perceptual similarity, nor is it based on grouping and regrouping objects and events experienced in the real world. Grouping yields nothing but groups of equal members, as in Level 5, whether these are based on contiguity, similarity, or substitutability. It does not yield hierarchical symbolic structures based on abstract analysis of cultural functions, as are represented at Level 6.

This argument appears similar to that put forth by Chomsky and

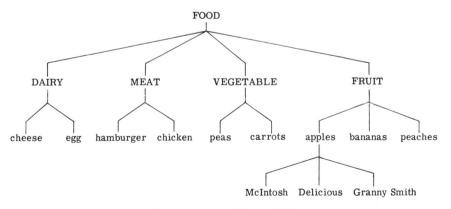

FIGURE 7.8   Level 6. Formation of hierarchical semantic structure.

others that the abstract structure of language is not accessible through experience. However, I will argue in the next chapter that the symbolic structure of the semantic system is available through the language and that the child acquires it as an additional level of representation that is "pulled out" of the conceptual level by exposure to the cultural–linguistic system during early to middle childhood.

The proposal, then, is that the conceptual system enables the child to "get in" to language and to use it appropriately; that language feeds back into that system, setting up new concepts and networks; and that language itself eventually "breaks free" of the conceptual system, although it maintains connections with it. Its "free elements" then combine freely into new structures that are not constrained by experience, and this system in turn sets up a more open and abstract conceptual system.

It should be stressed that relationships within the conceptual system are interdependent. The development of the ER as a differentiated structure depends upon the development of concepts and their emerging interrelational networks. In turn, the analysis and synthesis of internal structure and group formation are interrelated processes that are, by all evidence, well in place by the third birthday. No doubt some development of earlier concepts and language is necessary before the more derived structures become established.

There is no implication here that these are all the types of structures within the conceptual system. There are many other possibilities, including schemas of other kinds, narrative structures, theories, and games. Those sketched here seem to be those that have been considered most basic and have been the most studied. Their relationships are suggestive of relations that may lead to the formation of other temporary or more or less enduring structures.

Words in Concepts

During the years in which the conceptual system is developing and becoming established as a system, words are entered into the conceptual structures in the same way that other information is. Thus, words are *embedded* in concepts. The fact that concepts may replicate (and also differentiate and integrate) means that words may enter into different structures, but only insofar as the embedding concepts do. That is, concepts lead, words follow. Moreover, since the concept retains its connections to the events from which it has been derived, words are also constrained to contexts, albeit these contexts are generalized. This ensures that words are used successfully, but it also means that the child may have difficulty interpreting words in strange contexts.

Although words are conceived here to enter into concepts as other components do, both the word and the perceptual representation applicable to the concept appear to have special status as identifiers of the concept and as instantiators of it in novel contexts. This special status, as well as the indissoluble nature of the word–concept bond for object terms in early childhood, is evident in many ways. The research on nominal realism reviewed in Chapter 5 speaks to this issue in that children do not distinguish between the word for a thing and the thing itself. This has been shown in both Piaget's clinical interviews and in Markman's (1976) experimental research. One of the most dramatic demonstrations of the power of concept binding, I believe, is the research by DeVries (1969) in which children were presented with a live cat, which they identified as such, but which then was apparently turned into a dog by putting a dog mask on it. Preschool children affirmed that it was then a dog and had all the characteristics of a dog—it would bark, eat dog food, and so on. From one point of view, this experiment demonstrated their lack of conservation of identity. From another point of view, it indicated that the concept itself at this period is indissoluble: the perceptual characteristics identify the creature as a dog; this in turn implies the name and all the other essential characteristics of dogness. Another demonstration of the close word–concept–context bond is found in Ehrlich's (1979) report of children who deny that a ladle can be used for anything but serving soup (see the discussion in Chapter 6).

During this period of development children acquire huge vocabularies of lexical items compared to those with which they began at age two. Some of these may remain embedded in the event context in which they are used; most will be given a separate conceptual status. The use of a novel word by someone in an interpretable context indicates that there is a concept to be acquired, and thus a concept space is set up for it, even though very few of the empty spaces within it will be filled. Such a process is evident in the example from Emily in Chapter 2, who tried to understand in some way the new term "intercom." In that example her father provided a great deal of information about it: you buy it at Caldor's, you plug it in, and you listen to baby brother cry through it. Emily's prior experience enabled her to hang onto "buying it at Caldor's," for which she demonstrated a well-developed *buying* script. However, the rest of the information was garbled (plug in to Stephen, say "ahhh") and the term itself was lost. Nonetheless, however inadequate this concept may be, the term (and its importance to Daddy) generated the building of a concept that could be filled in as experience with the gadget grew.

To some degree the analysis in this chapter has demonstrated how constrained the individual conceptual system is by the context of experience. So long as concepts are derived from the representations of one's own experience, they will retain the limitations of that experience and their uses will be constrained by the event representations from which they were derived. Note, however, that it is not the case that the child cannot generalize to any new situation. Children, as well as adults, constantly call upon their established general ERs to interpret a new experience. Thus, they may use terms in what seem idiosyncratic ways if they analogize inappropriately to a new context. Their failures to use words appropriately are most frequently noted when an adult presents them with an uninterpretable context, one that has no analogy in their experience (except, as the case may be, in terms of very abstract features such as temporal relations).

Words in Events

The ER has been presented thus far as an abstract skeletal structure, one from which concepts of objects, persons, and actions can be derived and on the basis of which relationships can be defined. However, an important component of the event is not represented in this picture, namely, the language that is used within the event. It might be expected that from the point of view of the meaning system this would be the most important aspect of the event. Certainly, children must relate terms applied to actions and objects as they are experienced to their own conceptualizations as these emerge from those experiences. However, for the substantive terms we have considered thus far, this is a minor problem (in spite of its apparent philosophical difficulties, e.g., Quine, 1960). With respect to other types of language terms, however, there is a more difficult and intriguing role to be played in the representation of events.

We can consider the terms that cannot be given a conceptual representation per se (within the present definition of concept as a mental unit) to form a class that is different from the substantive terms represented in concepts derived from events. The former are primarily relational terms, used to relate two or more language structures but also to index important conceptual relationships. Such terms as "and," "or," "but," "before," "after," "first," "last," "big," "wide," "in," "under," "then," "there," "because" and "if," and also the inflectional morphemes such as "-ed," "-ing," and " 's" represent this class. Some are used as prepositions, as conjunctions, as adverbs or adjectives, or in several of these roles. Some (e.g., "more" and "up") are learned early in the language game, others (e.g., "because" and "if") considerably later. All of those mentioned, however, are found in preschoolers' speech samples. Many of them have been subjected to considerable experimental and theoretical analysis, most frequently within the framework of a semantic feature analysis.

The analysis of the development of the conceptual basis for language use and of concept binding outlined above is not meant to account for the child's use of these terms, as it does for object terms. To the extent that there are relational concepts underlying them, they are implicit, not explicit. As one evidence of this, children can use these words appropriately but cannot discuss them (Papandropoulou & Sinclair, 1974). In order to explain their uses, we must take into account the following observations and conclusions.

Given that children do learn and use relational terms correctly in context and that they are productive (i.e., not formulaic), conceptual relations of temporal order, cause–effect, size, direction, spatial relationship, conjunction, disjunction, contradiction, past, present, future, possibility, and necessity must be under the control of the 3-year-old, and conceivably the 1- or 2-year-old.

These relations are exemplified by adult usage within particular event contexts where the terms are used by adults. For example, the adult says: "Not now, after nap." "Drink your milk, then you can go out." "We can't go out because you're not dressed yet." (See Hood and Bloom, 1979, for further examples of causal statements by adults in everyday contexts; see Lucariello & Nelson, in preparation for both causal and temporal uses.)

Even though the contexted relations are understood by the child and the terms are acquired in application to these relations, they remain dependent upon event context for their use. That is, the child needs to understand the structure of the particular exemplified relation on a conceptual level independent of the language in order to use the term or interpret it correctly. Here again, the language depends upon the conceptual representation (in this case the event context); the relation cannot be reversed, that is, language does not yet structure the conceptual representation.

There are many indications in the literature of this one-way relationship in the use of relational terms (see French & Nelson, in press, for a review). One of the most cogent demonstrations is the Carni and French (1984) study, which showed that when all other factors were controlled, children interpreted "before" and "after" correctly when they understood the temporal structure of the event but not when they did not have such a prior understanding.

This is not to say that children themselves do not generalize from one context to another. Our analysis of their use of relational terms in event descriptions clearly shows that they do. Moreover, the analysis of the Emily data (Nelson, 1984b) shows how these terms are used in constructing narrative accounts of events even at 2 years. What children do not do is interpret the terms used by others to construct new interpretable relationships. That is, whatever representation of event structure the young child is using and generalizing from in verbalizing relationships is not readily transferrable to abstract or novel situations. Thus, there appear to be as yet unidentified situational constraints on the use of these relational terms by young children.

We have identified two classes of terms, one that can be given a conceptual representation and is concept-bound and one that represents conceptual relationships and is event-bound. The class of verbs (and perhaps some adjectives) seems to lie in between these two in that most verbs can be given a conceptual representation, but they are also essentially relational.

The data that are presently available are insufficient for suggesting a representational scheme at the conceptual level for relational terms or for suggesting a course of development that might apply to them. Despite the many studies of temporal terms, deixis, size adjectives, tense and aspect, and other related topics, we have nothing like the vast literature on development of object concepts and categorical taxonomies in young children on which to draw. Thus, it is premature to suggest what formulas children may use in their representations of such terms or how they may extract and generalize a particular relation from one representation to another. It does not seem premature, however, to suggest that these formulas work on pragmatic conditions of use rather than concepts as defined here.

One conclusion we can draw relates generally to the conceptual representation underlying the child's lexicon. Although it was possible—and even necessary—to lay out a number of different types of concepts and layers of representational structures, the various types were all found to develop very early (with the exception of the hierarchical tree), more or less as natural evolutions within the conceptual system. Within familiar and well-structured event contexts, children seem to form concepts readily and apply language terms to them and their relations easily. The conclusion here is that the conceptual structure supports the language and determines how the child will use it.

In a similar vein Tanz (1980), in her study of deictic terms, concludes that meaning is contextually determined for young children and notes that "This orientation toward the contextual determination of meaning is adaptive" in that children must constantly try to interpret language in relation to context. In convergence with the view taken here, she notes that "In adult language use . . . meaning emerges out of the integration of language and context. In child language acquisition meanings are *discovered* through the interpretation of integrations between language and context" (p. 164).

In summary, acquiring the meaning of a word involves, in part, learning to apply the word in appropriate contexts. The communicative function of the language and the conceptual representation of meaning converge because both are rooted in event contexts. Event representation supports both concept development and the interpretation of language. This convergence also suggests the breadth and limitation on the child's acquisition of shared meaning during early childhood. The event-based conceptual system provides common ground for understanding and producing language. However, the conventionalization of that system, which broadens the contexts of application, takes place through language and eventually provides the means by which language structures concepts as well. In the following chapter we shall trace the way in which lexical representation becomes differentiated from conceptual representation and thus how a particular language, culture, and history become represented in the individual's semantic system.

Summary

In this chapter an event-based conceptual system has been laid out and its development in early childhood described. It is claimed that this system can account for most of the developments, including the limitations, of children's concepts and their lexical uses summarized at the end of the last chapter. In particular, the contextual and conceptual constraints on language are accounted for in this system. Conceptual development alone cannot account for other semantic phenomena, however, in particular those phenomena displayed in the lexical organization of the language being acquired, including the hierarchical symbolic systems of the culture. These developments and their basis in language use are considered in the next chapter.

Notes

[1]Miller and Johnson-Laird (1976) described the relationship between the conceptual system and the lexical system as a mosaic, as follows:

> We assume that a semantic field consists of a lexical field and a conceptual core. A lexical field is organized both by shared conditions determining the denotations of its

words and by a conceptual core, by the meanings of what the words denote. A conceptual core is an organized representation of general knowledge and beliefs about whatever objects or events the words denote—about what they are and do, what can be done with them, how they are related, what they relate to. This lexical–conceptual relation is complex. To say that a lexical field covers a conceptual core like a mosaic is suggestive, but it greatly oversimplifies.

The mosaic metaphor captures much that is important: it is only in terms of the core that the choice of particular conditions to identify instances can be rationalized; it is only in terms of the core that a particular lexical concept can be assigned a location relative to other lexical concepts in that field . . . It is also necessary to realize that a conceptual core is an inchoate theory about something and that the same lexical field can cover very different theories. In particular, we must keep in mind that it is only in terms of the core that lexical concepts can be generalized and extended, or nonliteral uses of words interpreted. The mosaic can be stretched in some directions and not others; which stretchings can be interpreted depends not on the mosaic but on the conceptualization it covers. Theories of linguistic relativity to the contrary, thought is not forever bound by the words in which it must be expressed. (p. 291; reprinted by permission)

Although the mosaic metaphor is a bit obscure, the kinds of relations that Miller and Johnson-Laird are concerned with here are to a large extent those that must be considered in a developmental theory.

[2]For example, several components of an event may take place and be perceived as happening simultaneously, as when mother cooks while child eats. Language utilizes certain devices ("as," "while," "during," etc.) for expressing such configurations within its linear constraints.

[3]While the ER model should not be seen as providing the basis for a particular sentence order, it may provide the "natural order" for discourse. For example, in recounting events it is expected that the order of relating follows the order of occurrence unless some device is used to indicate that that order is being violated.

[4]See Kosslyn (1980) for evidence from studies of imagery along this line and a model that accounts for such effects.

[5]The similar notion that deliberate deception is an advanced form of conception was put forth by Premack and Premack (1983) in their discussion of limitations on the mind of an ape.

[6]In this connection Sigel (1983) noted that children as old as 7 or 8 do not include snakes or chickens in the animal category.

[7]"Meaning is constant across all members of a speech community" (Macnamara, 1982, p. 212).

8

Semantic Development:
From Denotation to Sense

The Need To Systematize Semantic Knowledge

Up to this point we have not considered in any detailed way what the third component of meaning—sense—is and how it becomes established in the child's meaning system. In the interpretation of language laid out here, the child begins with reference, the relation between words and things, quickly establishes denotation, the relation between words and concepts, and slowly builds a system based on sense, the relation between words and words. The completed system incorporates all three interrelated components, which serve different functions in the interpretation of meaning.

The first of these, reference, is, as Putnam (1975) notes, a matter of sociolinguistics—what the community chooses to include in a particular equivalence class that is given a name in the language. Children enter into the system of reference in partnership with (usually) parents or other caretakers who name things in their presence. Learning to share this aspect of meaning does not necessarily imply sharing other aspects, as Vygotsky (1962), Piaget (1962), and Anglin (1977) argued. It is possible to imitate a name used by others for an object without having any deeper understanding of the object class involved.

The second aspect, denotation, depends upon the establishment of a conceptual system that can be associated with language terms. This aspect involves a psychological state, the development of a psycholinguistic concept in collaboration with the linguistic community. As the previous chapter suggested, progress in achieving shared concepts is accelerated during the preschool years as the differentiation and integration of the experientially based conceptual system and experience of the language in use proceeds. That is, the establishment of the conceptual system is an individual matter, but its match to the culturally shared system is a collaborative matter accomplished largely through language in use.

The third aspect of meaning—systematic sense relations—is a sociopsycholinguistic achievement, the establishment of lexical relations among words themselves. It depends upon—but is not isomorphic with—the conceptual achievements outlined in the last chapter and also upon the implicit or explicit display of these relations by other language users.

As emphasized previously, meaning is not any one of these aspects alone, but rather all of them together are necessary conditions of a fully realized internalized meaning system. Their relation to each other changes with development as systems evolve. For this reason, one cannot find a single invariant principle, or set of principles, that explains either word meaning or word acquisition at all stages of development.

Although development of the conceptual system provides the child with the interpretive mechanism for understanding and using language in situations that can be appropriately contexted—through either objective or subjective (conceptual) context—this system by itself does not provide the basis for decontexted language use based solely on lexical relations. For this a semantic system that is unencumbered by all of the syntagmatic entailments of the conceptual system must be established. The emergence of such a system makes possible the manipulation of language terms without reference to situational context. It is the result of this development that shifts in performance on both semantic and verbal classification tasks at about 6 to 7 years are observed. These shifts can be attributed to the achievement of a system of semantic relations that is purely symbolic and semiautonomous, that is, it can operate independently of the conceptual system. This proposition and its implications are examined in this chapter. In addition, the developments within the semantic system feed back into the conceptual system and may bring about reorganization at that level as well.

Properties of the Semantic System

Although there is no general agreement on an appropriate linguistic description of semantics, there are certain generally agreed upon concepts and relations (Lyons, 1977) that should be made explicit before their application in development is considered.

Lexical Fields

The notion of lexical fields or domains organizing the lexicon is a product of structural linguistics, owing its origin to de Saussure and Sapir among others. It has received considerable use in linguistics, anthropology, and psychology, where such domains as color, kinship, flora, and fauna have been much studied. The general assumption, following de Saussure and Sapir, is that different languages lay different structures, through their terms and relations between terms, on top of a common "stuff." This general assumption leads naturally to the Sapir–Whorf hypothesis (put simply, "language structures thought;" e.g., Whorf, 1956).

No one denies that terms in the language are related in different ways and that certain domains of closely related terms can be discerned (e.g., kinship terms) that differ from culture to culture. The problem is whether this presents us with the inevitability of the Sapir–Whorf hypothesis in either its strong or its weak form (for a recent discussion see A. Bloom, 1981).

The view taken here may seem dangerously close to Sapir–Whorf in that I am claiming that acquisition of a level of lexical representation based on lexical relations restructures the conceptual level. That is, rather than being laid on a common "stuff" that exists "out there," I am suggesting it is laid on previously established conceptual stuff "in there" in the head. However, there is a way out of what seems like an untoward linguistic deterministic orientation, which has already been alluded to. Namely, the child's (and the adult's) conceptual system is complex and dynamic, existing not in one but in multiple representational systems, subject to continuing operations of analysis and synthesis. Thus, while the lexical system may be laid on the conceptual "like a mosaic" (Miller & Johnson-Laird, 1976), it cannot completely determine it, since the conceptual system is capable of absorbing the linguistic influence and reacting to it. The two are in dynamic interaction.

The basis for lexical fields is established in terms of different lexical relations, among them the following.

Similarity Relations

The most familiar and apparent of relations between words based on similarity is *synonymity*. Two lexemes (or words) are said to be synonymous when the selection of one rather than another has no effect on the message that is transmitted (or the truth value of the proposition). Of course, in some cases there may be subtle or not so subtle differences in the social or expressive components of a message by the choice of one or another of synonymous terms, and for this reason it may be claimed that there are no completely synonymous terms. However, such terms in English as "basement" and "cellar" (used alternatively by Emily [see Chapter 2] at 22 months), "purse" and "pocketbook," and "pants" and "trousers" are often used interchangeably even by young children. (Of course, some of these terms may be more archaic than others or used in different cultural–geographic settings; their common denotation is not affected thereby.)

Synonymous uses by young children raise the question as to whether there is any recognition on the part of the child who, for example, uses both "cellar" and "basement," that these two terms are lexically related to each other. This question is not easily answered simply by examining uses of the terms. Rather, the basis for the relation needs to be examined. Componential or feature theories assume that the lexical components constituting the words' meaning match completely, or nearly so in the case of synonyms. Alternatively, it might be that the child has established two equivalent concepts on the basis of their use in different event contexts, or that a single event contains alternative uses. There has been little or no study of the use or recognition of synonyms by young children, so these questions have not been addressed.

Contrasts

Opposition in the language is much more complex than interchangeability. *Antonymy* is the term used in linguistics for these relationships, and it refers to several different kinds of contrast, all dependent upon dichotomization. Lyons notes:

> We can leave to others to enquire whether the tendency to think in opposites, to categorize experience in terms of binary contrasts, is a universal human tendency which is but secondarily reflected in language, as cause producing effect, or whether it is the preexistence of a large number of opposed pairs of lexemes in our native language which causes us to dichotomize, or polarize, our judgements and experiences. It is, however, a fact, of which the linguist must take cognizance, that binary opposition is one of the most important principles governing the structure of languages. (Lyons, 1977, p. 271).

Children appear to learn early some pairs of contrasts such as "up–down," "good–bad," and "big–little." E. V. Clark (1973) showed that preschool children are sensitive to the opposition implied in that they will reply appropriately to one member of the pair with a contrasting term. Opposites are also among the most frequent paradigmatic responses in word-association tests for children (Heidenheimer, 1978b). Thus, unlike some other relationships, it may be that antonymy is established as a lexical relationship quite early. However, little systematic exploration has been done on this topic.

Opposites can be divided into "gradable" and "ungradable" categories. Gradable opposites always involve a comparison, while ungradable opposites divide the universe of discourse into two complementary subsets. For example, "male" and "female" may be considered ungradable in normal discourse. A person is not more "female" or less (although she or he may be more or less feminine); she either is or is not. Gradable opposites (like "feminine" and "masculine," "big" and "little," and "good" and "bad") refer to degrees of the quality in question. As Lyons points out, this distinction is bound to the logical implications of the use of these terms. The sentence "X is hot" implies "X is not cold." However, it is not the case that "X is not hot" necessarily implies "X is cold;" the gradability allows for degrees along a scale with the possibility of a neutral point where neither positive term applies.

Do children recognize the difference between gradable and ungradable contrasts? In particular, do they realize that terms such as "big" and "little" always imply a comparison to some standard, rather than an absolute assignment to a category of big things and little things? There is some evidence (Nelson & Benedict, 1974) that they do recognize the comparative sense of these terms even when used in their noncomparative forms (e.g., "big"). However, this is again an area that has been little explored. There is some feeling among linguists that even among normal adult speakers there is a tendency to attribute absolute qualities to the implicitly gradable terms of the language that are morphologically unrelated, such as "good" and "bad." Thus, to say of someone that he is not a good chess player may normally be taken to imply that he is in fact a bad chess player. If this is the case, we would not be surprised to find that children, too, interpret the terms in this way.

Opposition and contrast relate to the polarity relation in a natural way. Polarity has played an important role in some theories of semantic development (e.g., E. V. Clark, 1973), based on the finding that polar opposites in some early studies were confused in application by young children. When terms are related to each other as polar opposites, one is considered the positive term and the other the negative, and the positive term also often encodes the sense of the entire range of the quality in question (see H. H. Clark, 1970). Thus, we say "How big is it?" or "How good is it?" without any implication that "it" is big rather than small or good rather than bad, whereas we cannot ask the question "How little is it?" without an implication as to where "it" lies along the scale of bigness. Positive or negative poles are inherent in very many adjective and noun pairs, whether morphologically related (as in "friendly–unfriendly") or not.

Some of these pairs have been extensively studied in semantic development research, mainly for the purpose of determining whether they are confused in meaning and whether the positive pole term is invariably learned first, as the initial statement of the semantic feature theory suggested. As pointed out in Chapter 5, it seems fair to say that the story is more complicated than that theory initially suggested. Confusion on this issue is traceable to the neglect of the most basic question that needs to be posed, namely, are these terms systematically related to each other in the child's lexical system or are they more or less distinct? What is the course of development of their relations?

In summary, the relations of synonymy and antonymy have not been adequately studied in developmental research to date; thus, evidence for their establishment as basic relations in a semantic system is not available.

Hierarchical Relationships

Children's treatment of hierarchical relationships in the language and in cognition is central to many issues in cognitive and linguistic development, as indicated at many points previously. Hierarchical structures based on *hyponymic* relations play an important role in semantic theory, especially in defining semantic fields or semantic domains. In these terms "cow," for example, is said to be a hyponym of "animal," and "cow" and "horse" are said to be cohyponyms. While much of the discussion of these relations in semantics is similar to that in cognitive psychology, there are some additional points to be made. The hyponymic relationship, as Lyons (1977) points out, is based on the coordination of syntagmatic and paradigmatic structures. "A hyponym encapsulates the sense of some adjectival modifier and combines it with the sense of the superordinate lexeme" (p. 293). This is another way of stating that the relation is based on both similarity and contrast, leading to another implication: one can learn that two lexemes are cohyponyms without knowing anything else about them. A child can be told, for example, that a tulip is a kind of flower and know thereby that it is a cohyponym of daisy without knowing anything more about its relation to daisy, without knowing, that is, in what way they contrast. One would need to know that the tulip has a particular shape, mode of propagation, season of blooming, etc. in order to contrast it in some way with daisy. In other words, one needs to modify the superordinate noun with an adjective or adjectives to answer the question "What kind of flower is a tulip?" and thus to place it properly in the lexical tree.[1] An important implication here is this: "Hyponymy is a paradigmatic relation of sense which rests upon the encapsulation in the hyponym of some syntagmatic modification of the sense of the superordinate lexeme" (Lyons, 1977, p. 294).

There is no implication in the suggested structure of a hierarchical lexical tree (as in Figure 6.2) that there is a particular basic level, as cognitive psychologists have recently posited (Rosch *et al.*, 1976). The structure remains open to elaboration at many different levels, as the dotted line and gaps suggest. Nor is there an implication that any particular set of relations or contrasts are reflected at a given level. Moreover, there are terms (nouns as well as verbs, adjectives, and adverbs) that cannot be easily fitted into these hierarchical structures; we could think of them instead as belonging to non-hierarchical groups. This is particularly true of sets of common objects that have no established single lexeme in the superordinate position. "Cooking utensils" is one such group, where such terms as "knives," "pots and pans," and "casserole" would be grouped. One has to stretch even further to find an appropriate lexical tree for terms like "key" and "lock" or "window" and "door." "Parts of the house or building" is descriptive but fits a schematic or part–whole conceptual structure much more easily than a componentially composed lexical tree structure. These problems are not foreign to lexical semanticists, but they do pose important barriers to the easy integration of logically defined lexical and conceptual structures and relationships.

Contextual Relations

There are two types of contextual relations between word meanings, linguistic and nonlinguistic. The most important of the linguistic type is *anaphora,* or the referral of words within an utterance to prior words, as when a pronoun refers to a previously introduced noun. Anaphoric reference is in general a discourse problem rather than a strictly semantic one and will concern us little or not at all. It is, of course, an interesting and important problem in language development, since it requires that the child keep in mind the point of view of a listener as well as the content of previous statements (see, e.g., Maratsos, 1973a).

The most important category of extralinguistic relationships is *deixis.*

By Deixis is meant the location and identification of persons, objects, events, processes and activities being talked about, or referred to, in relation to the spatiotemporal context created and sustained by the act of utterance and the participation in it, typically, of a single speaker and at least one addressee. (Lyons, 1977, p. 637)

Personal and demonstrative pronouns, tense, and other grammatical and lexical markers relating the utterance to its spatiotemporal context all fall into the category of deictic terms. As noted in Chapter 6, these terms have been subjected to considerable examination in recent years, particularly by Clark and her colleagues, in the effort to determine how children coordinate the linguistic and extralinguistic worlds (e.g., E. V. Clark, 1978). Tanz (1980) reexamined some of these issues and pointed out that some aspects of the various deictic systems are grasped very early, for example, the personal pronoun system is generally mastered well before 3 years of age. On the other hand, some terms, such as "come" and "go" and "take" and "bring," which depend upon particular deictic conditions and roles, are not completely sorted out until 8 or 9 years. Deictic terms are of particular interest because they quintessentially represent relations between language terms and pragmatic conditions in the world, rather than world–world or word–word relationships. That children do appear to master at least some of these shifting relationships (e.g., the "I–you" contrast) at a very early age indicates that there is no essential difficulty in this particular *type* of relationship; the difficulty inheres in the complexity of particular application conditions. Deictic relations are important components of certain word meanings that are part of every child's basic vocabulary. They are of particular significance for their dependence on discourse context for interpretation. Thus, the role of context in learning and use may be best revealed in the study of such terms.

It is clear from this brief discussion that lexical relations are dependent upon general conceptual distinctions and that discerning the difference between understanding real-world relations (world–world), relations between real-world conditions and language terms (world–word), and those between the terms themselves (word–word) is not an easy matter.

Hierarchicalization of the Lexicon

Of the relations and structures discussed, the hyponymic has received the most attention in lexical research, as has its counterpart in conceptual structures, and much of this research has already been reviewed in Chapters 5 and 6. Here we consider how the lexical relation differs from the conceptual relations described in Chapter 7 and how it relates to those of the conceptual level.

It has been claimed, and this claim will be repeated here, that the hierarchical relationship is a symbolic one that is not and cannot be made apparent in the world of objects and events.[2] The different types of groups that children form—and their use of general names for these groups—can help to make this point clear. (1) One common type of group that children name is the *slot-filler group,* in which a general term stands in for items that could occur in a slot, as in "I like toast and meat and *food.*" Here *food* serves as a placeholder or variable; when other items fill the slot, it no longer has a place in the structure. (2) A second type of group is the collective term used to describe a part–whole structure. As Markman (1981) pointed out, children seem to use superordinates in a collective sense throughout the early childhood period. "Animals" may be used to refer to the whole collection represented by all the animals in the zoo. "Tiger" may then be viewed as a part of this collection but not as a member of the class *animal.* (3) Third, children may use a general term to refer to undistinguished members of a category, as when they use "bug" to refer to all small crawling things for which they have no other name.

In contrast, young children do not readily group things as types. They do not see that roses are a kind of flower, which is a type of plant. Although they may see that things can have more than one name (e.g., "flower" and "tulip" or "Bozo" and "dog"), the relationship between the two is not a hierarchical one. This should not be surprising, since the hierarchical class relationship cannot be demonstrated concretely—it can only be explained symbolically.

Suppose we set out to demonstrate to the child that cows, horses, cats, and dogs belong to the class of animals. Using toy farm animals we can make groups of cows, horses, dogs, and cats and ask the child to label them. Then we can form the group into a larger group and label it *animals.* We can induce the child to say that all the members belong to the larger group *animals,* and thus cows, horses, etc. are all part of the group *animals.* But what have we formed? A part–whole structure or collection. We have not formed a hierarchical structure such that "a cow *is* an animal" or "a horse is *a kind of* animal." This structure is logical or linguistic and is not accessible through objective demonstration. It rests on a relation between *terms* and not between objects.

There is sufficient evidence from young children to indicate that there is no limitation on the generality of their categories or their ability to form part–whole collections or slot-filler groups but that there is a limitation on their grasp of the hyponymic or class-inclusion relation. Is this a limitation on their logic, as Piagetian theory claims? Or, alternatively, is it a limitation on their representational system, which has not yet established a lexical system independent of the experientially derived conceptual system? A reasonable hypothesis is that when children can represent the relation, they will be able to use it.

Miller and Johnson-Laird's (1976) suggestion that the lexical system is "laid on" the conceptual system is misleading, particularly with respect to this relation. Recall that, at first, language terms are embedded in concepts and events. Thus, the lexical system cannot simply be spread over the conceptual system; rather, it must be differentiated from it. Indeed, understanding the relations that structure the lexical system depends upon the analysis of similarity and contrast within the conceptual system. Although there are indications that this analysis has proceeded prior to the formation of hierarchical relations, in the formation of analogies, for example, limitations on the analysis can be observed during this early period.

For example, the 3-year-old child may know that you wear coats and pajamas and may identify *clothes* as things you wear but still not include coats and pajamas in the category *clothes,* because *clothes* refers in his or her conceptual system to those things you put on in the morning (Saltz *et al.,* 1972). Or a child may know that both human mothers and cows give milk but not see the implication that they are both a certain type of animal. Or the child may know that he is a boy and that his father is a man but not see that they share the component ''male'' and that therefore he cannot grow up to be a mother. On the basis of data similar to these examples, Saltz and his colleagues (Saltz, 1971) concluded that young children have overrestricted categories. In a sense this is another way of looking at the same phenomenon, that young children form their semantic categories around those things that share real-world contexts, and therefore their categories tend to be small and fragmented. Their first hierarchical categories are a conceptual and semantic mix, still constrained by conceptual entailments but based on componential analysis and available for hyponymic structuring.

Where does the hyponymic structure come from? We have seen that it cannot be observed in the real world, nor does it emerge from perceptual or functional analysis of objects. Rather, the child must acquire the system from the language itself, and only after it is acquired can it be analyzed to determine what its basis is and how it can be expanded. This process takes place gradually during the preschool years, as the child is *told,* for example, that dogs and cats are animals and also that tigers and leopards are animals. The child may entertain many interesting hypotheses about why they are all animals (see Carey, in press), or the system may remain largely arbitrary in his mind for a long time. Nonetheless, the system begins as external fact; it only begins to organize internal relationships as the child begins to be able to extract the basis for the different domains and flesh out its representation through analysis of existing conceptual structure.

The implication here is that there is no problem for the child with the hyponymic relation *in the language*. There are two parts to this: (1) the semantic system must be differentiated from the conceptual system in order that terms can be reorganized independently of conceptual context, and (2) when this point is reached the system may be reorganized in terms of inclusion relations without difficulty. That the child may be able to handle such relations when they are freed of perceptual and conceptual context is evident in the greater ability of the young child to use categorical reasoning in verbal tasks than in tasks relying on perceptual support, for example, in responding to class-inclusion questions (see Chapter 6).

Learning the semantic structure of the language need not always be so explicit as in the animal example. It seems likely that children may reorganize their lexicons according to hierarchical relationships spontaneously once the basis for the system (shared and contrasting features) and its relational structure becomes evident. But without explicit guidance the child's system is likely to be somewhat idiosyncratic and incomplete. Despite their fascination with cars and trucks, for example, most children do not have a well-organized *vehicle* or *transportation* category even at school age, the reason presumably being that these superordinate terms are not commonly used with young children. This category is implicit, but because it is so the child is likely not to include in it boats and planes, as well as cars and trucks. These will remain separate until he or she learns in school that they are all forms of transportation and therefore are classified together.

There are, of course, innumerable ways in which things can be classified and reclassified, and most objects that we use belong to more than one semantic domain. For example, clocks are often included in the *furniture* category, but they also belong to the category *timepieces,* which includes watches, sun-dials, and hourglasses as well as clocks. Children show an early facility in categorizing and recategorizing (see Chapter 3 on extensions of early words); thus the underlying process is evident very early. However, the particular relations of dominance and inclusion used in the culture remain to be learned. Although prototypical category members in Rosch's (1975) scheme are just those that share distinctive perceptual features as well as motor movements and these properties are also the basis for early extension of terms, the classification system of the culture goes beyond this to define members that do not share these properties but share more abstract functions (e.g., cultural utility) as members of the same class. These classifications must be learned through language. The prototypical members retain their centrality in the semantic system presumably because they are the first to be identified as belonging to a particular domain.

An important part of the present proposal that has not yet been made explicit is that the differentiation of the lexical level from the conceptual establishes it as an autonomous system of free elements that can combine and recombine in different ways, of which the hierarchical structure is only one. Once free of the concept binding of early childhood, words can be used flexibly and freely, without necessarily implying the entailments of the conceptual level.

The fact that the semantic level can operate purely symbolically has important implications for using language and for certain types of verbal problem solving. Ordinary conversations can be carried on without accessing the conceptual level, so long as reference is made clear. For example, as discussed in Chapter 1, if I ask "Who ate the apple that was on the counter?," it is possible for you to interpret this question without accessing your concept of *apple, eat,* or *counter* but simply through bringing up your memory of a particular apple that was sitting on this particular counter not long ago and automatically computing your part or nonpart in the questioned event. Information about kinds of apples, parts of apples, growing conditions, ingestion, digestion, support principles, carpentry, etc., all essential to the concepts of *apple, eat,* and *counter,* do not enter into these computations. Thus, the free-element semantic system frees the language user from unnecessary conceptual complexity. Of course, in cases of doubt concepts are brought forth and examined, but frequently interpretation and production take place at a level of meaning that has become automatized. (See Carpenter & Just [1977] and Engelkamp [1983] for discussion of a related position and supporting research.)

The preschooler has not yet achieved this automatization of meaning "packets" in the form of words. As discussed in Chapter 7, tied to their concepts, words imply more necessary entailments than they do for the adult. Thus, in the phase of so-called nominal realism, children will insist that a dog cannot be called a cow (Piaget, 1929). Moreover, event contexts constrain the uses of words; thus, "before" refers only to sequentially clear situations and not to ambiguous ones (Carni & French, 1984). On the other hand, the conceptual content and its connections to other structures (e.g., the event representation) provides for wide-ranging associations that are not made in the semantic system. For example, a young child pronounces that a Band-Aid is like a spider (because it has long dangling things and mommy throws it in the

wastebasket) when this connection would be at best bizarre in the semantic system. The conceptual system and the semantic system are
therefore each constrained and each open, but in different ways. The
free-symbol system also enables the child to manipulate words independently of their concepts and thus to solve verbal problems, such as
the class-inclusion problem, more easily.

Let me clarify this position further by reviewing its basic premises.
(1) The young child's concepts are derived from schematic representations of events that embed objects, actions, instruments, and person
roles. The concept is structured and bounded as a unit with internal
content. (2) The organization of concepts in the conceptual system is
based on spatiotemporal contiguity in the event representation or on
substitutability within a slot in the event frame. Perceptual similarity
forms a separate connective system. (3) The organization of word meanings evolves during the years of early childhood to form a system separate from the conceptual system. In this semantic system words are
related to other words through abstract relations of similarity and contrast, as defined within the language. Words can then access perceptual
images and conceptual content and entailments but exist as free elements that can operate autonomously and can recombine to produce or
understand novel conceptualizations. The semantic system therefore
presents a new and potentially powerful tool of thinking in a decontexted mode or, rather, in any context that may be established, regardless of previous experience. It is also obvious that the symbolic mode is
essential for logical and mathematical manipulation as well as for scientific thinking.[3]

Internalization of the Lexical System

The question of how children come to internalize the lexical system
is not one that can be given a completely satisfactory answer here because it has not really been studied. Two routes can be suggested, however. First, it is possible that children subject their language to analysis
in much the same way that they do other aspects of their experience
and that a mechanism of implicit learning of lexical structure similar to
the implicit learning of grammatical structures identified by Reber and
his colleagues is at work (Allen & Reber, 1980; Reber & Allen, 1978;
Reber, Kassin, Lewis, & Cantor, 1979).

The possible power of implicit learning has yet to be fully explored.
Recent research on syntactic development has implicated covert or cryp-
tic processes of analysis and reorganization (e.g., Bowerman, 1976, 1982;
Karmiloff-Smith, 1979; Maratsos & Chalkley, 1980; Newport, 1981).

The semantic system may well develop through similar covert processes operating on language input rather than on experiential input and relating that input to the established conceptual system.

Not to be underrated, however, is the role of explicit instruction. Adults in all cultures no doubt teach children such things as how to classify plants in the forest or dinosaurs in books and how to determine who is related to whom in what way and what that implies. In our own culture, classification systems are highly valued to an extreme. We teach young children colors, shapes, sizes, ages, time, space, numbers, letters, taxonomies of animals, fruits, and so on, ad infinitum. Most of these systems are arbitrary—that is, they have little conceptual content for the child—but the child may begin to learn them early and thus set the framework for a meaningful system of semantic relationships. Note again that these classification systems can only be taught through language—they are not demonstrable in the real world without language or some other symbolic system.

Children between the ages of 4 and 10 often take great pleasure in mastering such systems, including hierarchical structures (see the nice case study by Chi [Chi, 1978; Chi & Koeske, 1983] of learning dinosaur names). Sometimes they go farther and design their own systems as a game or fantasy. But no one—so far as I know—has ever observed a nonhuman animal spontaneously engaging in hierarchical classification.[4] Although the issue is open (and not too much hangs on it), it seems likely that hierarchical structures must first be explicitly taught before a child sees their possibilities and begins to apply them to other structures. Once taught, it becomes evident that much of the language having to do with the physical (and to some extent the social) world falls into this kind of structure, and domains that might have been initially organized at the conceptual level as groups or collections may become restructured into better or poorer hierarchies.

It may help in considering how the semantic system is mastered to think of the child as acquiring a partial system mediated by both the adult's partial system and by the child's conceptual system. Figure 8.1 provides a schematic view of this relation. The important points to be seen in this diagram are (1) that the adult's representation is an incomplete structure in comparison with the cultural system, (2) that its display in speech is a partial and disconnected representation of the adult system, and (3) that what the child gets from this display is an incomplete, error-prone construction based on both prior (nonhierarchical) concepts and language use. However, as more hierarchical structures are constructed in this way, it seems likely that the child will find it easier to map his own concepts onto this model.

Cultural System (Langue)

Adult Representational System

Adult Presentation (Parole)

Child Semantic Representation

Child Conceptual System

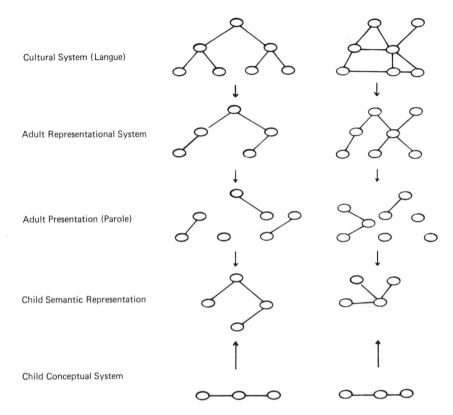

FIGURE 8.1   Mediation of the child's semantic system by the adult's partial representation and presentation system and the child's conceptual system.

Making the Implicit Explicit

A great deal of semantic growth and systematization depends upon making initially implicit relations and structures explicit. Again, adult input may be not only helpful but in some cases essential to this process.

One example of the process of making implicit knowledge explicit is that of providing definitions of terms. Anglin (1977) interpreted young children's responses to questions about the meaning of words to indicate that they had fragmented, imagic, idiosyncratic meanings; that, although their extensions of concepts were accurate, their intensions were immature and uncoordinated. However, my interpretation of similar data (see Chapter 6) was that children's knowledge of word meanings was similar in its content to that of adult's. Although each child gave a partial definition, together they produced complete explanations that matched those of the dictionary quite well, except for the omission of superordinate terms. This could be the result of the process of each child's incomplete accessing of implicit knowledge. Giving an adequate definition of a term requires reflection on one's knowledge of the uses of the term, organization of that knowledge into a conventional form, and production in verbal form. The last two of these steps may only develop in response to adult challenge and model. This thesis has been explicated by Watson (in press) and supported by her studies of children's definitions.

Making implicit knowledge explicit is a process that has been little studied, but it is assumed in many current models of development that rely on the notions of metacognition in its various forms (e.g., metamemory, metalinguistics). Keith Nelson and I (Nelson & Nelson, 1978) proposed that it was the final outcome of the development of any cognitive system and, in particular, of the various subsystems making up the language as a whole.

In summary, the process by which the child develops the semantic system depends not only upon the implicit structure displayed in the language, which must be related to the prepared conceptual representations, but also upon explicit teaching of symbolic systems. It is relevant to note that not all children in our culture are exposed equally to these cultural systems, nor do all cultures utilize the same or equivalent systems. Thus, children vary in the degree to which they master various types of symbolic structures and in the age at which these structures become systematized and operative at an automatized level.

The suggestion that meaning depends upon at least three different interpretive structures—perceptual, conceptual, and semantic—is one manifestation of the view that the mind is organized in multiple ways to serve multiple functions. In addition, it has been proposed that at both the conceptual and the semantic levels relatively permanent (but not impermeable) organizations of old knowledge exist, but that new constructions and reorganizations come into existence spontaneously as well as in response to new input. While all levels are flexible and dynamic in this way, the semantic level has the additional advantage of not being embedded in conceptual structures that imply additional contingencies and thus constrain meaning. Rather, it is purely relational, consisting only of labels and relations such as "is a type of," "belongs to," "has a," and "is the opposite of." Thus, the possibility for manipulating such elements and constructing new rearrangements is greater. Once constructed, the validity of the new relations must be tested by the implications of the conceptual structures that they reflect. To take a trivial example, *whale* may exist simultaneously in the *fish* category and in the *mammal* category in one's subjective lexicon. Which is used at any given time depends upon the context that it is tested against. If the wrong classification is called upon, a false logical proposition might be accepted, for example, "All fish lay eggs, therefore whales lay eggs." Syllogistic reasoning, analogical reasoning, class inclusion, and metaphor all depend upon relations in the semantic level in the present view.[5] The number of relations that exist at the semantic level is presumably limited but large enough to express all the possible logical relations between words within any given domain.

Relational Terms

In Chapter 7 it was suggested that relational terms such as "in," "there," "before," "and," and "because" were initially organized in terms of their conditions of use within event structures and that this constrained their use to the kinds of events that children had represented on the basis of prior experience. The research is quite clear that children gradually become freed of these experiential contexts and learn to interpret these terms appropriately in novel and arbitrary contexts between years 4 and 10. The explanation would again seem to be that these terms have become newly represented on a semantic level in which the relations they represent are abstract, rather than event contingent. Their meanings, of course, in most cases are interpretable in particular contexts (to the extent that they are deictic); however, these contexts need not bear a close relation to those the child has previously experienced.

The important point here is that when the semantic level becomes established on its own, it can operate both to establish a context and to project new knowledge onto the conceptual level. At the early stage the conceptual level determines what can be produced and how things will be interpreted. Thus, children whose conceptual system is not askew produce terms appropriately. However, their interpretation of terms used by others may be faulty whenever these uses do not fit the child's own experiential base.

Implications for Research

The present view has a number of implications for the way children learn words and solve tasks, some of which have been mentioned in passing. I consider here explicitly some of the research findings reviewed in Chapter 5 from the perspective of the present model. The major implications for which evidence is sought are as follows:

A shift in word *learning* during early childhood should be noticeable within domains that have become semanticized, from dependence on contextualized meanings to fitting terms within a sense system.

Word *meanings* should become relatively free of specific contexts as the semantic system is established.

Words should become less embedded in their conceptual contexts.

Relations between words should shift to reflect semantic rather than experientially derived bases.

Verbal *problem solving* should become easier, reflecting the autonomy of semantic relationships.

It should be apparent on the basis of the research reviewed earlier that all of these "predictions" are actually well-known effects, each associated with a different explanation. The question may be raised as to whether there are any unique predictions made by this model. The major implication not specifically contained above is that *only* cognitive tasks drawing on the semantic level will show a shift in performance between 4 and 7 years. Tasks that draw on perceptual processing, event representations, or conceptual representation should not be significantly affected (although there may be increases in speed or differences attributable to task interpretation, attention, memory span, etc.). Thus, some tasks that are generally assumed to reflect the same type of cognitive organization, such as classification by sorting and memory for taxonomically categorized lists, should in fact reveal performance differences related to their different organizing principles, the one reflecting conceptualization (based on spatiotemporal relations), the other semantic organization (based on abstract, hierarchical relations).

With these proposals in mind, let us reconsider the findings from several research paradigms.

Word Learning and Word Meaning

Referential Meaning

As argued throughout this book, at least three different principles are involved in word learning, and they are relied upon to differing degrees at different points in development. Referential meaning predominates in the very earliest stage, although it may be active at any point. Children's acquisition of words for pictures (e.g., "ostrich" or "submarine") is based on their referential properties alone, at least until they are able to internalize conceptual knowledge through language and understand something about the functional properties of ostriches and submarines.

That people of all ages can learn to use terms referentially without any deeper conceptual meaning is obvious. We observe it frequently in young children, who can learn to name dozens of automobile types with their appropriate brand names or will memorize 50 or more dinosaur types known only through pictures (see Chi & Koeske, 1983). While the subject in Chi's study learned more than the names, the dinosaurs could be divided into those that much was known about and those that little was known of; the latter were quickly forgotten. Children seem to enjoy this kind of learning. It does not stop with childhood, however. Recall the example given in Chapter 1 in which I see an exotic fruit in the supermarket and am told it is a papaya. I bring it home and this time I am asked "What is it?" I reply "It's a papaya." "What do you do with it?" "I don't know; all I know is it's called a papaya." My meaning for the term is referential only: I can refer to this food as a papaya, but I have no deeper knowledge of it.

Of course, as this example implies, terms used referentially often—perhaps usually—go on to acquire deeper meanings. After I open the papaya, eat some of it, look it up in the dictionary or the encyclopedia, or ask my knowledgeable friend about it, I will have acquired experience and knowledge on which to base a concept of the fruit. Terms that do not enter into a deeper knowledge system are soon forgotten, as Chi and Koeske's (1983) dinosaur study showed. Presumably this is the fate of many of the terms learned from picture books that have no other base. The ephemeral status of many first words (e.g., Bloom, 1973) no doubt reflects the instability of purely referential meanings.

It may be objected that we do not need a separate explanation for lexical acquisition in terms of referential meaning, since what is implied is simply the perceptual component of a concept—Miller and Johnson-Laird's (1976) perceptual paradigm. The distinction is useful, however, for the reasons given above, especially regarding the unstable ephemeral status of these terms and for characteristics of learning that seem important. Referential terms can be easily acquired to match a perceptual paradigm; they then set up a slot where a full concept should be—it is, as it were, a strong invitation to find out more about the thing named. When this information is obtained—however it is obtained—the conceptual slot is no longer empty, and the term has taken on denotational meaning.

Equally important is the fact that only object terms can be learned referentially. Pointing to objects or saying "this is X" names things. Actions, states, and properties, by their nature, have relational as well as informative connections. To say that someone is skipping or jumping is to *know* (to some degree) what skipping or jumping is. To say that an object is red or striped is to know (correctly or incorrectly) what it is to be red or to have stripes. These terms may have inaccurate meanings (and are quite likely to because of their nonobviousness), but they cannot be learned simply as names. (They can, however, be learned as part of a system—see below.) The well-known asymmetry between noun and verb learning is explicable on these grounds alone.

Denotational Meaning

Not all words, even at first, are learned as referential terms. As was argued in Chapter 3, the beginning language learner has begun to partition experience into concepts, and some words are learned that map onto these concepts directly. Denotational meanings have their basis in the individual's concepts—which are themselves derived from intersubjective experience—and they become further modified as they are used in interactions with others. Denotational meanings of terms include perceptual, functional, and other knowledge about the thing, act, state, or property, perhaps including typical examples or stereotypes. The individual's concepts are subject to continuing modification and accretion, as suggested in Chapter 7, that is, they are open. Of course, a concept like *dog* is unlikely to be much changed after childhood, but this does not mean that it is impermeable. During early childhood most word learning takes place through conceptual differentiation—learning names for the components of representations of one's experiences in the world.

Sense Meaning

The claim here is that the establishment of a lexical system per se is an achievement of the preschool period. Its manifestation is in terms of links between words within domains, that is, lexical relationships. Of course, these links have conceptual implications, but they require a different level of analysis, one in which relations between concepts may be asymmetrical. Hierarchical and non-hierarchical semantic domains make new kinds of systematic relations (derived from or at least consistent with the conceptual relationships) possible at both levels.

When these semantic domains (sense systems) are established, the child (and later the adult) has all three meaning components available—the referential, the denotational, and the sense based. Like perceptually based learning, learning from sense relationships (e.g., ''A wombat is a kind of animal'') also sets up slots where a concept may be formed, and if the concept is not subsequently established and related to other concepts, the word itself may be forgotten, even though its place in the lexical system remains.

Word learning at the denotational (conceptual) level is typical at all ages and can go in either direction. That is, a nonverbal conceptual element can be matched with a word that seems to fit it; or a word learned referentially, situationally, or through other words can open a conceptual slot that is available for receiving further information. Both processes take place from the beginning, or at least by 1½ years (see Chapters 2 and 3).

Word learning as part of a system is observed from about 2 years for subsystems such as the color domain.[6] Collections, hierarchies, and systems such as kinship begin early but continue to develop very late. Most of the research on the development of word meanings (for example, with relational terms such as "before" and "after" or "big" and "tall") has been in terms of their sense relations rather than their denotative meanings. It is at this level that distinctions between terms are made in the semantic feature or lexical contrast models (E. V. Clark, 1983). The fallacy in this line of research has been to suppose that the same principles apply to word learning no matter what type of word, what stage of development, or what the conditions of learning. It is not surprising, therefore, that componential theories have generally failed to predict the order of acquisition of terms (Carey, 1983).

Surprisingly few studies have attempted to teach new words. The best known of these is the study of the acquisition of the artificial color word "chromium" by preschool children. Children who learned this word fitted it into their system of color terms (making it equivalent to green or brown depending upon the availability of other terms), but Carey and Bartlett (1978) found no differences in acquisition as a function of the size of the children's color vocabulary. However, it seems that all children who learned the term had some prior color words, thus they presumably had some lexical system to fit the term to. Note, however, that the color domain is a system of perceptual categories; thus, it is not a good test of the conceptual–semantic distinction. The definitive study of word learning at different developmental points from the present theoretical position remains to be carried out.

Changes in Word Meanings

In one of the few proposals to suggest a shift in the basis of word meanings, Markman (1976) proposed that as children became aware of words at a metalinguistic level at about age 7 to 8 (presumably dependent on instruction in reading), word meanings became problematic in their own right (see Chapter 5). Her findings led her to suggest that children then adopted a referential theory of meaning, that is, they adopted the position that words must have a referent in the real world if they are to mean. Thus, they would respond to questions such as "If all giraffes disappeared from the world, would the word giraffe mean nothing or would it mean an animal with a long neck?" by saying that it would mean nothing. Such responses depend crucially on how the child interprets the critical term "mean," an interpretation that might shift depending upon how the term is used in the classroom. As Watson (in press) stressed, teachers put a good deal of emphasis on defining words in the course of the instruction that may lead to metalinguistic awareness.

The view here is that metalinguistic awareness hinges on the ability to reflect on language as an object in its own right, which is only possible after the achievement of the autonomous semantic level, when words are disembedded from concepts. The meaning of Markman's finding remains unclear, however, and additional studies are needed to determine how it may relate to the other developments described in this and the previous chapters.

Word meanings do change over the course of childhood, if the studies of children's definitions are taken as indications. They shift from functionally based definitions to definitions based on categorical relations (see Chapter 6). Watson (in press) argued that this shift reflects explicit teaching of definitional forms and the increasing ability of children to make implicit relationships explicit. While this is a plausible explanation, it is also true that these relations could not be learned and made explicit if the potential for them did not exist in the system. I have argued above that semantic relations are conventional, explicit, and to some degree taught, but that the basis for them must be developed in the child's conceptual system before they can be learned.

Disembedding and Changing Relations

Word Association and Other Semantic Memory Tasks

As summarized in Chapter 6, semantic relations (superordinates, coordinates, subordinates, opposites, and synonyms) are rarely given in word-association tests by children as old as 6 or 7 years. Younger children give contextually related responses, functions, actions, or perceptual associates. This shift in responding, on a task that demands quick responses, suggests that a different level of relationships (i.e., lexical) becomes established during middle childhood and becomes the most readily accessible level when words are presented.

Other tasks purporting to draw on semantic memory, such as recall of categorized word lists and release from proactive inhibition, also show shifts in responding during the early school years, such that children are able to take advantage of hierarchical categories that they did not before. Again, this suggests that these categories are newly established and have become automatic at the verbal level. While some categorical relations do appear to be utilized in verbal tasks in early childhood, these are explicable in terms of the child's understanding of situationally derived relations. In other words, they are paradigmatic conceptual relations derived from syntagmatic structures rather than the paradigmatic abstractions of the semantic hierarchies.

Class-Inclusion Tasks

The ability to answer correctly the question "Are there more roses or more flowers?" when the group consists of 10 roses and 3 daisies requires that the relation between words be understood. As Inhelder and Piaget (1964) claimed, it is necessary to be able to manipulate the logical relationship $A + A' = B$ and its inverse $B - A' = A$ and to conclude that $B > A$ and that A and A' are included in B. However, it is also necessary to know that roses are a type of flower, that *flower* stands in a dominant hierarchical position with respect to *rose*. Any other relationship would not lead to the same conclusion. For example, if a child uses the term "flower" as a collection of which roses are a part, she may be led to the correct answer for the wrong reason (cf. Markman, 1981).

Consider also the results of a number of lines of related research. Rosch *et al.* (1976) showed that 3-year-old children can classify by basic objects but not by superordinate classes. Macnamara (1982) showed that children treat superordinate terms as collectives. Markman (1981) demonstrated that children understand part–whole relations in collections before they understand class-inclusion relations. My research (Chapter 6) confirms the finding in word-association tasks that children understand the superordinate–subordinate relation before they do the reverse. Together these findings suggest that understanding the hierarchical relations between superordinate, subordinate, and coordinate is a late achievement that is dependent upon the ability to conceive of the terms independently of their conceptual underpinnings and to establish abstract relations between *terms,* not between concepts or objects. This is not to say that the semantic structure, when established, does not have implications for the conceptual structure; it obviously does. Moreover, the conceptual organization must provide the basis for the semantic relation to be established, as described in Chapter 7. That some part of the hierarchical system is established early is clear, but the organization of terms is not completed for some time, and until it is the child's handling of class-inclusion and other related tasks is unreliable and highly dependent upon task variables.

This brief review indicates that the proposed developmental model is consistent with research findings from a variety of theoretical and methodological paradigms. More research needs to be carried out to examine its implications for word learning and for the predicted difference in performance on verbal and nonverbal tasks.

Relation to Other Models

At this point the relation of the present proposal to other models in semantics, cognition, and development can be considered. It can be noted that the proposal is consistent with some of the developmental claims of Piaget (1970) in terms of the differentiation and coordination of conceptual systems, although the emphasis here is not on the underlying logic structure, as in Piaget's theory. In fact, the assumption here is that operations do not change with development but the representational levels do. In this respect it resembles to some extent Bruner's (1966) model. The strong working assumption here is that what gets represented in the system and in what form has major implications for all functions of the cognitive system.

In terms of differentiation and integration and of the development of layers of potential representational systems, the model draws on Werner (Werner, 1948; Werner & Kaplan, 1963). It is closest in its developmental assumptions, however, to Vygotsky (1962) (see below). It is apparent, then, that the proposal here draws from a number of different approaches to development in a synthesis that is meant to rise above simple eclecticism.

The system owes something as well to information processing and artificial intelligence (AI) models, in particular to those of Collins and Loftus (1975), Kintsch (1974), Miller and Johnson-Laird (1976), and Schank and Abelson (1977). None of these is a developmental model, however, none provides any clue as to how a system might be developed, and none attempts to take developmental data into account in any serious way.

The general argument here is that the relations of the semantic system depend upon the analysis of similarity and contrast of components *within* the conceptual system. Thus, the proposal appears to be consonant with other models of semantic development, including the semantic feature model (E. V. Clark, 1973), the lexical contrast model (E. V. Clark, 1983), and Bierwisch's (1981) lexical development model. It is, however, actually quite different from these in its developmental implications, in the following ways.

First, words are not acquired in terms of either features or contrasts. Conceptual components are implicit in the conceptual system but are not the building blocks of that system. A word may be learned that fits into the conceptual system, but the concept behind it may still lack components essential to its place in the semantic system. Moreover, a child may not recognize a similarity or contrast that is actually implicit in his concepts because the conceptual system is based on different organizing principles that do not make such similarities salient.

Second, and relatedly, contrasts and hierarchical domains emerge with development, dependent upon the joint effects of explicit instruction and implicit abstract analysis. They are not the basis for acquisition (at least at first), nor are they evident in the real world. Rather, they inhere in the semantic structure of the language and must be reconstructed anew by the child on the basis of simultaneous analysis of the language and the previously established conceptual system.

Third, the semantic system that eventually results is decontexted, composed only of elements and their relations to one another. The elements—terms of the language—are capable of invoking concepts and other parts of the cognitive system but are also capable of being manipulated independently of other parts. Thus, it is at the most abstract level content-free, a purely symbolic system. The relations have their basis in similarity and contrast between conceptual components but do not carry the content of these components. Thus "dog" and "cat" are related semantically as cohyponyms of "animal" but are not related at *that* level as small, furry creatures that like to be petted and fed scraps of human's food, as they may be in the child's conceptual system.

As noted previously, there are a number of proposals about semantic and syntactic development that have relied on the assumption that forms and structures are first acquired and later analyzed and resystematized. These studies bear out the proposal that language systems reorganize themselves during early to middle childhood. Bowerman's (1978a, 1982) studies of the emergence of errors in the application of noncausative verbs to causative uses suggest the emergence of a process of comparison of components and similarity matching that results in a new systematic form. Karmiloff-Smith (1979) documented the differentiation of functions for terms originally used plurifunctionally by preschool children, suggesting a new hierarchical structure. In the most elaborate model, Maratsos and Chalkley (1980) proposed a process of analysis and correlation of syntactic relations that results in the identification of form classes. In each of these descriptions, forms that are originally used correctly and in limited contexts are subject to further analysis in the light of further exposure to the parent language, which leads to further elaboration and a higher-level systematic structure. The general process envisaged is that of the *acquisition* of a form initially entered into a system followed by *analysis* of its meaning and use, followed by *resystematization* based on this analysis. The present model is consonant with these proposals with respect to its reliance on this general mechanism of development.

A model of semantic development put forth by Bierwisch (1981) explicitly recognizes the necessity of distinguishing the conceptual and the semantic representation in order to account for certain aspects of meaning. For example, he states: "The semantic structure SEM of a word determines a conceptual unit denoted by the word relative to a given context. To put it the other way round: SEM determines a family of related conceptual units, the differentiation of which depends on the context within which the word is interpreted." Thus, Bierwisch recognizes the importance of both conceptual distinctions and contexts of use. However, he does not go far enough. His ultimate goal of achieving a formal system applicable to development is defeated by his attempt to incorporate context. The developmental achievement must include the ability to interpret words transcontextually, in novel contexts as well as well-understood ones. Words must become capable of establishing context in addition to being determined by it. At the same time, the semantic structure must be independent of specific context. Although context is essential to meaning, it cannot be successfully entered into a formal specification of semantic structure. The multilayered, dynamic meaning system defeats such formalistic models, however elegant.

Carey (1982) followed up her critique of the componential and innate concept models with a proposal based broadly on the idea that semantic concepts derive from a person's (and a child's) current theories about the world. That is, they are not constrained by semantic features or contrasts, nor are they learned. Because of her strong reliance on cognitive development in terms of models of physical reality, her theory appears to be related to Piaget's, although it is not a Piagetian model in the strict sense. It appears that her proposal would be consonant with the present view of the conceptual level of development, although I cannot undertake a comparative evaluation at this point because I have not yet had access to a more complete description of her model.

Vygotsky's theoretical assumptions are quite congenial to the present model when given a broad interpretation. Vygotsky (1962) viewed language as essentially social and the internalization of speech as the establishment of verbal thought, reaching a higher plane than that achievable by preverbal thought, its appearance in development coinciding with the appearance of logical memory, hypothesis formation, and true concepts. Vygotsky's discussion of the difference between "scientific" concepts and "spontaneous" concepts is especially interesting in connection with the developments proposed here.

Vygotsky (1962) equates spontaneous concepts with unconscious mental operations (in the present proposal, implicit or cryptic operations). He notes: "Scientific concepts, with their hierarchical system of interrelationships, seem to be the medium within which awareness and mastery first develop, to be transferred later to other concepts and other areas of thought" (p. 92). This claim is consistent with the proposal set forth earlier that the semantic level enables the establishment of hierarchical systems and is dependent upon metaprocesses involving reflection on previously established systems.

Again:

> It seems obvious that a concept can become subject to consciousness and deliberate control only when it is part of a system. If consciousness means generalization, generalization in turn means the formation of a superordinate concept that includes the given concept as a particular case. A superordinate concept implies the existence of a series of subordinate concepts, and it also presupposes a hierarchy of concepts of different levels of generality. (p. 92)

He illustrates this claim with the changing relation between *flower* and *rose*, reminiscent of Piaget's class-inclusion problems. At first, says Vygotsky, the concept *flower* is no more general for the child than the concept *rose*, although more widely applicable. When *flower* becomes generalized the relation between the two terms changes and "a system is taking shape . . . the rudiments of systematization first enter the child's mind by way of contact with scientific concepts and are then transferred to everyday concepts, changing their psychological structure from the top down" (p. 93).

In Vygotsky's scheme, then, hierarchicalization and systematization are products of instruction. In partial illustration of this relation, he describes an experiment contrasting the use of logical terms ("because" and "although") with scientific and spontaneous concepts by 8- and 10-year-old children. Contrary to intuitive expectations, these relations are better understood in scientific than in spontaneous contexts, the reason being, according to Vygotsky, that the scientific concepts exist

within a system of logical relations, while the spontaneous concepts do
not.

In conclusion, he states

> that the *absence of a system* is the cardinal psychological difference distin-
> guishing spontaneous from scientific concepts. It could be shown that all the
> peculiarities of child thought described by Piaget (such as syncretism, juxta-
> position, insensitivity to contradiction) stem from the absence of a system in
> the child's spontaneous concepts. (p. 116)

Most of this discussion is consonant with the claims made here about
the development of the semantic system, although the emphasis here
is not on scientific concepts as a separate type of concept but on the
establishment of systematic paradigmatic relations. Unlike Vygotsky,
here the young child's conceptual system is not considered to be un-
systematic but, rather, to be organized around situationally based, syntagmatically derived relations.

In contrast to Vygotsky's claim that language is essentially social, Piaget's theory (e.g., Piaget, 1970) tends to view language as an individual construction of the system of logic. The present theory does not
conflict with the findings of Inhelder and Piaget (1964) on semantic-
type tasks and long-term memory. However, it posits a more direct relation between language and thought and, in particular, suggests that
a level of thinking "in" language is responsible for many of the effects
attributable in the Piagetian system to the establishment of concrete
operations. For example, changes in performance on verbal classification
tasks can be explained in this model by the establishment of the semantic system rather than through a new level of reasoning. The goal
of the Piagetian theory is to explain the development of logical thought.
The goal of the present model is to explain how meaning is developed.
The two are not reducible to each other, although there are some points
of both agreement and conflict in their assumptions and conclusions.

Radical Nativism

The most direct challenge to any developmental theory of semantics
or cognition is set forth by Fodor (1975, 1981) in his defense of radical
nativism. Fodor defends the proposition that concepts are built into the
human mind, genetically determined. His most recent (1981) statement
regarding the status of concepts and their innate character contains a
number of clarifications and extensions of his earlier position on this
matter. In order to understand his position, it is necessary to keep in
mind that he takes "concept" to be essentially the equivalent of word

meaning, or the meaning of a lexical item. Moreover, he distinguishes between lexical concepts (expressed in a single word) and phrasal concepts (those expressed through a combination of words). The argument, to Fodor, is whether all lexical concepts are primitive, unlearned, and without internal structure (and therefore innate) or whether (characterized as the empiricist view) some have internal structure and are learned piecemeal. An important assumption behind his proposal is that the only possible model of learning is hypothesis testing. Then, reasoning that in order to test a hypothesis that concept X is associated with word W, one must first generate a possible candidate concept, and to do so indicates an ability to form the concept without learning, he argues that *all* concepts must be present *a priori*.

There is, however, no evidence that children engage in hypothesis testing as a learning process in acquiring terms of the language or, particularly, in acquiring the superordinate terms that are essential to the fully developed semantic system. All the evidence we have shows that hypothesis testing is an advanced and explicit form of thinking, that children are poor at it until late childhood, and that children change the rules of their language—grammatical or lexical—slowly and reluctantly in the face of conflicting data (see, e.g., Bickerton, 1981). As Piaget (1962) states: "The natural state of the mind is belief, and doubt or hypothesis are complex, derived behaviors whose development can be traced between the ages of seven and eleven up to the level of formal operations" (p. 167).

To the empiricist's surprise, Fodor turns to the mental chemistry of James Mill and John Stuart Mill for enlightenment. He points out that in the nineteenth-century theory of *associationism,* simple concepts (ideas) were held to be *generated* by the *fusion* of two or more other simple concepts. That is, simple concepts can combine, not in a logical, constructive, additive fashion, but through an unspecified mental function that produces new (simple) concepts from old ones. This leads Fodor to the proposal that he wants to defend, namely, (1) that all lexical concepts are in this sense innate, (2) that some are triggered by exposure to relevant stimuli in the environment, and (3) that some are produced by the mental chemistry process. None are learned; none have internal structure.

Fodor (1981) then tackles the problem of why some primitive concepts appear to be acquired before others. He concludes that "the structure of the triggering hierarchy [that determines the order in which concepts are attained] isn't natural from any *philosophical* point of view, though it may be quite natural from the point of view of an ethologist." And,

> The idea that, as it were, ontogeny recapitulates epistemology, is *hope-less* . . . If, therefore, you want to know which concepts are in fact normally triggered by encounters with their instances, you can't find out by doing conceptual analysis, and you can't find out by doing epistemology. *You have to go and look.* (p. 313, italics in original)

Further,

> Since all primitive concepts must ipso facto be learned, it looks as though the innate structure of the mind is going to be very rich indeed according to the present proposal. Our ethology promises to be quite interesting even if our developmental psychology turns out to be a little dull. (p. 314)

This version of Fodor's solipsistic theory is tightly argued, and its conclusions are hard to resist (see Bickerton, 1981; Carey, 1982; Macnamara, 1982). However, as noted previously, since word meanings are based on cultural conventions, a theory that rejects learning or development of any kind must be wrong. Let us see why.

First, if the most basic (triggered) layer of concepts is innately specified for the species as a whole, then not only would concepts be attained in a certain order but the concepts so attained would necessarily be the same for all children. For example, the word "cow" (or its equivalent in other languages) would specify *cow* for all children exposed to the same instances. The instance would trigger the innate concept. (Of course, a child might make a mistake and take "cow" to refer to *horse* or some other simultaneously experienced percept.) However, all studies of early naming behavior by young children (see Chapters 2 and 3) show that this is not the case. Not only do children's basic concepts extend to different instances than adults' but they also vary from child to child. Moreover, children do not easily acquire (as they should under a triggering theory) concepts that must be considered basic, for example, the concepts *tall, brother,* and *animal,* to take a few (see Anglin, 1977; E. V. Clark, 1973; Macnamara, 1982).

While Fodor may be on the right track in endorsing ethology rather than epistemology and mental chemistry rather than logical construction, a real problem arises when the data from word learning (Chapters 3 and 5) is considered. Lexical concepts change with development, as all recent research has shown. This is not simply a renaming; rather, the concept *car* frequently narrows from a subset of all vehicles, including truck, to a subset that matches the adult extension of the term. Terms such as "clock" are often extended, at first, to a broad and seemingly illogical set before becoming narrowed to the appropriate class (Bowerman, 1976; Rescorla, 1980; see also Chapter 3).

Most seriously, Fodor's closed solipsistic view allows no room for social–cultural input, for teaching beyond corrective feedback of hypothesis testing, or, indeed, for any of the characteristics of an open system, which the human conceptual system can only be.[7] The cognitive processes that are involved in lexical acquisition must incorporate the products of encounters with the world in a more direct way (see also Dennett, 1978).

All this aside, one cannot dispute the dual claims that (1) in order to learn the meaning of a word, one must have a concept for that meaning, and (2) that people do not always access the internal structure of a concept—whatever that is—when they process speech. (The latter point is also made by Lyons, 1977.) This, however, does not mean that *children* do not. There are no equivalent experiments with young children, but the interpretation given to semantic research with children outlined above indicates that children do indeed access internal structure and experientially based context when they interpret speech. (All this takes time, of course, and children do appear to be slow processors.)

As I have argued, meaning exists at many levels, and interpretation may require different levels of processing. Building up conceptual representations adequate to the semantic structure of the language takes years and much interaction with language speakers. In the end (by 7 to 10 years), the child has concepts available to be mapped into a lexical system; thus Fodor's proposition (1) holds, but not from the beginning. When so mapped at the semantic level, proposition (2) holds as well. That is, the "empty cell" model implied by Fodor's reasoning holds for the semantic—or sense—level outlined here, a level available for ordinary fast interpretation and reasoning by older children and adults and flexibly linked to the richly textured conceptual level. However, this is an achievement of early conceptual development in collaboration with the linguistic community and not an *a priori* given.

Convergence and Nonconvergence

This brief consideration of some developmental (and antidevelopmental) models is sufficient to indicate that there is wide agreement among developmentalists on the emergence of a level of verbal thought that is qualitatively different from previous thinking at some point between 5 and 10 years of age (for other examples, see Bruner, 1966; Luria, 1976; and White, 1965). The claims made here with respect to the achievement of a distinctively semantic level of organization, semiautomatic, semiautonomous, and accessible to explicit operations—and therefore simultaneously fast and reflective—is in one sense simply another statement of these pervasive ideas. That it is related to the emergence of a new level of an organized semantic system used in all language processing may be novel. On the other hand, nondevelopmentally oriented theories—taken from linguistics, philosophy, artificial intelligence, or cognitive psychology—for the most part are not in accord with these propositions; rather, they attempt to fit all acquisition phenomena into a single model of human cognitive–linguistic structure. Nonetheless, it is important to recognize that the final level of development achieved by the system must be in accord with phenomena that are accounted for by models of the adult system, even if no one such model is presently adequate to the developmental phenomena.

At the same time, developmental considerations may have important implications for adult models. One such implication of the present proposal is its positing of layers or levels of representation. Simultaneous representation at perceptual, situational–contextual, conceptual, and semantic levels suggests reasons why contradictory theories of representation and processing in the human cognitive system may each contain some of the truth. Such simultaneous representation is generally consistent with a number of developmental theories, especially that of Werner (Werner, 1948; Werner & Kaplan, 1963).[8]

The findings that adults in psychological experiments may give evidence of prototypical conceptual structures composed of more or less typical members (Rosch et al., 1976) but may also find it perfectly sensible and "right" to provide necessary and sufficient features for category membership of even less typical members or to provide prototypes for well-defined categories (Gleitman, Armstrong, & Gleitman, 1983) are relevant to this position as well. Similarly, subjects may provide event features when asked to list characteristics of *lunch* but event scripts when asked the same about *eating lunch* (Rifkin, 1984). And, although they will provide neat predicability trees when given careful instructions to say whether a sentence makes sense (Keil, 1979), they will find sentences violating the constraints of the predicability tree interpretable when provided with less constraining instructions (Gerard & Mandler, 1983). The list of contradictory results (and their resulting contradictory theories) could be multiplied. The point is that these results can only be reconciled by recognizing that the cognitive system is multilayered and that words do not simply access either semantic representations or concepts, but may access at least these as well as percepts, representations of events, and specific episodic memories. All of these may enter into performance on a given task. Unfortunately, constraining subjects by giving them instructions presumed to be specific to a particular "layer" (e.g., Keil, 1979) presupposes the characteristics of that layer. The advantage of the developmental approach is that it provides a way of unpeeling the layers, so to speak, in order to view their characteristics as they develop.

Summary and Implications

In this and the previous chapter the effort has been to show that phenomena of conceptual and semantic development are inherently interrelated and that many of the cognitive characteristics attributed to the young child are a function of the still undifferentiated conceptual–semantic system. In turn, the greater facility of the child of 5 to 10 years in manipulating symbols, engaging in verbal reasoning tasks, working with hierarchical inclusion relations, and treating words in terms of their lexical relations rather than their conceptual contents are all held to be functions of the establishment of a level of purely symbolic semantic relationships. The differentiation of this level, it is claimed, has broad implications for cognitive tasks of all kinds that involve symbolization in language. Thus, the establishment of a semantic system has implications far beyond those of the processes of word learning and word meaning.

Moreover, because the system is culturally defined and culturally transmitted, the establishment of this system is dependent upon the child's interactions with knowledgeable others, who either through direct instruction or participatory interactions allowing implicit learning transmit the significant relationships of the system to the child. It is not until the child's conceptual system has developed appropriate structure, as described in Chapter 7, that these relationships can be identified within the child's own system and thus abstracted at a new level. Thus, the individual cognitive system, the culturally defined semantic system, and the social interaction with others all work together to establish a shared meaning system that incorporates sense relationships as well as denotation and reference.

Notes

[1]Verbs, adjectives, and adverbs do not lend themselves to these kinds of questions but can be fitted to hierarchical structures through nominalization or through modification by adverbs. Whether or not this is an appropriate semantic representation for the subjective lexicon has been questioned, however (see Huttenlocher & Lui, 1979).

[2]This may be taken as the classical nominalist position that general categories are not real but only exist as names. However, the position here is different in that it is the *relation* between superordinate and subordinate terms that is claimed to be essentially symbolic.

[3]This is not to denigrate the conceptual mode, which produces richer, more creative connections but is slower and more difficult to manipulate because of this. It should be noted that in this conception *symbolic* thought begins at age 6 or 7 in our culture, while *representational* thought begins in infancy (cf. Piaget, 1962; see also Bruner *et al.*, 1966).

[4]Object sorting does not qualify for the reasons given earlier. Symbol systems are essential to hierarchical classification.

[5]Analogy and metaphor are found in the young child's language and thought, but like the rest of the language system are at that point constrained by the conceptual system. Their mature uses, for example, X is to Y as A is to B, rely on the analysis of relationships, not on isolated features or situational context. It is interesting that Premack (Premack & Premack, 1983) found that only apes trained to use a symbolic system can solve problems of this kind.

[6]Although it is interesting that in American middle-class culture colors used to be learned at a later age—around 5 years according to Ilg & Ames (1955).

[7]Fodor: "The organism is a closed system proposing hypotheses to the world, and the world then chooses among them in terms explicated by some system of inductive logic." Wilden: "I am surprised that anyone should consider an organism a closed system . . . the organism is open in three senses: open to material forms of order, open to energetic forms of order, and open to informational forms of order" (Fodor, 1980, pp. 152–153).

[8]Werner and Kaplan (1963) outline three "fields" (perceptual–motor, lexical–conceptual, and symbolic–syntactic) that can be related to the tripartite meaning system suggested here. Discussing the connections in detail would take us too far afield, however.

IV

Conclusion

9

Cognition, Context, and Culture

Aspects of a Shared Meaning System

This book began with the assertion that semantic development represents a problem in the development of a shared meaning system. The complexities of this way of viewing the problem have occupied the ensuing discussion, and it is time to consider the broader implications of this view, the problems it entails, and the questions it leaves open.

First, it has been claimed that meaning is tripartite in nature and cannot be considered as a unitary concept. The evolved system consists of three parts: the cognitive representation of meaning, the communicative context of meaning, and the conventional meaning of words within the linguistic–cultural community. These three different ways of viewing meaning can also be seen as representing meaning for oneself, for one's communicative partners, and for the community at large. They have been characterized here within one view of semantics as representing denotation, reference, and sense, respectively. It is important not to confuse these different aspects of meaning, although each may play a necessary role on a given occasion of language use.

The cognitive representation of meaning involves an interpretive–expressive system that calls on all functions of the individual's cognitive system, including perception, memory, schematic representations of events, concepts, categories, lexicon, and grammar. The cognitive system is the concern of cognitive psychology, developmental psychology, and psycholinguistics. Because it undergoes development during infancy and childhood, its role in interpreting and expressing meaning also changes during this period. In particular, the development of the child's conceptual system plays an important part in the changing way that words mean over the early childhood period.

The communicative context of meaning determines specifically what a word may mean on a given occasion of use. Understanding meaning in these terms requires consideration of the different kinds of discourse contexts that may be involved, speech acts, conversational conventions, and personal agendas and intentions, among others. These are matters of social psychology, sociolinguistics, and pragmatics. They enter into semantic development because the child must come to understand how words are used and mean within particular contexts; moreover, as we have seen, context of use may determine whether a word is understood at all.

The conventional meaning determines how a word is commonly interpreted within a given cultural community and how this word relates to other words in the language. This aspect of meaning is the concern of linguistic semantics, philosophy, and anthropology. While conventional meaning is not all there is to semantic development, and while it has been claimed here that it is a late achievement of the child, it is nonetheless essential that the child master the basic structures and meanings as they are conventionally represented in the community.

The problem of achieving shared meaning differs for each of these meaning systems. The cognitive aspect requires coordinating one's concepts with those with whom one shares ideas. The contextual aspect requires coordinating one's interpretations of communicative contexts with those of others in different social situations. The cultural aspect requires bringing one's subjective lexicon into coordination with that of the linguistic community. While these requirements are different, they are also obviously interrelated.

The three aspects of meaning can then be seen to move in ever larger contexts from individual to the social group to the community at large.[1] However, in development the move proposed is different, that is, from social context to individual conception to conventional representation, or from reference to denotation to sense. This movement has been laid out in the previous chapters and will be briefly recapitulated in the next section.

At this point it should be noted that when viewed in this way, *the study of language development in general and semantic development in particular is basically a problem in the acquisition of culture.* As children learn to interpret the language in different contexts and to hone their concepts to fit the words as others use them, they are taking on aspects of the culture as it is symbolized in the language and in conversational structures acceptable to the community. Through talk children learn what important distinctions are made in the language and how words are related to each other. The cultural lessons of early childhood are often indirect but nonetheless effective in conveying what is and what should be in the community. The acquisition of lexical structure is one manifestation of the acquisition of cultural forms. Regrettably, acquisitions of this general kind have been little studied and are little understood.

The other side of this perspective is that the interiorization of cultural norms through language requires the cognitive representation of all three aspects of meaning: concept, context, and culture. Thus, the first (individual) aspect of meaning for self comes to incorporate the other two. It is to elucidate this result that the model of conceptual development put forth here has been worked out.

Lexical Development as a Cognitive Problem

Because development of meaning is an essentially interactive process, its study can be approached in many ways. The approach taken here is from the point of view of developmental psychology, emphasizing the development of the individual child while recognizing that the child exists within a system of personal relationships crucial to that development. The model of development set forth here is designed to meet the conceptual and semantic representational requirements of the developing meaning system. However flawed this model may turn out to be, the problems addressed will remain. These problems include: (1) an explanation for how children can share meaning without full understanding, (2) a description of how meanings are represented and how they change, and (3) an explanation of how knowledge of semantic structures arises. Without addressing these problems, understanding word learning and the development of word meaning is not possible.

The proposed model of representational development can be summarized in terms of phases and levels. There are three essential phases: (1) getting into language, the prelexical phase; (2) establishing shared meaning, the conceptual phase; and (3) developing a conventional system, the semantic phase. The following levels within the cognitive system are essential to this description (although they are not exhaustive of cognitive functions): the perceptual, the event representation, the conceptual (with various sublevels, as described in Chapter 6), and the semantic. (Note that no action level is proposed here; action exists within a different system of relationships.) These levels are not static or autonomous but are dynamic interactive knowledge structures. As the system develops content enlarges, organization increases, and relationships among the levels change. Essential to these changes is the assumption that the knowledge structures are subject to continuing analysis and synthesis processes, producing new relationships—in effect, new knowledge—even in the absence of new input. That is, the child's cognitive system is actively engaged in organizing knowledge. Word meanings expand and contract in accord with these organizations, and word learning is made possible as world knowledge becomes organized.

The Prelexical Phase

In the prelexical phase words do not have meaning per se. The child begins to respond to words and to use some words in well-practiced action schemes or in conjunction with routines or social formats. Children can be observed to understand the structure of certain routine events, for example, bath time. That is, they display expectancies with respect to the people and objects involved, the sequence of activities, and the reciprocity and contingency of actions. These expectancies go beyond the action schemes operating on objects; they involve as well actions and intentions of others and interrelationships of people and objects. It is proposed, therefore, that the child has representations of familiar events, or scripts. That is, the child has developed a level of event representations, although it appears that these are wholistic, not dissoluble into their parts. Thus, words may be used within them or to refer to the event as a whole but do not successfully refer to its parts.

The assumption of a level of event representations may appear unnecessary. In other models it has been claimed that action or gesture precedes and leads into the acquisition of words. Or, it is suggested that the communicative action games mothers play with babies (e.g., "give and take") support the acquisition of words. Or, it is claimed that mothers interpret children's vocalizations in terms of intentions that then become internalized by the child as meaning. None of these involves a level of representation, whether of events or of concepts. However, the claim here is that words do not attach themselves meaningfully to actions, whether the child's own or in conjunction with others. Meaning is not expressed in action; action does not represent meaning. Rather, meaning is a cognitive concept. When the child has a meaning for a word, this implies a mental representation of some kind. Although words may become attached to actions by the young child (e.g., saying "vroom" while pushing a truck across the floor) or by the adult (e.g., the soldier who responds by pulling the trigger when he hears "fire!"), they do not acquire meaning thereby. We do not accept that "vroom" means "push truck" or that "fire" means "pull trigger" except by stretching the ordinary meaning of meaning.

The essential claim here is that the child cannot get to language through action alone. Action must become represented on the cognitive level if it is to enter into the meaning system. In the present proposal, the level of event representations is the level at which actions, as well as people and objects, become represented. By the same token children cannot get into language solely by having their vocalizations interpreted by others. The child's intentions will remain inchoate unless they are articulated with a level of representation in which conditions in the world can be represented. It is possible for the child to learn word forms to use in communicative situations (e.g., ''I want'' or ''Thank you'') without any other cognitive representation, but these do not thereby acquire meaning on the cognitive level, although they may meet communicative context conditions. In short, understanding the world in action and conversing with an interpretive partner may be essential to the language-learning process, but they are not sufficient to establish a meaning system. The prelexical phase can be best understood in terms of words associated with actions or with communicative routines.

Note that the role of the event representation here is a paradoxical one; it serves to support the child's initial move into language use, and it serves as a source of concepts that are associated with words as the child moves into the meaningful use of language. Prior to the conceptual phase, the child may use words to name things, to accompany actions, and to refer to situations. The child must achieve the realization that meaning is based on concepts and not on context alone. Toward this end, words and referents interact to bring about the partition of the wholistic event representation and to allow the naming of concepts so partitioned (see Chapter 6).

This view of early development has two emphases that distinguish it from otherwise similar views. First, it emphasizes the essential role of the development of conceptual representation independent of but interactive with language development. Second, it emphasizes the child's *participation* in events as the source of conceptual knowledge rather than simply the child as agent of instrumental action. *Participatory interaction* is seen as essential to the child's acquisition of meaning, not only because language is used within interactive contexts but because these contexts provide the structures that make mutual interpretation possible; structures of action, causality, contingency, reciprocity, and role-taking are essential to understanding the meanings encoded in language. Without the social interactive basis for conceptualization, the child's meanings would be confined to concepts of small objects, and both language and thought as we know it would be thereby impossible.

The Conceptual Phase

The conceptual phase of lexical development begins with reference. There comes a point when the child understands that words are not just used in situations, they refer. It has been suggested here that the necessary underpinning for understanding reference is a level of mental representation. The child may begin by understanding that a word picks out or indexes a particular object; this can be achieved by a primitive (nonrepresentational) form of reference. To go beyond this limited understanding, the child needs to have a mental representation or concept to stand for what the word denotes or may be used to refer to. The child's source of such concepts is the event representation, which provides information about what things are used for within the general scheme. Partitioning concepts from event representations and learning words to signify them are processes that go hand in hand. Then, as concepts become independently represented, they may be combined with other concepts to form the basis for novel propositions in language.

The development of a separate level of independent concepts may also be challenged as unnecessary on the grounds that once the child learns the word–referent relationship, he is off and running and concept development has nothing to do with it. However, as reviewed in Chapter 3, research suggests that understanding the word–referent relationship is long in coming and that it is not an obvious relationship to most children younger than 18 months or so. Understanding (that is, responding appropriately) and even using words may take place without the understanding of reference per se. Once reference is grasped, however, it supports rapid learning of object names. What delays its understanding? The answer put forth here is that reference cannot be established at the perceptual level alone; the conceptual level is needed in order for the child to understand that concepts determine what can be referred to by a word.

Considerable development of the system takes place within the conceptual phase, including the analysis of concepts and the relating of concepts to each other both syntagmatically and paradigmatically, resulting in new conceptual organizations. These developments are reflected in the changing abilities of preschool children to use hierarchical relationships in the language and to relate words out of context. That words still remain tied to concepts and event representations is revealed in a number of research findings, most strikingly for object names in the phenomenon of nominal realism and for relational terms in their correct use only in well-understood contexts (see Chapter 5). Thus, the period of conceptual meaning enables the child to share meanings appropriately in familiar situations with familiar others, but the fact that meanings still inhere in the child's concepts delays the attainment of a level of conventional meanings. As children exchange meanings with others during this period, their concepts become more like those of others in their social world (i.e., more socialized), but they may still be "childish" (i.e., unconventional).

One way of viewing the ensuing development is to suppose that as the child's concepts become more and more socialized, they come into line with the semantic system of the parent language. However, there are both psychological and linguistic arguments against this proposal. First, it is psychologically unrealistic to assume that the individual's conceptual system and event representation system somehow dissolve into a monolithic semantic system. Both of these established components of the cognitive system are needed to account for the interpretation of language (among other things) by adults as well as children. Second, while conceptual knowledge is necessary to the interpretation of language in use, there is clearly a level of semantic relationships that is not dependent upon the individual's mental state but rather is defined in the language independent of any individual. (This is presumably the aspect of meaning that Macnamara [1982] states must be constant across all members of a speech community, but the present use of the term considers this aspect to be only one part of meaning.) However, for the child to grasp the language as a whole, this level of meaning must be attained in addition to the subjective interpretation of words within the individual conceptual system.

The Semantic Phase

The development of an independent semantic level was considered primarily in terms of the establishment of hierarchical systems of words within lexical fields. While this is the clearest example, based on the available empirical literature, there are certainly other types of structures and relationships that are learned in and are dependent upon language itself. When this level is achieved, words can be manipulated independently of concepts. Language becomes an autonomous and automatic system. The child can begin to think *in* language and *about* language. Obviously, words do not lose their conceptual meanings, but words and concepts no longer stand in a one-to-one relationship to each other. Further, words can be learned *from* language, not only in nonlinguistic contexts, and the abstractness of the semantic level leads to the establishment of meanings of relational terms that are no longer contextually determined. The claim here is that all of these phenomena are related and all are the result of the establishment of a separate semantic level of representation not previously present. Beyond the identification of these phenomena, however, development within this level has not been considered in this discussion. No doubt it is subject to considerable change during the school years.

Lexical Development as a Social Context Problem

The child learns and uses language in specific social contexts. As discussed in Chapter 2, the child's understanding of these contexts is essential to understanding how words are used within them. Thus, psychologically, interpretation of context precedes interpretation of words. That this is true by no means implies that understanding context makes the interpretation of language clear or easy. As has been often noted, any context may lead to any number of different statements, questions, exclamations, or commands. For this reason the repetitive use of certain language forms in consistent contexts may enable the child to identify these forms and their referents in this situational context.

Context is a complex notion. It is all too easy to assert that context supports language or that language becomes decontextualized without specifying what aspect of context is operating in these processes. As has been emphasized throughout, the notion of context can only be considered within a model of how the child comes to represent different contexts. Thus, context cannot be disentangled from mental representation.

This point can be made from a different perspective by noting that contexts are ephemeral; only by understanding how the child's mind gets hold of, holds onto, and organizes the regularities in contexts can one understand how context plays a role in supporting language use. Here the script model put forth in Chapter 2 plays an essential role. The notion is that through participatory interaction the child builds up scripts for familiar events that include action as well as language. These mental representations of situations enable the child to take her place in interactions within these contexts. As language is used to refer within scripted situations, the child can begin to interpret shared reference and may partition the script into its component parts, forming concepts of those things referred to. Thus, word, context, and concept work together to enable the child to move into meaningful language, language that may be used outside of its original context.

The contexts in which language is used with young children are relatively limited. The most studied is the dyadic play situation but, as noted in Chapter 4, this situation may not be typical of children's experience. Caretaking routines appear to provide conditions within which children can get a handle on both the situational structure and language use. Of equal importance and interest is the fact that the language used within similar contexts by different mothers provides different language experiences that result in different acquisition patterns for different children. Some mothers provide referential language, whether they are naming pictures in books or eating lunch, while others provide formulaic models of "what to say" that are appropriate within different social contexts. Research suggests that the referential model is more likely to facilitate the move into conceptual, meaningful language use on the child's part.

Of course, even though children may learn to use language within familiar family-based contexts, sooner or later they must extend their meanings to uses within the larger community, whether that includes preschools, playgrounds, city streets, schools, or work places. How children make these transitions has not been much examined, at least not from a cognitive or language-centered view. One result of these extensions is the necessity of accommodating conceptual meanings that may have been quite restricted to word use within larger social groups. This move is a move toward greater conventionalization. That this is not an unproblematic move is evident in the case studies of children who develop "private languages" that serve for some years within their families, or perhaps only with their siblings, but that cannot be understood outside these groups (e.g., Luria & Yudovich, 1959), thus requiring remedial training for the children involved. Eventually, children are exposed to the abstract demands of language in the school context, a social context that has its own unique properties. School language may provide the impetus for the organization of the highly conventionalized semantic structures that become evident by 7 or 8 years of age. This is a problem that the present discussion cannot give adequate consideration to, however.

In any event, by mid-childhood most children have begun to use words with consistent meanings across situational contexts and are able to reflect on their meanings in order to provide definitions out of the usual context of use. This by no means suggests that meaning has become decontextualized; rather, it implies that context can be used to aid in interpreting meaning on a particular occasion of use but does not constrain meaning to that or any other particular context.

Lexical Development as a Cultural Problem

Culture, like language, is a relatively enduring set of practices realized within a symbolic system. Like language, it varies, while exhibiting universal functions. Thus, like language, it must be acquired. In particular, whatever the universal structures of culture or language, the meanings associated with particular forms must be mastered by children who grow up within a given cultural–linguistic community. Language is, of course, a form of culture as well as a carrier of culture. The lexicon of a language is in this sense a cultural given. Individuals may acquire some part of it, but no individual masters all of it.[2] Putnam's (1975) emphasis on the division of linguistic labor brings out the point that adults, as well as children, have only partial knowledge of the conventional meanings of a language. On the other hand, children begin from scratch to master meaning structures, and they do it without knowing the complexities and the systematic properties of the problem. The resources they begin with are, in fact, inadequate to the task, and much of what they learn turns out to be wrong and must be abandoned. For example, they must abandon the notions that all rounds things are called "ball," that all tall things are "big," that all big things are "old," and so on.

It might seem that it would be an advantage to the child to begin with some notion of hierarchical structures or with a set of semantic features with which to parse meanings rather than beginning with contextualized reference and experience-based concepts, both of which lack generality, much less universality. Yet, while each child's experience is a sample from the culture at large, nonetheless that experience provides a variable base within which understanding of language forms can become established. Abstraction and universal meanings are not essential to young children. What is essential is acquisition of knowledge of how their own part of the world works. Once this knowledge is acquired, it can be analyzed for general features and patterns, and these features and patterns can be matched to the more abstract structures that are exhibited in and often directly taught through language.

The suggestion that the lexical structure of the language may depend to a large degree upon didactic teaching, unlike the grammatical structure which, from all evidence, does not, implies that that structure is conventional and culture specific. Of course, there are universal distinctions (Greenberg, 1966) such as plant and animal, male and female, parent and child. There may be as well, as Lyons (1977) suggests, a universal tendency to think in terms of bifurcating contrasts, which is reflected in lexical structures. Nonetheless, none of these examples is specific to the language; rather, they appear to reflect basic ways of structuring human thought and experience. Indeed, because lexical knowledge must reflect cultural knowledge, it must be dependent to some extent upon teaching. Moreover, from first word to first grade to college classroom, much of teaching by parent and teacher is concerned with instilling knowledge of the relevant lexicon. It is commonly observed that parents rarely correct the young child's grammar, but they frequently correct the young child's word use. The child's errors in naming, while sometimes tolerated (as when the 15-month-old calls both dogs and cats "doggie"), appear to be highly salient to parents, who attempt to substitute correct terms for inappropriate ones whenever possible.

It is in the area of the hierarchical taxonomies of the language that the notion that lexical structure is taught appears to be controversial. There is apparently a very strong conviction on the part of many psychologists that hierarchical thinking is a basic characteristic of the human mind, and that the fine points of such structures may have to be acquired, but that the ability to form nested categories and classes as such is a human given (e.g., Macnamara, 1982). This view has to deal with the evidence that young children do not appear to understand categories in the same way that older children and adults do (see Chapter 5). Young children can group objects and think in terms of collections, but general terms such as "animal" are used collectively and not to refer to decomposable classes. In the face of this evidence, one may fall back upon the Piagetian argument of the development of logical classification; or, one may rely on some version of a maturation argument; or, one may accept the present argument that such structures depend upon the manipulation of symbolic forms and that the achievement of such manipulation is a joint function of demonstration by others and an abstraction of lexical terms from their conceptual base. This position does not deny that the child's mind has the potential for forming and manipulating hierarchical structures, but it emphasizes the dependence of this ability also upon the potential of the symbolic form of human language. In this regard language may be thought of as a prosthetic device for human thinking; written symbols—words, numbers, or other symbols—afford an even greater elaboration of the possibilities of such hierarchical classifications.

Some years ago Deese (1969) suggested that "natural" hierarchies might be constrained to a single level. This suggestion is similar to Rosch's (1975) identification of a "basic level" of categorization. If we interpret "natural" or "basic" to mean unaided by cultural–linguistic imposition, these proposals are quite consonant with that put forth here. But I would go further to suggest that in order to be used flexibly and in elaborate classification schemes, words must be free of conceptual implications. Thus, development within the cognitive system is necessary as well. It may be that in unschooled, nonliterate cultures such development does not take place. This seems to be the import of Luria's

(1976) observations of the practical classifications of peasants in postre-volutionary Russia.

In our own complex society a great deal of effort is expended on bringing children into the complexities of modern technologically based classification systems. This effort begins at home, is extended in pre-schools, where attributes of color and shape are taught and categories such as *clothes, food,* and *animals* are explicitly emphasized, and cul-minates in grade-school classrooms. Even television is not exempt, as brief exposure to programs such as Sesame Street, aimed at young chil-dren, quickly confirms.

"The structures of culture, whether primarily referential, like lan-guage, or primarily figurative, like ritual, are highly formalized . . . in order that they may be learned and reproduced with a high degree of conformity to norms despite the passage of time and the entry and exit of individuals from the culturally constructed scene" (Foster & Brandes, 1980, p. 271). It is the argument here that the formalisms of lexical structure are taught and that children are brought into the conformity to norms only gradually as they learn these formalizations. However, the formalizations build upon preformal structures that have their source in the child's conceptualization of experience, this in turn being influ-enced by how parents structure and talk about that experience. The final product is the result of this complex interaction between social context, concept, and culture.

In summary, we can put the matter in the following terms. Culture, like language, is a relatively enduring symbolic system. The context of language use is ephemeral, nonenduring. Event representations, con-cepts, and words are the individual's way of dealing with the enduring and the ephemeral simultaneously, making the ephemeral enduring and finding enduring cultural order in ephemeral presentations.

Conclusion: The Problems of Semantic Development

In Chapter 1 eight questions were set out with the claim that these must be addressed by a theory of semantic development. Some of these have received clear answers, while others remain as problems to be ad-dressed in future work. By way of a summary of where we have come and where we may go from here, I present brief answers to these ques-tions here.

1. *How is knowledge of the world organized and conceptualized by the child and how does this system develop?* As stressed throughout,

the child's meaning system operates by converging on an interpretation from the conceptual system and from the context of use to assign a unique meaning that is shared between speakers on any given occasion. Given that knowledge of the world and its conceptualization may differ between speakers and, in particular, between child and adult, understanding the development of the conceptual system is necessary to understanding how words are given meaning.

The development of the child's conceptual system was considered in some detail in Chapters 3 and 7 and has been reviewed above. Briefly, the system evolves from representation of whole events to partitioned concepts related to one another through contextual event relations to analysis of whole concepts into components that form the basis for a new level of relations. Relations between concepts are initially syntagmatic, and the first paradigmatic relations are based on substitutability in events. Componential analysis makes possible the identification of paradigmatic relations based on contrasts and similarity between concepts, which in turn provide the basis for the structuring of a specifically lexical system of relationships. The continued existence of a level of event representations provides the basis for interpretation of context.

2. *How are language terms learned at different points in development?* This question has been considered at various points, and the proposals were summarized in Chapters 7 and 8. Basically, the claim is that words are learned from their contexts of use. When the child first begins to learn a few language terms, they may be learned only through reference to an immediately apparent object or situation or they may be learned as part of the structure of an event. However, by midway into the second year, words may be learned in reference to concepts that have been disembedded from the representation of event context, and at this point the word will be embedded as part of the concept structure. Words may be attached to preexisting concepts, but concepts may also be constructed to fit newly learned words. Only later when the lexical system is differentiated can words be learned solely from their use in linguistic contexts without experientially based conceptual content, as they may be in school.

3. *How are language terms used at different points in development? How does use affect meaning?* As implied in the answer to the previous question and throughout this discussion, learning, meaning, and use are closely related. At first, the child may confine use of terms to a particular context and for a particular referent or a particular communicative function. In early childhood terms may continue to be used in more restricted contexts than adult meaning allows. In Chapter 7 the effect of context on use during this period was seen to be different for

relational terms than for substantive terms. The former were said to be event-bound and the latter concept-bound during early childhood. This means that generalization across event contexts determines use of relational terms, while the composition of concepts determines how substantive terms can be used. It was pointed out that deriving meaning from use makes it possible for a child to confine her own word use to appropriate contexts, thus avoiding numerous errors, even when the child's meaning of a term only partially matches that of the adult's. Thus, the effect of use on meaning is to confine productive uses to a narrower range of contexts than for the adult and to lead to possible misinterpretations of meaning in unfamiliar contexts. When semantic representation frees the word from its conceptual base, terms may be used across strange as well as familiar contexts. Thus, the child first learns to use context to interpret meaning and later uses meaning to interpret context.

4. *How are word meanings constructed at different points in development?* In the present conception meaning is an interpretive–intentional system that subsumes all three components of meaning—reference, denotation, and sense. This tripartite system depends upon, respectively, perception, conception, and lexicon. Words are given meanings in contexts through reference, that is, what is being pointed to perceptually or linguistically; through denotation, calling upon the conceptual system to establish what is conceptually implied by and entailed by the term; through sense, calling upon the lexical system to establish the place of the word in relation to other words; or through all three systems interactively. That words can be appropriately interpreted in context and can be used to express intentions in appropriate contexts requires (1) that the user can establish a cognitive context that matches in relevant ways the parameters of the experiential context, (2) that the term can be given some interpretation by its user through its perceptual, conceptual, or lexical relationships, (3) that that interpretation matches the requirements of the established context, and (4) that that interpretation is shared by the conversational partner or partners. Each new use (interpretive or intentional) has the potential for adjusting the term's perceptual, conceptual, or lexical representation. Thus, operations of the system are consistent over development.

What changes with development is the potential use of the different parts of the interpretive system and the composition of these parts. The perceptual system plays a role from the outset, the conceptual system becomes available as language is being learned, and the lexical system only becomes established after language is in use. Thus, in the fully developed system word meanings are constructed within all three systems (when relevant), but in the still developing system word meanings may depend upon only one or two of the relevant constituents.

5. *How are language terms organized and related to each other at different points in development and how does this organization change?* In line with the tripartite nature of the system proposed here, language terms are assumed to be organized within different systems during development. At the outset terms are organized within event representations. During the subsequent period of early childhood, substantive language terms are organized within concepts, and their relations to one another are those established within the conceptual system, derived from experiential contexts. Later, the lexical level becomes differentiated and relations between terms reflect the paradigmatic relations of componential similarity and contrast. One system does not replace the next; rather, the system as a whole becomes more complex, allowing for multiple representations for different functional purposes.

6. *How are the domains of conceptualization and semantics related to one another and how do these relations change with development?* The model proposed views the domains of conceptualization and semantics as undifferentiated in early childhood, becoming differentiated and interactive as the lexical level becomes separated from the conceptual between 3 and 5 years. When lexical domains and relational sytems based on paradigmatic analysis of conceptual components are established, words can be used and interpreted independently of their conceptual and event-based connections. Hierarchical relations between words are established, metalinguistic operations can be performed, and words may be entered into lexical "slots" that give them an interpretation on the basis of their relations to other words.

7. *How do these relations affect performance on language tasks at different points in development?* Research on comprehension, memory for word lists, definitions, word associations, category production, nominal realism, and metalinguistic tasks was reviewed in Chapter 5, and performance changes were observed in all of these paradigms during early to mid-childhood. The differentiation of conceptual and lexical systems during this period was shown in Chapter 7 to account for these changes in the following ways. Correct production of relational terms is first confined to event contexts that match the child's event representations, while comprehension in contexts without such support is error prone, indicating the event binding of these terms that are not yet established on a separate semantic level. Hierarchical categories in list recall and related paradigms is poor in early childhood unless based on event slot-filler categories. Definitions in early childhood reflect conceptual content but not lexical relations of the paradigmatic type. Word

associations reflect situational and other syntagmatic conceptual relations but not paradigmatic relations until school age. Category-production tasks reveal small, fragmented categories, presumably based on slot-filler categories. Nominal-realism questions reveal the indissoluble word–concept bond in early childhood, which dissolves by 7 or 8 years. Metalinguistic tasks (e.g., "What is a word?") are not understood by young children, who have not yet disembedded their lexical representations from the event-based conceptual level.

In contrast to the difficulties that young children have on these (somewhat strange) language tasks is their facility in using terms appropriately in context. The proposal here is that their event representations and conceptualizations support their spontaneous uses in appropriate ways, but that the analysis of those uses that would provide a more abstract level of relation representation is a delayed process that takes place only after use in context is well established.

8. *How does developmental change in the system take place?* As always in a developmental model, this is the most difficult question to address and the one that leaves the greatest room for further investigation. The following processes were suggested as accounting for changes in the system:

1. Implicit learning of structure is an established but as yet poorly understood process that must be invoked to account for the child's representation and abstraction of the structure of events, including the language used within them.
2. Analysis of representations yields first concepts from events and later components of concepts, and later still comparison of components. It is assumed that such analysis at a deep level is an ongoing function of the cognitive system that accounts, in general, for cognitive organization, intuitive thought, and some kinds of creative problem solving.
3. Integration of components yielded by the analysis produces new combinations and reorganizations of concepts. Integration of new experiences and uses into the old system induces changes that may be either minor or major.
4. Direct instruction from others may instigate, hasten, or facilitate the process of organization. Although direct instruction is unsuccessful when the child's own system is not yet developed, it may be highly successful when a sufficient basis for a particular system is in place.

The proposal that the acquisition of cognitive systems is a process with its own general principles of development was set forth in the cognitive pendulum theory (Nelson & Nelson, 1978). Lexical development is a special case of such development and as such would be expected to follow the general course from broad, general rules to specific, separate rules to integration of rule systems, followed by increased flexibility and explicit processing. The general thesis that the development of a system follows its own structural imperatives, moving toward greater integration, automaticity, and flexibility is implicit in the developments described here.

Making sense, then, is a never-ending problem involving context, concept, and culture, for the child as well as the adult. To share meaning on any particular occasion requires that one share context, world knowledge, and knowledge of the language system with communicative partners. As a child's mastery of these sources of knowledge expands, her ability to make sense, to self and to others, increases accordingly. But these sources are not independent: They feed back on each other, supporting new levels of sense-making as development proceeds and as the child takes her place in ever-widening cultural contexts.

Notes

[1]A different way of looking at how meaning moves from smaller to larger context is from word to sentence to discourse. We cannot consider here how this notion of linguistic context of meaning crosscuts the psychological–sociological–anthropological course we have outlined.

[2]This may not hold for primitive cultures, but it clearly holds for modern technological cultures like ours.

Bibliography

Abelson, R. P. (1981). Psychological status of the script concept. *American Psychologist, 36*(7), 715–729.

Acredolo, L. P. (1979). Laboratory vs. home: The effect of environment on the 9-month-old infant's choice of spatial reference system. *Developmental Psychology, 15,* 585–593.

Ainsworth, M. D. S., & Bell, S. M. (1974). Mother–infant interaction and the development of competence. In K. Connolly & J. Brown (Eds.), *The growth of competence.* New York: Academic Press.

Al-Issa, I. (1969). The development of word definitions in children. *Journal of Genetic Psychology, 14,* 25–28.

Allen, D. A. (1977, March). *The development of propositional speech in young children.* Paper presented at the Society for Research in Child Development Biennial Conference, New Orleans, LA.

Allen, R. (1983). *The influence of information context and activity frames on the very young child's interpretation of conversational messages.* Unpublished doctoral dissertation, City University of New York, New York.

Allen, R., & Reber, A. S. (1980). Very long term memory for tacit knowledge. *Cognition, 8,* 175–185.

Amidon, A., & Carey, P. (1972). Why five-year-olds cannot understand before and after. *Journal of Verbal Learning and Verbal Behavior, 11,* 417–425.

Andersen, E. S. (1975). Cups and glasses: Learning that boundaries are vague. *Journal of Child Language, 2,* 79–104.

Anderson, A. L. N., & Prawat, R. S. (1983). When is a cup not a cup? A further examination of form and function in children's labelling responses. *Merrill-Palmer Quarterly, 29,* 375–385.

Anderson, J. R. (1978). Arguments concerning representations for mental imagery. *Psychological Review, 85,* 249–277.

Anglin, J. M. (1977). *Word, object, and conceptual development.* New York: Norton.

Anglin, J. M. (1983). Extensional aspects of the preschool child's word concepts. In T. Seiler & W. Wannenmacher (Eds.), *Concept development and the development of word meaning.* New York: Springer-Verlag.

Ashmead, D. H., & Perlmutter, M. (1980). Infant memory in everyday life. In M. Perlmutter (Ed.), *Children's memory*. San Francisco: Jossey-Bass.

Austin, J. S. (1962). *How to do things with words*. Oxford: Oxford University Press.

Barrett, M. D. (1978). Lexical development and overextension in child language. *Journal of Child Language, 5,* 205–219.

Barrett, M. D. (1982). The holophrastic hypothesis: Conceptual and empirical issues. *Cognition, 11,* 47–76.

Bartlett, E. J. (1976). Sizing things up: The acquisition of the memory of dimensional adjectives. *Journal of Child Language, 3,* 205–219.

Bartlett, E. J. (1977). The acquisition of the meaning of color terms: A study of lexical development. In P. Smith & R. Campbell (Eds.), *Proceedings of the Stirling Conference on the Psychology of Language*. New York: Plenum.

Bartlett, F. C. (1932). *Remembering: A study in experimental and social psychology*. Cambridge, England: Cambridge University Press.

Bates, E. (1976). *Language and content: The acquisition of pragmatics*. New York: Academic Press.

Bates, E. (1979). *The emergence of symbols*. New York: Academic Press.

Becker, J. A., Ross, S. R., & Nelson, K. (1979). Stimulus mode and concept formation in pre-school children. *Developmental Psychology, 15,* 218–220.

Benedict, H. (1976). *Language comprehension in 10–16 month old infants*. Unpublished doctoral dissertation, Yale University, New Haven, CT.

Benedict, H. (1979). Early lexical development: Comprehension and production. *Journal of Child Language, 6,* 183–200.

Benelli, B., D'Odorico, L., Levorato, M. C., & Simion, F. (1977). Formation and extension of the concept in a prelinguistic child. *Italian Journal of Psychology, IV,* 3.

Berko-Gleason, J. (1978). Talking to children: Some notes on feedback. In C. Snow & C. A. Ferguson (Eds.), *Talking to children*. New York: Cambridge University Press.

Berlin, B. (1978). Ethnobiological classification. In E. Rosch & B. B. Lloyd (Eds.), *Cognition and categorization*. Hillsdale, NJ: Erlbaum.

Berlin, B., & Kay, P. (1969). *Basic color terms: Their universality and evolution*. Berkeley, CA: University of California Press.

Bernstein, B. (1970). A sociolinguistic approach to socialization: With some reference to educability. In F. Williams (Ed.), *Language and poverty*. Chicago: Markham.

Bever, T. (1970). The cognitive basis for linguistic structures. In J. Hayes (Ed.), *Cognition and the development of language*. New York: Wiley.

Bickerton, D. (1981). *Roots of language*. Ann Arbor, MI: Karoma.

Bierwisch, N. (1970). Semantics. In J. Lyons (Ed.), *New horizons in linguistics*. Baltimore: Penguin Books.

Bierwisch, N. (1981). Basic issues in the development of word meaning. In W. Deutsch (Ed.), *The child's construction of language* (pp. 341–387). London: Academic Press.

Bjorklund, D. F., & Zaken-Greenberg, F. (1981). The effects of differences in classification style in preschool children's memory. *Child Development, 52,* 888–894.

Blake, I. K. (1979, March). *Early language use and the black child: A speech–act analysis of mother–child inputs and outputs*. Paper presented at the biennial meeting of the Society for Research in Child Development, San Francisco, CA.

Bloom, A. (1981). *The linguistic shaping of thought: A study in the impact of language on thinking in China and the West*. Hillsdale, NJ: Erlbaum.

Bloom, L. (1970). *Language development: Form and function in emerging grammars.* Cambridge, MA: MIT Press.

Bloom, L. (1973). *One word at a time: The use of single word utterances before syntax.* The Hague: Mouton.

Bloom, L., & Lahey, M. (1978). *Language development and language disorders.* New York: Wiley.

Bloom, L., Lahey, M., Hood, L., Lifter, K., & Friess, K. (1980). Complex sentences: Acquisition of syntactic connections and the semantic relations they encode. *Journal of Child Language, 7,* 235–261.

Bloom, L., Lightbown, P., & Hood, L. (1975). Structure and variation in child language. *Monographs of the Society for Research in Child Development, 40*(2).

Bonvillian, J. D., & Nelson, K. E. (1982). Exceptional cases of language acquisition. In K. E. Nelson (Ed.), *Children's language* (Vol. 3). Hillsdale, NJ: Erlbaum.

Bornstein, M. H. (1975). Qualities of color vision in infancy. *Journal of Experimental Child Psychology, 19,* 401–419.

Bornstein, M. H. (1981). Two kinds of perceptual organization near the beginning of life. In A. Collins (Ed.), *Minnesota Symposium on Child Psychology,* Vol. 14 (pp. 39–91). Hillsdale, NJ: Erlbaum.

Bousfield, W. A. (1953). The occurrence of clustering in the recall of randomly arranged associates. *Journal of General Psychology, 49,* 229–240.

Bower, G., Black, J. B., & Turner, T. J. (1979). Scripts in memory for text. *Cognitive Psychology, 11,* 177–220.

Bowerman, M. (1973). Structural relationships in children's utterances: Syntactic or semantic? In T. E. Moore (Ed.), *Cognitive development and the acquisition of language.* New York: Academic Press.

Bowerman, M. (1976). Semantic factors in the acquisition of rules for word use and sentence construction. In D. M. Moorehead & A. E. Morehead (Eds.), *Normal and deficient child language.* Baltimore: University Park Press.

Bowerman, M. (1978a). Semantic and syntactic development: A review of what, when, and how in language acquisition. In R. L. Schiefelbusch (Ed.), *Bases for language intervention.* Baltimore: University Park Press.

Bowerman, M. (1978b). The acquisition of word meaning: An investigation of some current conflicts. In N. Waterson & C. Snow (Eds.), *Development of communication: Social and pragmatic factors.* New York: Wiley.

Bowerman, M. (1982). Reorganizational processes in lexical and syntactic development. In E. Wanner & L. R. Gleitman (Eds.), *Language acquisition: The state of the art.* London and New York: Cambridge University Press.

Braine, M. D. S. (1963). The ontogeny of English phrase structure: The first phase. *Language, 39,* 1–14.

Braine, M. D. S. (1976). Children's first word combinations. *Monographs of the Society for Research in Child Development, 41* (Serial No. 164).

Brannigan, G. (1979). Some reasons why single word utterances are not. *Journal of Child Language, 6,* 411–423.

Braunwald, S. R. (1978). Context, word and meaning: Towards a communicational analysis of lexical acquisition. In A. Locke (Ed.), *Action, gesture and symbol: The emergence of language* (pp. 485–529). New York: Academic Press.

Bretherton, I., Bates, E., McNew, S., Shore, C., Williamson, C., & Beeghly-Smith, M. (1981). Comprehension and production of symbols in infancy: An experimental study. *Developmental Psychology, 17,* 728–736.

Bretherton, I., McNew, S., Snyder, L., & Bates, E. (1983). Individual differences at 20 months: Analytic and holistic strategies in language acquisition. *Journal of Child Language, 10,* 293–320.

Brewer, W. F., & Stone, J. B. (1975). Acquisition of spatial antonym pairs. *Journal of Experimental Child Psychology, 19,* 299–307.

Bronowski, J., & Bellugi, U. (1970). Language, name and concept. *Science, 168,* 669–673.

Brown, R. (1956). Language and categories. In J. S. Bruner, J. J. Goodnow, & G. A. Austin (Eds.), *A study of thinking.* New York: Wiley.

Brown, R. (1958). How shall a thing be called? *Psychological Review, 65,* 14–21.

Brown, R. (1973). *A first language: The early stages.* Cambridge, MA: Harvard University Press.

Brown, R., & Berko, J. (1960). Word associations and the acquisition of grammar. *Child Development, 31,* 1–14.

Brown, R., & Lenneberg, C. H. (1954). A study in language and cognition. *The Journal of Abnormal and Social Psychology, 49,* 454–462.

Bruner, J. S. (1966). On cognitive growth: I. In J. S. Bruner, R. Olver, & P. Greenfield (Eds.), *Studies in cognitive growth.* New York: Wiley.

Bruner, J. S. (1975a). From communication to language—A psychological perspective. *Cognition, 3,* 255–287.

Bruner, J. S. (1975b). The ontogenesis of speech acts. *Journal of Child Language, 2,* 1–19.

Bruner, J. S. (1978, March). *The acquisition of language: The Berlyne Memorial Lecture.* University of Toronto, Toronto, Canada.

Bruner, J. S. (1983). *Child's talk: Learning to use language.* New York: W. W. Norton.

Bruner, J. S., Goodnow, J., & Austin, G. (1956). *A study of thinking.* New York: Wiley.

Bruner, J. S., Olver, R. R., & Greenfield, P. M. (1966). *Studies in cognitive growth.* New York and London: Wiley.

Campbell, R. N. (1979). Cognitive development and child language. In P. Fletcher & M. Garman (Eds.), *Language Acquisition.* New York: Cambridge University Press.

Carey, S. (1982). Semantic development: The state of the art. In E. Wanner & L. R. Gleitman (Eds.), *Language acquisition: The state of the art* (pp. 347–389. Cambridge, England: Cambridge University Press.

Carey, S. (1983). Constraints on the meanings of natural kind terms. In Th. B. Seiler & W. Wannenmacher (Eds.), *Concept development and the development of word meaning.* New York: Springer-Verlag.

Carey, S. (in press). *Childhood animism revisited: On the acquisition of natural kind terms.* Cambridge: Bradford Press.

Carey, S., & Bartlett, E. (1978). Acquiring a single new word. *Papers and reports on Child Language Development* (No. 15, pp. 17–29). Department of Linguistics, Stanford University, Stanford, CA.

Carni, E. (1982). *The ups and downs of "before" and "after": Contextual controls of understanding.* Unpublished doctoral dissertation, City University of New York, New York.

Carni, E., & French, L. A. (1984). Contextual constraints on the comprehension of *before* and *after. Journal of Experimental Child Psychology, 37,* 394–403.

Carpenter, P. A., & Just, M. A. (1977). Reading comprehension as the eyes see it. In M. A. Just & P. A. Carpenter (Eds.), *Cognitive processes in comprehension.* New York: Wiley.

Carter, A. L. (1979). Prespeech meaning relations: An outline of one infant's sensorimotor morpheme development. In P. Fletcher & M. Garman (Eds.), *Language Acquisition* (pp. 71–92). New York: Cambridge University Press.

Casby, M. W. (1979). Comparison of static form and dynamic action as the basis of children's early word extensions. *Kansas Working Papers in Linguistics, 4*(2), 71–77.

Cassirer, E. (1953). *Language and myth*. (Susanne K. Langer, Trans.), New York: Dover.

Chi, M. T. H. (1978). Knowledge structures and memory development. In R. S. Siegler (Ed.), *Children's thinking: What develops?* Hillsdale, NJ: Erlbaum.

Chi, M. T. H., & Koeske, R. D. (1983). Network representation of a child's dinosaur knowledge. *Developmental Psychology, 19,* 29–39.

Chomsky, N. (1976). *Reflections on language*. Glasgow, Scotland: Fontana.

Chukovsky, K. (1968). *From 2 to 5*. Berkeley, CA: University of California Press.

Church, J. (Ed.). (1966). *Three babies*. New York: Random House.

Clark, E. V. (1971). On the acquisition of the meaning of *before* and *after*. *Journal of Verbal Learning and Verbal Behavior, 10,* 266–275.

Clark, E. V. (1973). What's in a word? On the child's acquisition of semantics in his first language. In T. E. Moore (Ed.), *Cognitive development and the acquisition of language*. New York: Academic Press.

Clark, E. V. (1975). Knowledge, context, and strategy in the acquisition of meaning. In D. Dato (Ed.), *Georgetown University Round Table on Language and Linguistics*. Washington, D.C.: Georgetown University Press.

Clark, E. V. (1978). From gesture to word: On the natural history of deixis in language acquisition. In J. S. Bruner & A. Garton (Eds.), *Human growth and development*. Oxford: Clarendon.

Clark, E. V. (1983). Meanings and concepts. In P. H. Mussen (Eds.), *Carmichael's manual of child psychology (Vol. 3): Cognitive development* (edited by J. H. Flavell & E. M. Markman). New York: Wiley.

Clark, H. H. (1970). The primitive nature of children's relational concepts. In J. R. Hayes (Ed.), *Cognition and the development of language*. New York: Wiley.

Clark, H. H. (1973). Space, time, semantics and the child. In T. E. Moore (Ed.), *Cognitive development and the acquisition of language*. New York: Academic Press.

Clark, R. (1974). Performing without competence. *Journal of Child Language, 1,* 1–10.

Clarke-Stewart, K. A. (1973). Interactions between mothers and their young children. Characteristics and consequences. *Monographs of the Society for Research in Child Development, 38*(6–7).

Cohen, L., & Strauss, M. (1979). Concept acquisition in the human infant. *Child Development, 50,* 419–424.

Coker, P. L. (1978). Syntax and semantic factors in the acquisition of *before* and *after*. *Journal of Child Language, 5,* 261–277.

Coker, P. L., & Legum, S. E. (1975). An empirical test of semantic hypotheses relevant to the language of young children. In *Working papers on the kindergarten program: Quality assurance*. Los Alamitos, CA: SWRL for Educational Research and Development.

Cole, M., Hood, L., & McDermott, R. (1982). Ecological niche picking. In U. Neisser (Ed.), *Memory observed: Remembering in natural contexts*. San Francisco. Freeman.

Collins, A. M., & Loftus, E. F. (1975). A spreading activation theory of semantic processing. *Psychological Review, 82*(6), 407–428.

Corrigan, R. (1978). Language development as related to stage 6 object permanence development. *Journal of Child Language, 5,* 173–189.

Corrigan, R. (1979). Cognitive correlates of language: Differential criteria yield differential results. *Child Development, 50,* 617–631.

Cramer, P. (1974). Idiodynamic sets as determinants of children's false recognition errors. *Developmental Psychology, 10,* 86–92.

Daehler, M. W., Lonardo, R., & Bubatko, D. (1979). Matching and equivalence judgments in very young children. *Child Development, 50,* 170–179.

Daehler, M. W., Perlmutter, M., & Myers, N. (1976). Equivalence of pictures and objects. *Child Development, 47,* 96–102.

Deese, J. (1967). Meaning and the change of meaning. *American Psychologist, 22,* 641–651.

Deese, J. (1969). Behavior and fact. *American Psychologist, 24,* 515–522.

de Forest, M. (1984). *Crib talk.* Unpublished doctoral dissertation. La Jolla: University of California at San Diego.

de Laguna, G. A. (1963). *Speech: Its function and development.* Bloomington, IN: Indiana University Press. (Original work published 1927).

Dennett, D. C. (1978). *Brainstorms.* Cambridge, MA: Bradford Books.

Denney, N. W., & Ziobrowski, M. (1972). Developmental changes in clustering criteria. *Journal of Experimental Child Psychology, 13,* 275–282.

de Saussure, G. (1959). *Course in general linguistics.* New York: McGraw-Hill. (Original work published 1915).

de Vos, L., & Caramazzo, A. (1977, March). *The role of form and function in the development of natural language concepts.* Paper presented at the biennial meetings of the Society for Research in Child Development. New Orleans, LA.

DeVries, R. (1969). The development of object constancy. *Monographs of the Society for Research in Child Development, 34* (3, Serial No. 127).

Dewey, J. (1894). The psychology of infant language. *Psychological Review, 2,* 63–66.

Donaldson, M. (1978). *Children's minds.* New York: Norton.

Dore, J. (1974). A pragmatic description of early language development. *Journal of Psycholinguistic Research, 4,* 343–350.

Dore, J. (1975). Holophrases, speech acts and language universals. *Journal of Child Language, 2,* 21–40.

Dore, J. (1978). Conditions for the acquisition of speech acts. In I. Markova (Ed.), *The social context of language.* New York: Wiley.

Dore, J., Franklin, M. B., Metler, R. T., & Ramer, A. L. H. (1976). *Journal of Child Language, 3,* 13–28.

Douglas, M. (1978). *Natural symbols: Explorations in cosmology.* London: Barrie & Jenkins.

du Boucheron, G., & Cotillon, J. M. (1978). Les enfants organisient-ils hierarchiquement les concepts des objets? *Cahiers de Psychologie du Sud-Est, 21,* 17–35. (Cited in Ehrlich, 1979).

Ehrlich, S. (1979). Semantic memory: A free-elements system. In C. R. Puff (Ed.), *Memory organization and structure* (pp. 195–218). New York: Academic Press.

Eimas, P. (1974). Linguistic processing of speech acts by young infants. In R. L. Schiefelbusch & L. L. Lloyd (Eds.), *Language perspectives: Acquisition, retardation and intervention.* Baltimore, MD: University Park Press.

Engelkamp, J. (1983). Word meaning and word recognition. In Th. B. Seiler & W. Wannenmacher (Eds.), *Concept development and the development of word meaning.* New York: Springer-Verlag.

Entwisle, D. R. (1966). *Word associations of young children.* Baltimore, MD: Johns Hopkins.

Ervin, S. M. (1961). Changes with age in the verbal determinants of word association. *American Journal of Psychology, 74,* 361–372.

Fagan, J. F., III. (1978). Infant recognition memory and early cognitive ability: Empirical, theoretical and remedial considerations. In F. D. Minifie & L. L. Lloyd (Eds.), *Communicative and cognitive abilities—Early behavioral assessment*. Baltimore, MD: University Park Press.

Faulkender, P., Wright, J., & Waldron, A. (1974). Generalized habituation of concept stimuli in toddlers. *Child Development, 45*, 1002–1010.

Feifel, H., & Lorge, I. (1950). Qualitative differences in the vocabulary responses of children. *Journal of Educational Psychology, 41*, 1–18.

Ferguson, C. A. (1977). Baby talk as a simplified register. In C. E. Snow & C. A. Ferguson (Eds.), *Talking to children: Language input and acquisition*. New York: Cambridge University Press.

Ferrier, L. (1978). Word, context and imitation. In A. Locke (Ed.), *Action, gesture and symbol: The emergence of language*. New York: Academic Press.

Fillmore, C. J. (1976). The need for a frame semantics in linguistics. In *Statistical methods in linguistics*. Stockholm: Skriptor.

Fillmore, C. J. (1980, August). Formulas and part-assemblies. Paper presented to the Cognitive Science Conference, Yale University, New Haven, CT.

Fillmore, C. J., Kempler, D., & Wang, W. S.-Y. (1979). *Individual differences in language ability and language behavior*. New York: Academic Press.

Fillmore, L. W. (1979). Individual differences in second language acquisition. In C. J. Fillmore, D. Kempler, & W. S.-Y. Wang (Eds.), *Individual differences in language ability and language behavior*. New York: Academic Press.

Flavell, J. H. (1970). Concept development. In P. Mussen (Ed.), *Carmichael's manual of child psychology* (Vol. 1, 3rd ed.). New York: Wiley.

Flavell, J., & Ross, L. (Eds.) (1981). *Social cognitive development*. London and New York: Cambridge University Press.

Fodor, J. A. (1975). *The language of thought*. New York: Crowell.

Fodor, J. A. (1980). On the impossibility of acquiring "more powerful" structures. In Piatelli-Palmarini (Ed.), *Language and learning: The debate between Jean Piaget and Noam Chomsky*. Cambridge, MA: Harvard University Press.

Fodor, J. A. (1981). *Representations*. Cambridge, MA: MIT Press.

Foster, M. L., & Brandes, S. N. (Eds.). (1980). *Symbol as sense: New approaches to the study of meaning*. New York: Academic Press.

Freeman, N. H., Lloyd, S., & Sinha, C. G. (1980). Infant search tasks reveal early concepts of containment and canonical usage of objects. *Cognition, 8*, 243–262.

Frege, G. (1960). On sense and reference. In P. Geach & M. Black (Eds.), *Philosophical writings of Gottlob Frege* (2nd ed.). Oxford: Blackwell.

French, L. A., & Brown, A. L. (1977). Comprehension of *before* and *after* in logical and arbitrary sequences. *Journal of Child Language, 2*, 247–256.

French, L. A., & Nelson, K. (1982). Taking away the supportive context: Preschoolers talk about the "then and there." *The Quarterly Newsletter of the Laboratory of Comparative Human Cognition, 4*, 1–6.

French, L., & Nelson, K. (in press). *Ifs, ors and buts about the use of relational terms by young children*. New York: Springer-Verlag.

Funk & Wagnall's. (1968). *Standard College Dictionary*. New York: Funk & Wagnall.

Furrow, D. R. (1980). *Social and asocial uses of language in young children*. Unpublished dissertation, Department of Psychology, Yale University, New Haven, CT.

Furrow, D., & Nelson, K. (1984). Environmental correlates of stylistic differences in language acquisition. *Journal of Child Language, 11*, 523–534.

Furth, H. G. (1969). *Piaget and knowledge: Theoretical Foundations*. Englewood Cliffs, NJ: Prentice-Hall.

Gardner, H., Winner, E., Beckhafer, R., & Wolf, D. (1978). The development of figurative language. In K. E. Nelson (Ed.), *Children's language* (Vol. I). New York: Gardner.

Gelman, R., & Gallistel, C. R. (1978). *The child's understanding of number.* Cambridge, MA: Harvard University Press.

Gelman, R., & Spelke, E. (1981). The development of thoughts about animates and inanimates: Implications for research on social cognition. In J. Flavell & L. Ross (Eds.), *Social cognitive development.* New York: Cambridge University Press.

Gentner, D. (1978). On relational meaning: The acquisition of verb meaning. *Child Development, 49,* 988–998.

Gerard, A. B., & Mandler, J. M. (1983). Ontological knowledge and sentence anomaly. *Journal of Verbal Learning and Verbal Behavior, 21,* 507–523.

Geschwind, N. (1970). The organization of language and the brain. *Science, 170,* 940–944.

Gibson, E. J., Owsley, C. J., & Johnston, J. (1978). Perception of invariants by five-month-old infants: Differentiation of two types of motion. *Developmental Psychology, 14,* 407–415.

Gleitman, L. R., Armstrong, S. R., & Gleitman, H. (1983). On doubting the concept "concept." In E. K. Scholnick (Ed.), *New trends in conceptual representation: Challenges to Piaget's theory?* Hillsdale, NJ: Erlbaum.

Glick, J. (1978). Cognition and social cognition: An introduction. In J. Glick & K. A. Clarke-Stewart (Eds.), *The development of social understanding.* New York: Gardner.

Goldstein, K., & Sheerer, M. (1941). Abstract and concrete behavior. An experimental study with special tests. *Psychological Monographs, 53* (2, Whole Number 239).

Gopnik, A. (1982). Words and plans: Early language and the development of intelligent action. *Journal of Child Language, 9,* 303–318.

Gopnik, A., & Meltzoff, A. W. (1984). Semantic and cognitive development in 15 to 21 month old children. *Journal of Child Language, 11,* 494–514.

Graesser, A. C., Woll, S. B., Kowalski, D. J., & Smith, D. A. (1980). Memory for typical and atypical actions in scripted activities. *Journal of Experimental Psychology: Human Learning & Memory, 6*(5), 503–515.

Graves, Z., & Glick, J. (1978). The effect of context on mother–child interaction: A progress report. *The Quarterly Newsletter of the Institute of Comparative Human Development, 2*(3), 41–46.

Greenberg, J. H. (Ed.). (1966). *Universals of language* (2nd ed.). Cambridge, MA: MIT Press.

Greenfield, P., & Smith, J. (1976). *The structure of communication in early language development.* New York: Academic Press.

Grieve, R., & Hoogenraad, R. (1979). First words. In P. Fletcher & M. Garman (Eds.), *Language acquisition* (pp. 93–104). Cambridge: Cambridge University Press.

Gruendel, J. M. (1977). Referential extension in early language development. *Child Development, 48,* 1567–1576.

Gumperz, J. J., & Tanner, D. (1979). Individual and social differences in language use. In C. J. Fillmore, D. Kempler, & W. S.-Y. Wang (Eds.), *Individual differences in language ability and language behavior.* New York: Academic Press.

Hagen, J. W., Jongeward, R. H., Jr., & Kail, R. V., Jr. (1975). Cognitive perspectives on the development of memory. In H. Reese (Ed.), *Advances in child development and behavior* (Vol. 10). New York: Academic Press.

Halliday, M. A. K. (1975). *Learning how to mean.* London: Edwin Arnold.

Heidenheimer, P. (1978a). A comparison of the roles of exemplar, action, coordinate, and superordinate relations in the semantic processing of 4 and 5 year old children. *Journal of Experimental Child Psychology, 25,* 143–159.

Heidenheimer, P. (1978b). Logical relations in the semantic processing of children between 6 and 10: Emergence of antonym and synonym categorizations. *Child Development, 49,* 1245–1246.

Higgins, E. T., McGarry, J., & Huttenlocher, J. (1975, March). *The effect of categorical relatedness on young children's object naming.* Paper presented at the Biennial Meeting of the Society for Research in Child Development, Denver, CO.

Hood, L., & Bloom, L. (1979). What, when, and how about why: A longitudinal study of early expressions of causality. *Monographs of the Society for Research in Child Development, 44.*

Horgan, D. (1978). How to answer questions when you've got nothing to say. *Journal of Child Language, 5,* 159–165.

Horgan, D. (1981). Rate of language acquisition and noun emphasis. *Journal of Psycholinguistic Research, 10,* 629–640.

Horton, M. S., & Markman, E. M. (1980). Developmental differences in the acquisition of basic and superordinate categories. *Child Development, 51,* 708–719.

Hudson, J., & Nelson, K. (1984). Play with language: Overextensions as analogies. *Journal of Child Language, 11,* 337–346.

Huttenlocher, J. (1974). The origins of language comprehension. In R. L. Solso (Ed.), *Theories in cognitive psychology.* Potomac, MD: Erlbaum.

Huttenlocher, J., & Lui, F. (1979). The semantic organization of some simple nouns and verbs. *Journal of Verbal Learning and Verbal Behavior, 18,* 141–162.

Huttenlocher, J., Smiley, P., & Charney, R. (1983). The emergence of action categories in the child: Evidence from verb meanings. *Psychological Review, 90,* 72–93.

Ilg, F. L., & Ames, L. B. (1955). *Child behavior.* New York: Dell.

Inhelder, B., & Piaget, J. (1964). *The early growth of logic in the child.* New York: Harper & Row.

Kagan, J., & Klein, R. E. (1973). Crosscultural perspectives on early development. *American Psychologist, 28,* 247–261.

Karmiloff-Smith, A. (1979). *A functional approach to child language.* Cambridge: Cambridge University Press.

Katz, J. J. (1972). *Semantic theory.* New York: Harper & Row.

Kay, D., & Anglin, J. M. (1982). Overextension and underextension in the child's expressive and receptive speech. *Journal of Child Language, 9,* 83–98.

Kay, P. (1976). *Constants and variables of English kinship semantics.* Working Paper No. 45, Language Behavior Research Laboratory, University of California, Berkeley, CA.

Keil, F. C. (1979). *Semantic and conceptual development: An ontological perspective.* Cambridge, MA: Harvard University Press.

Keil, F. C. (1983). Semantic inferences and the acquisition of word meaning. In Th. B. Seiler & W. Wannenmacher (Eds.), *Concept development and the development of word meaning.* New York: Springer-Verlag.

Kessen, W. (Ed). (1975). *Childhood in China.* New Haven, CT: Yale University Press.

Kessen, W., & Nelson, K. (1978). What the child brings to language. In B. T. Presseisen, D. Goldstein, & M. H. Appel (Eds.), *Topics in cognitive development* (Vol. 2). New York: Plenum.

Kintsch, W. (1974). *The representation of meaning in memory.* New York: Wiley.

Kosslyn, S. M. (1980). *Image and mind.* Cambridge, MA: Harvard University Press.

Kuczaj, S. A. II (Ed.) (1982). *Language development: Language, thought, and culture* (Vol. 2). Hillsdale, NJ: Erlbaum.

Kuczaj, S. A., II. (1983). *Crib speech and language play.* New York: Springer-Verlag.

Labov, W. (1973). The boundaries of words and their meanings. In C.-J. N. Bailey and R. W. Shuy (Eds.), *New ways of analyzing variation in English.* Washington, D.C.: Georgetown University Press.

Le Compte, G. K., & Gratch, C. (1972). Violation of a rule as a method of diagnosing infants' levels of object concept. *Child Development, 43,* 385–396.

Leiderman, P. H., Tulkin, S. R., & Rosenfeld, A. (1977). *Culture and infancy: Variations in the human experience.* New York: Academic Press.

Leonard, L. B. (1976). *Meaning in child language.* New York: Grune & Stratton.

Leopold, W. F. (1939). *Speech development of a bilingual child: A linguist's record: Vol. 1. Vocabulary growth in the first two years.* Evanston, IL: Northwestern University Press.

Lewis, M. M. (1951). *Infant speech.* London: Routledge & Kegan Paul.

Lieven, E. M. (1978). Conversations between mothers and young children: Individual differences and their possible implications for the study of language learning. In N. Waterson & C. Snow (Eds.), *The development of communication: Social and pragmatic factors in language acquisition.* New York: Wiley.

Lippman, M. Z. (1971). Correlates of contrast word associations: Developmental trends. *Journal of Verbal Learning and Verbal Behavior, 10,* 392–399.

Lucariello, J., & Nelson, K. (1982a, April). *Context and categories in young children's memory.* Paper presented at the Southeastern Conference on Human Development, Baltimore, MD.

Lucariello, J., & Nelson, K. (1982b, March). *Situational variation in mother–child interaction.* Paper presented at the International Conference on Infant Studies, Austin, TX.

Lucariello, J., & Nelson, K. (in press). Slot-filler categories as memory organizers for young children. *Developmental Psychology.*

Lucariello, J., & Nelson, K. (in preparation). *Naming things in context.* New York: City University of New York Graduate Center.

Luria, A. R. (1976). *Cognitive development: Its cultural and social foundations.* Cambridge, MA: Harvard University Press.

Luria, A. R., & Yudovich, F. I. (1959). *Speech and the development of mental processes in the child.* London: Staples Press.

Lyons, J. (1977). *Semantics* (Vol. 1). Cambridge: Cambridge University Press.

Macnamara, J. (1982). *Names for things.* Cambridge, MA: MIT Press.

Mandler, J. M. (1979). Categorical and schematic organization in memory. In C. R. Puff (Ed.), *Memory organization and structure* (pp. 259–302). New York: Academic Press.

Mandler, J. M. (1983). Representation. In J. H. Flavell & E. Markman (Eds.), *Cognitive development,* Vol. 3 of P. Mussen (Ed.), *Manual of child psychology* (4th ed.). New York: Wiley.

Maratsos, M. P. (1973a). The effects of stress on the understanding of pronominal co-references in children. *Journal of Psycholinguistic Research, 2,* 1–8.

Maratsos, M. P. (1973b). Decrease in the understanding of the word "big" in preschool children. *Child Development, 44,* 747–752.

Maratsos, M. P., & Chalkley, M. A. (1980). The internal language of children's syntax: The ontogenesis and representation of categories. In K. E. Nelson (Ed.), *Children's language* (Vol. 2). New York: Gardner.

Maratsos, M. P., Kuczaj, S. A., III., Fox, D. E. C., & Chalkley, M. A. (1979). Some empirical studies in the acquisition of transformational relations: Passives, negatives and the past tense. In W. A. Collins (Ed.), *Children's language and communication*. Hillsdale, NJ: Erlbaum.

Marin, O. S. M., Saffran, E. H., & Schwartz, M. F. (1976). Dissociations of language in aphasia: Implications for normal functioning. In S. R. Harnad, H. D. Steklis, & J. Lancaster (Eds.), *Origins and evolution of language and speech* (pp. 868–884). New York: New York Academy of Sciences.

Markman, E. M. (1976). Children's difficulty with word–referent differentiation. *Child Development, 47,* 742–749.

Markman, E. M. (1981). Two different principles of conceptual organization. In M. Lamb & A. Brown (Eds.), *Advances in developmental psychology* (Vol. 1). Hillsdale, NJ: Erlbaum.

Markman, E. M., Horton, M. S., & McLanahan, A. G. (1980). Classes and collections: Principles of organization in the learning of hierarchical relations. *Cognition, 8,* 227–241.

Markman, E. M., & Seibert, J. (1976). Classes and collections: Internal organization and resulting holistic properties. *Cognitive Psychology, 8,* 561–577.

McCall, R. B. (1977). Challenges to a science of developmental psychology. *Child Development, 48,* 333–334.

McCarthy, D. (1954). Language development in children. In L. Carmichael (Ed.), *Manual of child psychology* (2nd. ed.). New York: Wiley.

McCune-Niccolich, L. (1981). The cognitive bases of relational words in the single word period. *Journal of Child Language, 8,* 15–34.

McDonald, L., & Pien, D. (1982). Mother conversational behavior as a function of interactional intent. *Journal of Child Language, 9,* 337–358.

McNeill, D. (1970). *The acquisition of language.* New York: Harper & Row.

McShane, J. (1979). The development of naming. *Linguistics, 17,* 879–905.

Mervis, C. B., & Mervis, C. A. (1982). Leopards are kitty-cats: Object labeling by mothers for their thirteen-month-olds. *Child Development, 53,* 267–273.

Miller, G. A. (1967). Psycholinguistic approaches to the study of communication. In D. L. Amr (Ed.), *Journeys in science: Small steps . . . great strides.* Alberquerque, NM: University of New Mexico Press.

Miller, G. A. (1978). The acquisition of word meaning. *Child Development, 49,* 999–1004.

Miller, G. A., & Johnson-Laird, P. N. (1976). *Language and perception.* Cambridge, MA: Harvard University Press.

Moran, L. J. (1974). Comparative growth of Japanese and North American cognitive dictionaries. *Child Development, 44,* 862–865.

Moulton, J., & Robinson, G. (1981). *The organization of language.* New York: Cambridge University Press.

Mundy-Castle, A. (1980). Perception and communication in infancy: A cross-cultural study. In D. R. Olson (Ed.), *The social foundations of language and thought.* New York: Norton.

Neimark, E. (1974). Natural language categories: A failure to replicate. *Child Development, 45,* 508–511.

Nelson, K. (1969a). The organization of free recall by young children. *Journal of Experimental Psychology, 8,* 284–295.

Nelson, K. (1969b). *Word and phrase learning by young children.* Unpublished manuscript, Yale University, New Haven, CT.

Nelson, K. (1973a). Some evidence for the cognitive primacy of categorization and its functional basis. *Merrill-Palmer Quarterly Journal of Behavior and Development, 19,* 21–39.

Nelson, K. (1973b). Structure and strategy in learning to talk. *Monographs of the Society for Research in Child Development, 38* (1–2, Serial No. 149).

Nelson, K. (1974a). Concept, word, and sentence: Interrelations in acquisition and development. *Psychological Review, 81,* 267–285.

Nelson, K. (1974b). Variations in children's concepts by age and category. *Child Development, 45,* 577–584.

Nelson, K. (1975a). Individual differences in early semantic and syntactic development. *Annals of the New York Academy of Sciences, 263,* 132–139.

Nelson, K. (1975b). The nominal shift in semantic–syntactic development. *Cognitive Psychology, 7,* 461–479.

Nelson, K. (1976). Some attributes of adjectives used by young children. *Cognition, 7,* 461–479.

Nelson, K. (1977a). The conceptual basis for naming. In J. Macnamara (Ed.), *Language learning and thought.* New York: Academic Press.

Nelson, K. (1977b). The syntagmatic–paradigmatic shift revisited: A review of research and theory. *Psychological Bulletin, 84,* 93–116.

Nelson, K. (1977c). Cognitive development and the acquisition of concepts. In R. C. Anderson, R. J. Spiro, & W. E. Montague (Eds.), *Schooling and the acquisition of knowledge.* Hillsdale, NJ: Erlbaum.

Nelson, K. (1978a). How young children represent knowledge of their world in and out of language. In R. S. Siegler (Ed.), *Children's thinking: What develops?* (pp. 255–273). Hillsdale, NJ: Erlbaum.

Nelson, K. (1978b). Semantic development and the development of semantic memory. In K. E. Nelson (Ed.), *Children's language.* New York: Gardner.

Nelson, K. (1979a). Explorations in the development of a functional semantic system. In W. Collins (Ed.), *Children's language and communication, child psychology* (Vol. 12) (pp. 47–81). Hillsdale, NJ: Erlbaum.

Nelson, K. (1979b). The role of language in infant development. In H. H. Bornstein & W. Kessen (Eds.), *Psychological development from infancy.* Hillsdale, NJ: Erlbaum.

Nelson, K. (1981a). Individual differences in language development: Implications for development and language. *Developmental Psychology, 17,* 170–187.

Nelson, K. (1981b). Social cognition in a script framework. In J. Flavell & L. Ross (Eds.), *Social cognitive development.* New York: Cambridge University Press.

Nelson, K. (1982). The syntagmatics and paradigmatics of conceptual representation. In S. Kuczaj (Ed.), *Language development: Language thought and culture* (pp. 335–364). Hillsdale, NJ: Erlbaum.

Nelson, K. (1983a). Concepts, words and experiments: A rejoinder. *Merrill-Palmer Quarterly, 29*(4), 387–394.

Nelson, K. (1983b). The derivation of concepts and categories from event representations. In E. Scholnick (Ed.), *New trends in conceptual representation: Challenges to Piaget-theory* (pp. 129–149). Hillsdale, NJ: Erlbaum.

Nelson, K. (1983c). The conceptual basis for language. In Th. B. Seiler & W. Wannenmacher (Eds.), *Concept development and the development of word meanings.* New York: Springer-Verlag.

Nelson, K. (1984a). The context of language development. Paper presented to the Linguistics Section of the New York Academy of Sciences.

Nelson, K. (1984b). The transition from infant to child memory. In M. Moscovitch (Ed.), *Infant memory.* New York and London: Plenum Press, p. 103–130.

Nelson, K. (in press). *Event knowledge: Structure and function in development.* Hillsdale, NJ: Erlbaum.

Nelson, K., & Benedict, H. (1974). The comprehension of relative, contrastive and absolute adjectives by young children. *Journal of Psycholinguistic Research, 3,* 333–342.

Nelson, K. E., & Bonvillian, J. D. (1978). Early language development: Conceptual growth and related processes between 2 and 4½ years of age. In K. E. Nelson (Ed.), *Children's language* (Vol. 1). New York: Gardner.

Nelson, K., Engel, S., & Kyratzis, A. (in press). The evolution of meaning in context. *Journal of Pragmatics.*

Nelson, K., Fivush, R., Hudson, J., & Lucariello, J. (1983). Scripts and the development of memory. In M. Chi (Ed.), *What is memory development the development of?* In J. Meacham (Ed.), *Contributions to human development monograph series.* Basel, Switzerland: S. Karger.

Nelson, K., & Gruendel, J. M. (1981). Generalized event representations: Basic building blocks of cognitive development. In A. Brown & M. Lamb (Eds.), *Advances in developmental psychology* (Vol. 1). Hillsdale, NJ: Erlbaum.

Nelson, K., & Kessen, W. (1978). Concept development in the first two years. Unpublished report to Carnegie Corporation. Department of Psychology, Yale University, New Haven, CT.

Nelson, K., & Lucariello, J. (in press). The development of meaning in first words. In M. Barrett (Ed.), *Children's single-word speech.* Chicester, England: Wiley.

Nelson, K. E., & Nelson, K. (1978). Cognitive pendulums and their linguistic realizations. In K. E. Nelson (Ed.), *Children's language* (Vol. 1). New York: Gardner.

Nelson, K., Rescorla, L., Gruendel, J., & Benedict, H. (1978). Early lexicons: What do they mean? *Child Development, 49,* 960–968.

Nelson, K., & Ross, G. (1980). The generalities and specifics of long-term memory in infants and young children. In M. Perlmutter (Ed.), *Children's memory: New directives for child development.* San Francisco: Jossey-Bass.

Newport, E. (1981). Constraints on structure: Evidence from American sign language and language learning. In W. A. Collins (Ed.), *Minnesota symposium on child development* (Vol. 14). Hillsdale, NJ: Erlbaum.

Newport, E. L., Gleitman, H., & Gleitman, L. R. (1977). Mother, I'd rather do it myself: Some effects and non-effects of maternal speech style. In C. E. Snow & C. A. Ferguson (Eds.), *Talking to children.* London: Cambridge University Press.

Ninio, A. (1983). Joint book reading as a multiple vocabulary acquisition device. *Developmental Psychology, 19,* 445–451.

Ninio, A., & Bruner, J. S. (1978). The achievements and antecedents of labelling. *Journal of Child Language, 5,* 1–16.

Nowliss, G. H., & Kessen, W. (1976). Human newborns differentiate differing concentrations of sucrose and glucose. *Science, 191,* 865–866.

O'Connell, B., & Gerard, A. (in press). Scripts and scraps: The development of sequential understanding. *Child Development.*

Ogden, C. K., & Richards, I. A. (1946). *The meaning of meaning* (8th ed.). London: Routledge & Kegan Paul. (Original edition published in 1923.)

Olver, R. R., & Hornsby, J. R. (1966). On equivalence. In J. S. Bruner, R. R. Olver, & P. M. Greenfield (Eds.), *Studies in cognitive growth.* New York: Wiley.

Oviatt, S. L. (1982). Inferring what words mean: Early development in infants' comprehension of common object names. *Child Development, 53,* 274–277.

Papandropoulou, I., & Sinclair, H. (1974). What is a word? *Human Development, 17,* 241–258.

Penk, W. E. (1971). Developmental changes in idiodynamic sets of children's word associations. *Developmental Psychology, 5*, 55–63.

Peters, A. M. (1977). Language learning strategies: Does the whole equal the sum of the parts? *Language, 53*, 560–573.

Peters, A. M. (1983). *The units of language acquisition.* New York: Cambridge University Press.

Petrey, S. (1977). Word associations and the development of lexical memory. *Cognition, 5*, 57–72.

Piaget, J. (1962). *Play, dreams and imitation in childhood.* New York: Norton.

Piaget, J. (1963). *Origins of intelligence.* New York: Norton.

Piaget, J. (1969). *Judgment and reasoning in the child.* New Jersey: Littlefield, Adams & Co.

Piaget, J. (1970). Piaget's theory. In P. H. Mussen (Ed.), *Carmichael's manual of child psychology* (3rd ed., Vol. 1, pp. 703–732). New York: Wiley.

Piaget, J. (1971). *The child's conception of time.* New York: Ballantine. (Originally published in 1927.)

Piaget, J. (1976). *The child's conception of the world.* Totowa, NJ: Littlefield, Adams. (Original published 1929.)

Popper, K. R. (1972). *Objective knowledge: An evolutionary approach.* London: Oxford University Press.

Posner, M. I., & Keele, S. W. (1968). On the genesis of abstract ideas. *Journal of Experimental Psychology, 77*, 353–363.

Posner, M. I., & Warren, R. E. (1972). Traces, concepts, and conscious constructions. In A. W. Melton & Z. Martin (Eds.), *Coding processes in human memory.* Washington, D. C.: Winston & Sons.

Prawat, R. S. & Cancelli, A. A. (1977). Semantic retrieval in young children as a function of type of meaning. *Developmental Psychology, 13*, 354–358.

Prawat, R. S., & Wildfong, S. (1980). The influence of functional context on children's labelling responses. *Child Development, 51*, 1057–1061.

Premack, D., & Premack, A. J. (1983). *The mind of an ape.* New York: Norton.

Putnam, H. (1975). *Mind, language and reality.* New York: Cambridge University Press.

Pylyshyn, Z. (1981). The imagery debate: Analogue vs. tacit knowledge. *Psychological Review, 87*, 16–45.

Quine, W. V. O. (1960). *Word and object.* Cambridge, MA: MIT Press.

Ramer, A. (1976). Syntactic styles in emerging language. *Journal of Child Language, 3*, 49–62.

Ramey, C. T., Farran, D. C., Campbell, F. A., & Finkelstein, N. W. (1978). Observations of mother–infant interactions: Implications for development. In F. D. Minifie & L. L. Lloyd (Eds.), *Communicative and cognitive ability—Early behavioral assessment* (pp. 397–442). Baltimore, MD: University Park Press.

Ratner, N., & Bruner, J. S. (1978). Games, social exchange and the acquisition of language. *Journal of Child Language, 5*, 391–401.

Reber, A. S., & Allen, R. (1978). Analogic and abstraction strategies in synthetic grammar learning: A functionalist interpretation. *Cognition, 6*, 189–221.

Reber, A. S., Kassin, S. H., Lewis, S., & Cantor, G. W. (1979). *On the relationship between implicit and explicit modes in learning of complex rule structures.* Unpublished manuscript, Department of Psychology, Brooklyn College, Brooklyn, NY.

Reber, A. S., & Lewis, S. (1977). Toward a theory of implicit learning: The analysis of the forms of a body of tacit knowledge. *Cognition, 5*, 331–361.

Rescorla, L. A. (1976). *Concept formation in word learning.* Unpublished doctoral dissertation, Yale University, New Haven, CT.

Rescorla, L. A. (1980). Overextension in early language development. *Journal of Child Language, 7,* 321–335.

Rescorla, L. A. (1981). Category development in early language. *Journal of Child Language, 8,* 225–238.

Reznick, J. S., & Kagan, J. (1983). Category detection in infancy. In L. P. Lipsitt & C. Rovee-Collier (Eds.), *Advances in infancy research* (Vol. 2). Norwood, NJ: Ablex Publishing Corporation.

Ricciuti, H. N. (1965). Object grouping and selective ordering behaviors in infants 12 to 24 months old. *Merrill-Palmer Quarterly, 11,* 129–148.

Richards, M. M. (1979). Sorting out what's in a word from what's not: Evaluating Clark's semantic features acquisition theory. *Journal of Experimental Child Psychology, 27,* 1–47.

Riegel, K. F. (1970). The language acquisition process: A reinterpretation of related research findings. In R. Goulet & P. Baltes (Eds.), *Theory and research in life span developmental psychology.* New York: Academic Press.

Rifkin, A. (1984). Evidence for a basic level in event taxonomies. Manuscript submitted for publication.

Rosch, E. (1973). On the internal structure of perceptual and semantic categories. In T. E. Moore (Ed.), *Cognitive development and the acquisition of language.* New York: Academic Press.

Rosch, E. (1975). Cognitive representation of semantic categories. *Journal of Experimental Psychology: General, 104,* 192–233.

Rosch, E. (1978). Principles of categorization. In E. Rosch & B. Lloyd (Eds.), *Cognition and categorization.* Hillsdale, NJ: Erlbaum.

Rosch, E., & Mervis, C. B. (1975). Family resemblances: Studies in the internal structure of categories. *Cognitive Psychology, 7,* 573–605.

Rosch, E., Mervis, C. B., Gray, W. D., Johnson, D. M., & Boyes-Braem, P. (1976). Basic objects in natural categories. *Cognitive Psychology, 8,* 382–439.

Rosenblum, T., and Pinker, S. A. (1983). Word magic revisited: Monolingual and bilingual children's understanding of the word–object relationship. *Child Development, 54,* 773–780.

Ross, G. (1980). Concept categorization in 1 to 2 year olds. *Developmental Psychology, 16,* 391–396.

Ross, G., Nelson, K., Wetstone, H., & Tanouye, E. (in press). Acquisition and generalization of novel object concepts by young language learners. *Journal of Child Language.*

Ruff, H. A. (1978). Infant recognition of the invariant form of objects. *Child Development, 49,* 293–306.

Rumelhart, D. E. (1979). Some problems with the notion of literal meanings. In A. Ortony (Ed.), *Metaphor and thought.* New York: Cambridge University Press.

Rumelhart, D. E., & Ortony, A. (1977). The representation of knowledge in memory. In R. C. Anderson, R. J. Spiro, & W. E. Montague (Eds.), *Schooling and the acquisition of knowledge.* Hillsdale, NJ: Erlbaum.

Sachs, J. (1983). Talking about the there and then: The emergence of displaced reference in parent–child discourse. In K. E. Nelson (Ed.), *Children's language.* Hillsdale, NJ: Erlbaum.

Saltz, E. (1971). *The cognitive basis of human learning.* Homewood, IL: Dorsey.

Saltz, E., & Sigel, I. E. (1967). Concept overdiscrimination in children. *Journal of Experimental Psychology, 73,* 1–8.

Saltz, E., Soller, E., & Sigel, I. E. (1972). The development of natural language concepts. *Child Development, 43,* 1191–1202.

Saussure, F. de. (1959). *Course in general linguistics.* New York, NY: The Philosophical Library, Inc.

Scarlett, H., & Press, A. (1975). An experimental investigation of the phenomenon of word realism. *Merrill–Palmer Quarterly, 21,* 205–226.

Schank, R. C., & Abelson, R. P. (1977). *Scripts, plans, goals and understanding.* Hillsdale, NJ: Erlbaum.

Schiefflin, B. (1979). Getting it together: An ethnographic approach to the study of the development of communicative competence. In E. Ochs & B. B. Schiefflin (Eds.), *Developmental pragmatics.* New York: Academic Press.

Scholnick, E. (Ed.). (1983). *New trends in conceptual representation.* Hillsdale, NJ: Erlbaum.

Scribner, S. (1974). Developmental aspects of categorized recall in a West African society. *Cognitive Psychology, 6,* 475–494.

Searle, J. R. (1969). *Speech acts: An essay in the philosophy of language.* Cambridge, England: Cambridge University Press.

Shatz, M. (1978a). On the development of communicative understanding: An early strategy for interpreting and responding to messages. *Cognitive Psychology, 10,* 271–301.

Shatz, M. (1978b). The relationship between cognitive processes and the development of communication skills. In B. Keasy (Ed.), *Nebraska symposium on motivation.* Lincoln, NE: University of Nebraska Press.

Shatz, M. (1983). Communication. In P. H. Mussen (Ed.), *Handbook of child psychology,* 4th ed., Vol. III of *Cognitive development* (J. H. Flavell & E. M. Markman, Eds.). New York: Wiley.

Sigel, I. E. (1983). Is the concept of the *concept* still elusive or What do we know about concept development? In E. K. Scholnick (Ed.), *New trends in conceptual representation: Challenges to Piaget's theory.* Hillsdale, NJ: Erlbaum.

Smiley, S. S., & Brown, A. L. (1979). Conceptual preference for thematic or taxonomic relations: A nonmonotonic age trend from preschool to old age. *Journal of Experimental Child Psychology, 28,* 249–257.

Smith, E. E., & Medin, D. L. (1981). *Categories and concepts.* Cambridge, MA: Harvard University Press.

Smith, L. B., & Kemler, D. G. (1977). Developmental trends in free classification: Evidence for a new conceptualization of perceptual development. *Journal of Experimental Child Psychology, 24,* 279–298.

Snow, C. E. (1972). Mothers' speech to children learning language. *Child Development, 43,* 549–565.

Snow, C. E. (1977). Mothers' speech research: from input to interaction. In C. E. Snow & C. A. Ferguson (Eds.), *Talking to children: Language input and acquisition.* New York: Cambridge University Press.

Snow, C. E., & Goldfield, B. (1983). Turn the page, please: Situation-specific language acquisition. *Journal of Child Language, 10,* 551–569.

Spelke, E. S. (1982). Perceptual knowledge of objects in infancy. In J. Mehler, M. Garrett, & E. Walker (Eds.), *Perspectives on mental representation.* Hillsdale, NJ: Erlbaum.

Starr, S. (1975). The relationship of single words to two-word sentences. *Child Development, 46,* 701–708.

Steinberg, B. M. (1974). Information processing in the third year: Coding, memory, transfer. *Child Development, 45,* 503–507.

Steinberg, E. R., & Anderson, R. C. (1975). Hierarchical semantic organization in 6-year-olds. *Journal of Experimental Child Psychology, 19*, 544–553.

Strauss, M. S. (1979). Abstraction of proto-typical information by adults and 10 month old infants. *Journal of Experimental Psychology: Human Learning and Memory, 5*, 618–632.

Strohner, J., & Nelson, K. E. (1974). The young child's development of sentence comprehension: Influence of event probability, nonverbal context, syntactic form, and strategies. *Child Development, 45*, 564–576.

Sugarman, S. (1978). Some organizational aspects of preverbal communication. In I. Markova (Ed.), *The social context of language*. New York: Wiley.

Sugarman, S. (1981). The cognitive basis of classification in very young children: An analysis of object ordering trends. *Child Development, 52*, 1172–1178.

Sugarman, S. (1983). *Children's early thought: Developments in classification*. New York: Cambridge University Press.

Tanz, C. (1980). *Studies in the acquisition of deictic terms*. Cambridge, Cambridge University Press.

Tenney, Y. (1975). The child's conception of organization and recall. *Journal of Experimental Child Psychology, 19*, 100–114.

Thomson, J. R., & Chapman, R. S. (1977). Who is Daddy revisited: The status of two-year-olds' overextended words in use and comprehension. *Journal of Child Language, 4*, 359–375.

Tomasello, M., & Farrar, M. J. (1984). Cognitive bases of lexical development: Object permanence and relational words. *Journal of Child Language, 11*, 477–494.

Tomasello, M., & Todd, J. (1983). Joint attention and lexical acquisition style. *First Language, 4*, 197–212.

Tomikawa, S. A., & Dodd, D. H. (1980). Early word meanings: Perceptually or functionally based? *Child Development, 51*, 1103–1109.

Trabasso, T., Isen, A., Dolecki, P., McLanahan, A. G., Riley, C. A., & Tucker, T. (1978). How do children solve class inclusion problems? In R. Seigler (Ed.), *Children's thinking: What develops?* Hillsdale, NJ: Erlbaum.

Tulving, E. (1972). Episodic and semantic memory. In E. Tulving & W. Donaldson (Eds.), *Organization and memory*. New York: Academic Press.

Vygotsky, L. S. (1962). *Thought and language*. Cambridge, MA: MIT Press.

Vygotsky, L. S. (1978). *Mind in society: The development of higher psychological processes* M. Cole, V. John-Steiner, S. Scribner, & E. Souberman (Eds.). Cambridge, MA: Harvard University Press.

Watson, R. (in press). Toward a theory of definition. *Journal of Child Language*.

Wells, G. (1980). Apprenticeship in meaning. In K. E. Nelson (Ed.), *Children's language* (Vol. 2). New York: Gardner.

Werner, H., (1948). *Comparative psychology of mental development*. New York: Science Editions.

Werner, H., & Kaplan, B. (1963). *Symbol formation: An organismic–developmental approach to language and the expression of thought*. New York: Wiley.

Wertsch, J. V. (1978). Adult–child interaction and the roots of metacognition. *The Quarterly Newsletter of the Institute for Comparative Human Development, 2*, 15–18.

Wertsch, J. (1985). *Culture, communication and cognition*. London & New York: Cambridge University Press.

Wexler, K. (1982). A principle theory for language acquisition. In E. Wanner & L. R. Gleitman (Eds.), *Language acquisition: The state of the art*. New York: Cambridge University Press.

White, S. H. (1965). Evidence for a hierarchical arrangement of learning processes. In L. P. Lipsett & C. C. Spiker (Eds.), *Advances in child behavior and development* (Vol. 2). New York: Academic Press.

Whorf, B. L. (1956). *Language, thought and reality* J. B. Carroll (Ed.), Cambridge, MA: MIT Press.

Winner, E. (1978). New names for old things: The emergence of metaphoric language. *Papers and Reports on Child Language Development, 15,* 7–16. Department of Linguistics, Stanford University, Stanford, CA.

Wittgenstein, L. (1953). *Philosophical investigations.* New York: Macmillan.

Wolf, D., & Gardner, H. (1979). Style and sequence in symbolic play. In M. Franklin & N. Smith (Eds.), *Early symbolization.* Hillsdale, NJ: Erlbaum.

Wolman, R. N., & Barker, E. N. (1965). A developmental study of word definitions. *Journal of Genetic Psychology, 107,* 159–166.

Woodward, H., & Lowell, F. (1916). Children's association frequency tables. *Psychological Monographs, 22*(5, Whole No. 97).

Author Index

Numbers in italics show the page on which the complete reference is cited.

Subject Index

DEVELOPMENTAL PSYCHOLOGY SERIES

Continued from page ii

.